My Song Is of Mercy

Writings of Matthew Kelty,
Monk of Gethsemani

Selected and edited by Michael Downey

A SHEED & WARD BOOK

ROWMAN & LITTLEFIELD PUBLISHERS, INC.
Lanham • Boulder • New York • Toronto • Oxford

Published by Sheed & Ward
An imprint of Rowman & Littlefield Publishers, Inc.
A wholly owned subsidiary of The Rowman & Littlefield Publishing Group, Inc.
4501 Forbes Boulevard, Suite 200
Lanham, MD 20706

PO Box 317
Oxford
OX2 9RU, UK

Distributed by National Book Network

Library of Congress Cataloging-in-Publication Data

Kelty, Matthew.
    My song is of mercy : writings of Matthew Kelty / selected and edited by Michael
Downey
        p. cm.
    Contents: Flute solo — Talks and Sermons.
    ISBN 1-55612-606-9 (alk. paper)
    1. Kely, Matthew. 2. Trappists—United States—Biography. 3. Trappists—New
Guinea—Biography. 4. Monastic and religious life. I. Downey, Michael. II. Title.
BX4705.K375A3   1994
271'.12502—dc20   94-30801
                                                                       CIP

Printed in the United States of America.

♾ ™ The paper used in this publication meets the minimum requirements of
American National Standard for Information Sciences—Permanence of
Paper for Printed Library Materials, ANSI/NISO Z39.48-1992.

Contents

Editor's Introduction

*I*t was while on sabbatical at the Abbey of Gethsemani in Trappist, Kentucky, that I first met Matthew Kelty. Each night just after Compline, guests from the Retreat House would gather in the chapel to listen to the conferences of the chaplain, Father Matthew. He would begin his remarks by reading poems, telling stories about what was going on inside the monastery or about the rising cost of a small cup of coffee at McDonald's. In short order the retreatants would be buckled over in laughter, clearly in violation of the grand silence which begins at the close of Compline. Then would follow a reading of one of his sermons written for a different occasion, with running commentary in light of current events described in the day's *Wall Street Journal,* or the current issue of *Time* or *The National Catholic Reporter.* Those who pass through Gethsemani are taken by him: his candor, lack of affectation, childlikeness, willingness to listen long and lovingly, and his utter trust in God. I have grown to love him as a brother and a father. Indeed he became something of a father to me during the painful ordeal of my own father's illness and death.

It is his supple spirit that endears him to so many. When his convictions and theological positions seem more typical of an earlier mindset, they are never put forth with the arrogance of a crusty curmudgeon. His every sentence, written or spoken, springs from a deep and abiding conviction about God's mercy. Matthew Kelty speaks a language of mercy. And so I have judged it fitting to take the title of this volume from the opening of Psalm 101.

My Song Is of Mercy includes a revised version of *Flute Solo,* reflections written during Holy Week 1973 while Father Matthew was living as a solitary in Papua New Guinea. Since it first went out of print several years ago there has been a steady flow of requests for a second edition. Editing the revised version of *Flute* provided occasion for me to read many of Matthew Kelty's conference talks, sermons, book reviews, and letters. I saw quickly that *Flute Solo* and Kelty's *Sermons in a Monastery* (Kalamazoo, Michigan: Cistercian Publications, 1983), as well as *Letters from a Hermit* (Springfield, Illinois: Templegate, 1978), provide only a very small portion of the writings of the man and the monk Matthew. And so alongside *Flute* I have gathered into one volume a wide range of writings spanning the 1970s through Christmas 1993. I have arranged them chronologically, since there seemed no other way to organize such a wide range of writings covering vastly different topics in several different genres. In the case of sermons, citations for the gospel readings are provided where appropriate.

My hope is that this volume will offer the opportunity for *lectio divina,* a slow and contemplative reading that leads to ever-fuller participation in Christ's mysteries.

Several people have been most generous in their kindness and support as this project was underway. Above all I thank Timothy Kelly, OCSO, Abbot of Gethsemani. My gratitude to him and the monks of Gethsemani is beyond telling. If not for the interest and encouragement of Sheed & Ward these writings would still be in hard-to-decipher script, and stuffed in file folders in the chaplain's room at the Abbey of Gethsemani. Robert Heyer at Sheed & Ward welcomed my idea for a collection of Matthew Kelty's writings, and has been willing to wait as other more immediate tasks continued to take priority over this one in which I have taken such delight. Andy Apathy, managing editor at Sheed & Ward, has provided valuable assistance at every stage of the work. No one has been more patient in the course of this undertaking than Matthew Kelty himself. He knows that the best words are those that spring from silence, even if it has been my tardiness that has caused his words to steep in silence just a little longer.

Michael Edward Downey
Gethsemani
Good Friday 1994

Note from the Author

A theologian named Michael Downey came into my life. And made a difference.

He spent a sabbatical at the Abbey of Gethsemani and one thing led to another, my being Retreat House chaplain, he long-time guest. This collection of homilies from the last few years, plus a re-issue of *Flute Solo* of more than a few years ago, is one fruit of our relationship.

So here is something new, something old, all carefully prepared by one who knows how. I am grateful to him.

It is now 12 years since I returned from a stint as solitary in Papua New Guinea. The original *Flute Solo* marked the beginning of that experience in Holy Week of 1973.

People still ask me: why did you return to the abbey? The answer is probably simpler than even I at first realized: I thought it time to do so, moved by the same Spirit, I hope, that led me there in the first place. Nine years seemed enough of a good thing. I was, after all, a guest of the Divine Word missionaries there, though alone on a hill, and beholden to them in all the ways that made the venture possible. I will not forget my indebtedness to them and the Holy Spirit Sisters and the people there, so kind to me. It was all very beautful, and made real ultimately because the monks of Gethsemani permitted it. Common courtesy suggested that I not presume too much and answer some inner voice whispering that it might be time to go home and lend a hand. We get somewhat fewer and somewhat older as monks, and one more can always help.

And coming home was literally that, not as if it were some traumatic sacrifice. It is a beautiful life here too. I am baffled that so few seem to see that, am puzzled that we are not overwhelmed with would-be monks. In the midst of so much light, darkness.

But the darkness will pass. It always does. Meanwhile we prepare for better days with the confidence of the sower in spring. Great days are ahead. One sows with such hope for the good of the land and its people.

We look to far fields too and witness the growth of monastic life in other parts of the world. There will be monks in Papua

New Guinea one day. It will be fun to remind them that a monk of Gethsemani was there long ago singing psalms on a hill by the sea on the north coast. One could have done worse. Praise God!

Matthew Kelty, OCSO
Gethsemani
Holy Week 1994

Flute Solo

Flute Solo

*Q*uite by accident I stumbled onto a happy word in a Greek dictionary, *monaulia*, "flute solo." But it has another definition as well, "the solitary life," since the root word means both "flute" and "house," and the *monos* characterizes the solo flute and the person living alone, the solitary. It is a beautiful combination, for both are a kind of poetry. Certainly neither has any great practical value, yet the world would be less charming for want of the flute, less tolerable if there were no hermits.

I am not a flutist, yet I have a flute and I play it, play it for no purpose and for no ears save God's and my own. That being so, there is no need of artistry or skill and I can sing my tune without fear of correction or disapproval, let alone of another showing me how it should be done. If accomplished play is a good thing, and it is, it is perhaps also true that the way to skill is the end of joyous freedom. It is pleasant and easy to pray by flute and I do much of it. There is some element of pathos in the instrument that is dear to me, something humble and modest in its song. Even when the tune turns out rich and running, there is the sound of the bird in it, clean and selfless. I don't want to learn to play the flute; I prefer it this way. Beyond my incapacity to get far, there is the fear of my small joy being driven away by concern for doing it well and turning a natural act into a performance.

There are those gifted persons who can combine their gift with arduous training and still remain free, a superb accomplishment. Others often cannot, and the pleasure is soon stifled in the achieving. I suppose more persons would sing if they were not so fearful that others would criticize. Perhaps more would pray if they were not so sure it took skill and practice, or be hermits if they were not led to think it out of the question.

Lots of people would like to be able to play something, create a bit of music for themselves. Most want to pray, too. And if not everyone wants to be a solitary, there are not many who have not now and again tasted in lonely hours a solace not elsewhere come by.

We can be talked out of things. Scorn and ridicule are effective weapons and they get considerable use, nor is it only professionals who look with unveiled pity on awkward efforts. Others do so as well. I favor the attitude that permits the child to try his or her hand at many things, many ways, many times. And the adult.

The solitary runs into a lot of suspicion spoken and unspoken. It is in the air, an aspect of the climate. People get so that they fear to be alone. Worse, they think it wrong to want to be.

And yet there are so many lonely people. I sometimes feel that's all there are. That we are all solitaries. In a way, it's true. I am the only one of me there is; there could be no solitude greater than that. I came alone. I depart alone. And if I did not exist, nothing else would, even God, as far as I am concerned.

Yet faith tells me that this solitude is not real, that in our aloneness we come from God, are in God, are on the way to God. Further, that we shall one day be one with the one God, so sharing his solitude. Yet that same faith assures us that God's solitude is a community of love. So what looks lone turns out not to be.

Which is why solitude is so good. By means of entering into it, you discover it's not like you were told. It is not lonely in that way. It is lonely, but when you live with it a while, it turns on you, it opens up, it unfolds.

God dwells in the heart of every person, but he dwells there in quiet. He is a very shy God, quiet as a rainbow, and like a rainbow, kin to rain and to sunshine, pointing out hidden gold, sign of a word of promise given after a quarrel, a promise never to be revoked. His presence takes a little while to grow on you, but once the noisy rattling of our tongues, our hands, our head has cleared, one comes to love it. True, there is nothing to see; no word is spoken, no music heard. There is no sweet scent, no subtle influence. What is, is of another kind.

But if you leave it too soon—and everyone will tell you to hurry on, to move on, to come on—if you surrender to guilt and agree with the voices outside, then the heart returns to its old unhappiness, the old fare, the old routine. Yet suffering ever so small a touch of that dark light, it is certain you will return. Do.

Sometimes it helps to do a little something while you are at it, like the flute, as long as it be free and not an exercise. And only for a while, just long enough to taper off the din of a world come in with you. It does not take long. Sometimes a quiet craft, or painting, or drawing. Or the beads. Sometimes a candle will help, a Madonna. Even a bit of incense. Some darkness.

There ought to be a sanctuary, a place where a guilty person could go and know he or she could not be touched. There ought to be a place to hide, not from the eyes of others, but from my own eyes, too totally centered on what is outside. We need an escape from concern, the eternal fussing and fretting with externals. There is an inside to everything and if you know only the outside, then knowledge is schizoid. Most madness comes from living half a life. The best half is within. Or better said, the better half, speaking in terms of the marriage that is you.

It is the dark that gives point to our fears, for in the dark not yet used to, we see too much. The first thing you see on looking into a deep well is your own face and this is at least disconcerting, sometimes annoying. Longer looking reveals what is further down in the well. Even there we are vexed to discover another face which is also ours. Yet, one can grow accustomed to it, and, in a sense, it is a mistake not to, since it, too, is yourself.

Even while you are still with the flute, the past may come up, total recall without pretense, and not always pretty. It is not good to overdo it at first, but you may as well adjust to the fact that there will be more of this.

To want to leave now is understandable, but is still a matter of regret, for you are just on the point of getting to know you. The wise one, instead, would smile quietly, take up the flute again, thinking all the while, musing on it all.

There are places a person can go, a scene he or she can create, a haven for the heart. The reason they seem scarce is that no one wants them; there is small demand. But lovers always manage to find a place to go where they can be alone for a while. So can you. Playing the flute in public, like love on the street, lacks the grace it should have, the intimate depth.

Venture

The devious route by which one comes directly to what one was meant to be remains as much a puzzle looked back upon as looked forward to. There must be within the human person some hidden compass directing us where to go. One could easily speak of it as destiny, some prearranged program, did not one feel that it was all accompanied by response, even more by personal choice and election.

The other night I had a dream. I was walking along a wooded path much like a track working its way cross-country here in New Guinea. After some time the path came to a multiple juncture with other paths leading out in several different directions, one much like the other. In the dream I had no notion which path I was to take. I eventually took one and followed it a long way. It brought me to a figure dressed as a bishop who then robed me in priestly vestments of very sumptuous quality.

My dream was very true to life, for if I followed a call to the priesthood, I have always sensed the fact that it was as much someone else's doing as my own. I seemed to follow some instinct in entering a missionary society, and never once in the course of long training had I any doubt I was where I belonged. Before the novitiate was completed I had expressed my interest in becoming a contemplative monk several times, but on each occasion was counseled that there appeared to be nothing to indicate that I should move in that direction. So I did not, and once admitted to vows, never considered it again.

Since years later I did become a monk, it is interesting to reflect on these early desires and the way everything worked out. There is no doubt that had I known in my youth about monastic life, that is what I would have entered upon. At the same time, from this vantage point, it is clear to me that it was far better that I did not do so at that time.

There was an introversion to my character that was pronounced; had it been allowed to develop it is not likely it would have been healthy. There was much about life in minor and major seminary in a totally active order that was contrary to my taste, yet necessary and good for me. I had to adapt and to adjust in order to survive, and so cultivated out-going qualities with zest. I was no good at all in sports; I think because I did not have the basic aggression necessary, or, if I did, could not express it in that way. But there were many other activities and I was involved in most of them: publications, drama, music, debate, clubs, and committees. We had endless discussions, arguments, exchanges, and I developed a flair for quick retort and effective ridicule and sarcasm. Since manual labor in that particular era at the seminary was perhaps in higher repute than the intellectual life (World War II was on, labor was short, and we had an open invitation to help on the big farm—a new world to many of us), I managed to acquire some prowess in that, too, and enjoyed working with horses and pigs, in garden and flour mill. In my studies I was about average and had to work hard, not really knowing how to study.

Today, the seminary training that we underwent is looked back on as something depraved and bizarre. True, there was a good deal wrong with it, but at the time, few of us felt so and we took it all in with enthusiasm. There were only a few rumblings of the revolution to come and we did not understand them. We thought of ourselves as competent, alive, and aware—did we not speak forthrightly on such progressive issues as liturgy in English, cooperatives, back-to-the-land and organic farming, indigenous art forms in mission lands? And we looked forward with joy and confidence to the mission work we would be assigned.

There was a great sense of close fraternity in that enclosure which was fostered by almost every factor of the life: a heavy routine of public prayer and liturgy, an almost constant being together, a great sense of sharing in a common ideal. We found it stimulating and we stimulated one another. It occurs to me now that we had innumerable celebrations of one kind or another: programs or plays or speakers, musicals, banquets, picnics, get-togethers, hikes, outings, investitures, professions, ordinations, the cycle of liturgical feasts. Our time was tightly controlled and day followed day in spartan discipline. I frankly loved it and I sensed most of us did. We complained endlessly about the administration, the faculty, the prefects of discipline, but that was as much a part of the life as ritual. And through it all ran a spiritual current that only added to it and bound it together.

It was a "good seminary" and we were proud of it. We were further proud to be members of a worldwide missionary group and felt ourselves superbly blessed in that. We looked on students in diocesan seminaries and even in other orders and societies with a kind of sympathy, quite assured that what they had could not possibly come up to ours.

It was a fabulous creation, really, and over it hung some aura of God's and the Church's blessing; it was divinely right. The tight control that Rome kept on us was only further proof that evidently we were important.

Eventually, the whole thing fell apart, though many years later.

I was appointed to New Guinea and I was pleased. It was far away, had a romantic appeal, involved a primitive people I imagined I could relate to more easily than to some cultured nation like Japan. But the actuality proved something of a disaster. I was told to assist an older missionary in a bush station. I entered the work with gusto and was, I believe, adequate. The scenery was new to me and I enjoyed the change; making bush trips on horseback, erecting primitive chapels and dwellings. I wrote letters, taught school, gave instructions, baptized and married and anointed, dispensed medicine. And was lonely.

The step from the vigorously outgoing community of the seminary to the quiet life in the bush could not have been more extreme. I had had no contact with solitude for more than a dozen years, and was immediately brought back to the days of my childhood when I much preferred my own company, enjoyed being by myself.

I began to have serious misgivings about my life in New Guinea and grew somewhat frightened. The pastor used to go off on two- or three-week bush trips and I would run the main station while he was gone. When he returned, we would be together a week or so, and then I would take off for my series of outstations and be gone about the same length of time. That is the way we worked. At first we had few books and papers, no radio, no music, no icebox, little familiar food. We managed well enough, but it was arduous; we expected it to be that way.

But I had not reckoned with loneliness. Sometimes when evening was coming on I could feel a great dark cloud settling on my soul like an oppressive weight. It was much like the rain coming in the night; you could hear it working its way across the jungle, the oncoming roar of torrents beating down on all that rich foliage. I worried, prayed about it. I went to the chapel one night and told the Lord: "You see how things are. You love me. If this is not going to work, get me out of here." With our training and attitudes we would never have asked for a change, certainly not so soon. It was thought proper to ask God, however.

Within ten days of that prayer I received word from my bishop that I had been recalled to the motherhouse in the United States to edit the mission magazine of the society. It was the first word I had on the subject. I had been in New Guinea a few months over three years.

Editing the magazine was another thing altogether, but I enjoyed it. In those days we did not concern ourselves with proper training as much as they do today. It was assumed that our seminary had prepared us adequately. Our courses were innumerable and we had touched on a formidable array of subjects. The assumption was that once ordained you ought to be able to manage as teacher, farm manager, head of a printing plant, a school, a parish, a mission station. By dint of hard work, good luck, and past background, we did wonderfully well. But there was a lot of bungling. A new superior with new ideas offered me a course in journalism, but along with that I was to edit the magazine and serve as assistant at a local parish. When I saw the extent of the material the course covered, and that much of it would be of no use in my work, I decided not to enroll and settled down to editing the magazine as best I could.

The magazine had been begun early in the century as a propaganda piece and means of support and had served the Society well; publication continued until 1960. It was all printed on our own press by the Brothers in the Society. As time went on, it became evident that rising costs, new approaches to fund-raising, and the plethora of small Catholic publications were going to force us to call a halt. The halt was called abruptly by a peremptory order from Rome, which is the way things were done in those times. While the last issue was on the press, the plant caught fire at two o'clock one January morning and burned to the ground. I escaped from my quarters only by grace of a kindly Providence.

During the eight years with the magazine my thoughts had often returned to New Guinea and I had an affectionate nostalgia for it. Still, the predominant remembrance was the solitude. I never forgot it; it had left a deep mark.

Meanwhile, community life, as one of the priests of the seminary, was somewhat less than what I had known there as a student. Most of the priests were quiet, busy people involved with their classes, their study, their writing, their parochial work. Communal relations were good, but I dearly missed the intensity of the life I had once known. Now and then I preached retreats and enjoyed the work, as I liked helping out in parishes regularly.

Even though I was but dimly aware of it, my life was really falling apart. The New Guinea experience had been a first shattering. As time went on I began to sense something unreal and artificial, something basically untrue and dishonest in the way I lived. My busy, active, outgoing pursuits were somehow not genuine, but put-on, acquired, a sort of pretending. This growing insight really unsettled me. I began to sense a new sort of loneliness and panic.

I sought to make friends among the priests and did so, came to know many of the seminarians, made many deep and lasting friendships. They were a great help to me. Further, I began to enjoy drinking, by myself, with others, to a disturbing degree. By the time the magazine was terminated and the press had burned to the ground, I knew I had come to a serious point in my life.

Every now and then the flames of an old love would return and I would again find myself thinking about being a monk. I wondered if that was not what I was supposed to be. I did little or no reading about it, made no inquiries. Once in a while I would meet someone who had just made a retreat at Gethsemani, the Trappist monastery in Kentucky, and I would listen to their comments with great attention. 1 really knew little about the place or the life there—did not even want to know. But the conviction grew that that was where I belonged.

One of my good priest friends died after a long and sad illness. He was dear to me; we used to go fishing together once in a while in the north woods. My situation grew tense and sometimes I did not know what to do. I remember going to his grave one night and, bursting into tears, asking him in God's name to help me. He did.

After the folding of the magazine and the press fire from which I escaped, I had a strange interlude of freedom. I had the conviction that I was at a crossroad in my life and that some sort of resolution was called for. Rather suddenly I decided to make a retreat at Gethsemani. I went with nothing particular in mind, yet I knew instinctively what was going to happen.

The place frightened me thoroughly; completely captivated me. After a few days of fear and indecision, I asked to be admitted to the community. They accepted me, quietly, without fuss, neither much impressed nor unduly remote. It was all matter-of-fact and unexcited. Yet I knew a door had slammed shut behind me.

I returned to the seminary, told them what I had done, asked for permission to enter the abbey. The attitude was one of amusement and incredulity. They assured me of my love for people, for the active life, my talent for preaching, for involvement in works of all kinds. To myself I remarked that they did not know what they were talking about. I typed out a letter to Rome, slipped it under the cloth of the altar of the Virgin for her feast of December 8, then mailed it. The answer was a half-hearted one, but affirmative.

I was getting ready to go, delayed only by previously arranged engagements for some sisters' retreats, when the fire broke out in the press. It was a shocking experience and only emphasized what I had already sensed of the dramatic moment of that period of my life. I injured my foot badly in hot asphalt in escaping from the burning building and it took a while to heal. While the wound was still serious I gave one retreat in Dayton

and a second to some novices in northern Wisconsin. While returning from the latter I had another taste of death. The train was
racing toward Chicago bright and early that sunny wintry morning, still in the country, when it struck a large truck at a remote
crossing. When the train finally stopped and backed up to the
scene of the accident, they came to the diner and brought me out
into the bitter cold and bitter sight of three bodies flung around
the snow and under the twisted wreck. I could smell death and
blood while I held one man in my arms as he went into eternity.
The second was a blond young boy in leather boots and leather
jacket. I baptized him with melted snow. The third was dead. A
long while later an ambulance came and took them away; we got
back into the train and went on our way. When we left the train
in Chicago I saw the damage done to the front of the locomotive;
I felt a worse damage and knew in my heart that I was more
afraid of God than ever, and remembered cold blood on the
snow.A few days later I left on the night train for Louisville. The
evening before we had a social evening in the priests' recreation
room and I had all I could get to drink.

Olive Garden

*I*n the sixties Gethsemani was an intense experience; stepping
into it was stepping into an entirely different country. It was
death again. My whole identity dissolved and disappeared. At
forty-five I had a certain role in life. I knew and was known. I
had a history, a community I had grown up with and been associated with on all levels. Once I closed the abbey gate behind me,
all that was gone. Here I was not known, meant nothing at all to
anyone. The silence that muffled everything immersed me in my
nonentity. The place was a maze of complex rites, customs, ritu-
als, modes, and manners that everyone except me seemed to
make use of unconsciously, with no effort. There was obviously
an intense communication among the group, but it was done
mostly by sign language and I knew no sign. January meant that
the house was cold, filled with an odor I had never known before, born of damp wool, incense, and pine-sol. The dozen or so
novices were a varied lot; two priests, a couple of youngsters just
out of high school, some college graduates, an artist, an engineer,

a man from Ford Motor Co., and a man from United States Steel. They all seemed a bit brittle and strained. The novice master was Thomas Merton (Father Louis); at ease, offhandish, sharp, somewhat British. It was an ordeal.

The routine had weight. The choir was long and Latin, complex to stay with, exasperating for one's desperate efforts to locate proper pages in the huge volumes; the monks knew much of the office by heart and were spared the page shuffling. The food was sparse, generally lukewarm, if not cold, and the refectory monstrously ugly. The whole complex looked neglected; the church had needed painting at least for a decade; most areas needed cleaning. The grounds surrounding the abbey were nondescript and the immediate backyard a muddy farmyard every time it rained. We slept in little cells in an open dormitory, the air in winter both icy and unashamedly old. Except when doing manual labor, we were always dressed as monks, exactly how depending on specific regulations, even at night. And at work we wore long robes of denim tied around the middle with a belt, and a scapular or hood. There were all sorts of distinctions in what postulants, novices, professed Brothers or professed choir members wore, and this varied again as to season. At that time we were still wearing medieval socks, leggings, long home-fashioned drawers and undershirts. In winter it was all flannel and wool and one was glad for that.

The novice master was not hesitant about making demands. Every morning after prime and chapter, he would assign us our work. It was rarely the same job two days running. If you could type, you might end up doing some stencils for one of the articles he was working on, and that, often enough, on a bright sunny day when something outdoors would have been a pleasure. On a dark wintry morning with the temperature in the twenties and a stiff wind coming down from Canada, you would as likely as not be sent to clear brush from some exposed patch of pine. Three hours of that after a breakfast of coffee and bread was a good taste of reality.

We had a conference or lecture by the master every day before noon. We always looked forward to it. For one thing, the room was warm. The material was always interesting and Thomas Merton's presentation had great charm. He loved variety. And he had a very kind, gentle spirit in his toughness; he loved good wit and had eyes often merry.

All in all, it was a dreadful period for me. Yet, I loved it, all of it. I was appalled to think the master might find me unacceptable and was almost ecstatic when I learned much later that I was doing all right and would be received. I had a most obnoxious ego, an inflated front, that must have shocked him. He let it pass, taking a good crack at it now and then. Once he came down on me head-first, total-thrust, full-power. I never forgot it. I did not realize what he was about except in the vaguest way, and I did not know how to help myself. He worked on me. He showed me how.

We had interviews with Father Louis every two weeks or so, for about thirty minutes. They were priceless. He was interested, and even if you thought yourself quite deserving of the interest, he still took you seriously, knew how to guide you. He was very patient. I do not see how he put up with me, so conceited, so cocksure, so thin a veneer of education and pomposity. He used to smile when I would reveal some awareness of what I looked like, and say, "Lots of priests are like that. That's the way they make them."

I learned. I shall never forget him. I am grateful to God for those two-and-a-half years, and for frequent contacts afterward.

As it stated in my request for admission, I went to Gethsemani for a deeper spiritual life, a more intense community life, a life of apostolic prayer. All of which I received in full measure. They delivered.

Yet the greatest gift I had not asked for, had not expected. That gift was an understanding of the role of solitude in monastic life, in a person's life. It was Thomas Merton who taught me this, both in the days I was a novice under his direction, as also in later years in a study of his writings. Probably the most significant work of this man lay in his return to the solitary aspect of monasticism. The results of this awakening, this rediscovery, have only begun to be manifest. I am sure it is only a beginning.

It is necessary to see how original he was in this. By reason of his own charisma and his study of early sources of monastic life, he brought back to life this element that had practically disappeared. It was neither easy nor pleasant, for many opposed him.

Thomas Merton was arguing not merely for a revival of the eremitic life within the order, but also for a return to the spirit of solitude which from earliest times had been characteristic of monastic life, of Cistercian life. His writings and studies on this were many and good.

Now, some years after his death and the spreading of his teaching, it is somewhat difficult to recapture the situation on which he dwelt, for Gethsemani has since undergone both an external and internal renovation that is phenomenal. But at that time monastic life there, as at most monasteries of the kind for the past several centuries, had been warped in favor of community. Monks literally did everything in common: their prayer, their work, their reading, their sleep. They were together always. They were rarely, if ever, alone. Together with this intense communal life went silence. Up until a few years ago, there was generally no talk at all, save to a few superiors in governed situations. Even communication by signs was limited by rule. It was this silent community that was conceived as the ideal, and that is the way the monks lived for several generations. Against this backdrop were the protracted sessions in choir, long hours of work—much of it arduous—and times for reading. The tone of discipline was sometimes harsh, even cruel. Yet abbots were known to be kindly, and the way things worked out was to identify strictness with the rule, the life, the order, while the abbot, subject as was anyone else to this rule, did only what he had to do as gently as he might. The combination of a gentle abbot and a tough rule seems to have been accepted as about as good a combination as could be had.

The monks wanted it that way. They were happy men, hard, determined, ascetic, generous. They had what they came for and were pleased. If some were wounded by the regimen, that was not the fault of the regimen.

Merton put his finger on a weak spot. He knew that as long as that weakness was not corrected, all was not well. Monastic life is not just a group of ascetics, people accustomed to hard labor, indifferent to scant food, great stretches of formal prayer and liturgical ceremony, multiple observances and customs in a controlled environment. To some extent it is all that, but that is not the whole of it.

For years, an introduction to the monastic life consisted simply of learning your way around. One did as the others did. Since he considered one element lacking, Merton began to supply it. I believe he felt that when too much emphasis is placed on rigor and hardship, there is likely to be a development of the very sort of ego and false personality that is the basic enemy of growth in God. The regimen often made the monks tough, but toughness does not necessarily equal spirituality. A corps of disciplined ascetics may be an impressive achievement, yet have little to do with monasticism. God may not be able to deal with them.

Monks must first of all be persons made whole by union with their own reality and God's. Too much self can inhibit such union. Merton sensed that what was lacking was solitude. With shrewd insight born of grace and gifted mind, he spent his life proving his thesis and I believe he succeeded. Whether monks will heed his teaching remains to be seen. Rock the boat he surely did; he troubled the waters. Things can no longer be the same.

He did not think that living in a silent community was necessarily an adequate expression of solitude, though this had long been maintained. He thought the person in monastic life needed real solitude; that is, time alone. And further, and even more important, he needed to be schooled in what to do with that exposure. The greatest lesson Thomas Merton taught me was the fruitful use of solitude.

In this I was helped immeasurably by Carl Jung. I ran into his works in the library—at that time kept in the "reserved" section. I was spellbound by what I read. I still am; I have a dozen volumes of Jung here with me. His understanding of the "way we work" is a great gift to humankind. To my mind, or better, what he has done for me, is to translate ancient monastic teachings into terms I can relate to. They come to life through him.

The other great factors in what understanding I have of what it is to be a monk came through contact with a primitive culture in Papua New Guinea. I am ignorant of anthropology, but even a casual observer can perceive in primitive life a quality that we in the West lack; almost everything the native does is religious. If that be too sophisticated, then say that these indigenous people live in two worlds: the world of the visible, the world of the invisible. They are always in touch with another world not of matter. Building a house, making a garden, fashioning a drum, going on a hunt, having a feast, getting married, coming into adulthood, going to war—all these and many other activities are always—or used to be before we came—accompanied by ritual, by a mystic aspect, a relation to the spirits. Even if their concept of the spirits is not too elevated, even if somewhat limited in tone, the fact remains that to the people of Papua New Guinea this world contains much more than we can see. Even if much of this ritualism is concerned with placating inimical spirits, or working out bargains with them, it is contact with a world beyond.

We, on our side, think that the undeveloped nature of the primitive spirit world puts us in a superior position; we know better than to think our ancestors can help our garden grow. We live in a totally material world and fancy ourselves advanced.

Father Louis believed that solitude was essential. He sensed that the discipline involved in exposing self to reality could first of all only be done alone; further, that it ran no risk of developing an ego; that it would lead one to an experience of one's own poverty and sinfulness and thus to a realization of God's mercy; and, thence, to a compassionate love for humanity. But if this inner journey is not made, one's grasp of one's own being must be grievously limited, with the consequent weakened recognition of God's mercy. Genuine love for neighbor is of one kind with love for one's self and is rooted in reality.

Merton did not indicate anything specific except that permission ought to be extended to monks who expressed some desire for solitude and manifested some aptitude for it. In his own case, he was explicit in his request for a hermitage and was eventually granted it. He lived to see the abbot who for so long found it difficult to adjust solitude to the Cistercian tradition, also established in a handsome hermitage some miles south of the abbey. In Gethsemani, as throughout the order, there has been a revival of interest in the solitary life, and hermits and hermitages are no longer rare.

I certainly had not cultivated my inclination for the solitary life when I entered Gethsemani. On the contrary, I felt my need was precisely the opposite; an even more intense community. Nor did I originally respond to Merton's own interest, even though we novices gladly helped ready the ground for his hermitage on the wooded hill. His teaching on solitude impressed me deeply, however, and I found his writings on the subject full of implications for me.

However, in my first years at the abbey, I did manage to find myself a little hut where I could sometimes spend a few hours; these hours meant a great deal to me and were very good. Later I moved into an abandoned pumphouse at the foot of the dam at the end of one of the monastery's many ponds. It was a delightful spot, and though it was damp, I made it into something idyllic. The new abbot permitted me to spend one day and night there each week; also to celebrate the Eucharist in it.

I can scarcely describe how much the little hut meant to me. At the time, I was in charge of the abbey shoe shop, repairing shoes and providing monks with new shoes, boots, galoshes when they needed them.

Because afternoons were more convenient hours for the monks to come, I worked then and could go for part of the morning to the house near the lake. I got hold of one of the big old Latin psalters and did my office from it, and later acquired from a pawn shop a flute which I used to take with me to the lake (Joyous Lake, I named it) and play, a setting as sweet as I have ever known, since the water is totally surrounded with woods (some of the trees planted by Merton) and to the rear are gentle hills. The echoes from the flute were enchanting. Kentucky is fond of blue mists and a delicate haze often draped everything. Now and then there were wild ducks or a deer. I had the joy of this place several years. I called it Heartbreak House.

It was during these hours that there began to grow in me a longing for a life totally committed to solitude. This development came very slowly, for I much loved the life of the abbey, enjoyed the company of the monks, the liturgy. It always grieved me that some of the monks thought the solitary nursed a grudge against the community. That was not my case; I loved the abbey and still do. It is simply a matter of doing what you feel you must because called to do so.

It seemed to me also that if I was going to be a solitary, it could only be a real solitude if I left the abbey and went some place far away. There is naturally a great advantage in being near the abbey for practical reasons, such as food and clothing, care when sick—even old age and death must be reckoned with. A return on feast days and other occasions would also be a grace. Still, I felt that a solitary ought to bear the brunt of it all and not soften it by settling nearby. But this is only my view.

I began to think of likely places. There are some hermits in Vancouver, for the bishop there offers hospitality, and somone in my situation would need a bishop's permission. Ireland came to mind, center of monks and hermits centuries ago, and an abbot there seemed to think it might be possible.

One day, walking out to the hermitage, the idea of New Guinea came to me, so I wrote to a bishop there. I frankly did not expect a positive answer. He is a good missionary bishop, effective, experienced. I assumed he would thank me for my interest, ask for my continued prayers, and conclude it would perhaps be best if I remained in my monastery and as a monk there be a source of blessing for him and his mission.

His answer came back soon enough. He told me to come as soon as I could.

So I went to the abbot. I told him that I had a bishop who not only offered me hospitality, but who also guaranteed to let me live as a solitary, who would help me get settled, and who would also help me in maintaining myself, considering me simply as part of the mission work. We then began a long series of interviews in which I presented my story, the development of my solitary calling over the past years. He listened with an interest that seemed to slacken as time went on. Eventually I asked him outright if he would permit me to go. He said that he would not.

With that my dream collapsed, for I had long since determined that I would never act on this call without his blessing. As I saw it, if God could give the grace of a solitary vocation to a monk of Gethsemani, he most certainly could inspire the abbot of Gethsemani to cooperate with it. If God chose not to, then the circuit was not complete and I was not about to short it. I had solemnly sworn to obey the abbot and I saw no point whatever in remaining a monk if I were not willing to abide by that. I could always terminate the agreement, but I could not keep it and break it at the same time. So the matter was dropped and life went on as before. What will be, will be, I thought, if God is in it.

Piedmont Interlude

For three years I lived in a small, experimental monastery in the woods of the Piedmont in North Carolina, established from Gethsemani. It was a very great grace.

The venture was experimental by reason of its size—no more than six monks—as well as its life. For one thing, the worship was of a very simple nature: psalmody in the night, in the morning, in the evening. Mass followed the morning service. We picked up our own breakfast and supper and took them alone, silently. The meal at noon was in common, a prepared meal, with conversation, although talk at table is not traditional in a Cistercian house. Morning hours were spent in work, mostly to earn a living, but also in doing the necessary chores, since we had goats, chickens, a garden, and woods, and to the running of the place, taking care of guests.

The setting was excellent. A small town was only seven miles away, yet we were sufficiently off by ourselves to assure peace and quiet. While the scene was charming, it was in no sense dramatic. The monastery was made up of a cluster of frame buildings of stained redwood; a chapel, a main building with library, reading room, kitchen, refectory, washroom, and three guest rooms; and six cabins scattered in the adjacent pines for the individual monks, each with one room about twelve feet square serving as bedroom and study. Behind the main buildings was a workshop and at the other end of the property a rather discordant note—a mobile home.

The mobile home served as a weaving studio. Here we had several floor looms, most of them four harness forty-eight-inch models; one had twenty-four harnesses. We were able to obtain abundant yarn in a local plant from which we wove ponchos and scarves for sale. The proceeds went into maintaining ourselves. We had more or less stumbled into weaving, but it turned out to be a fortunate step. Carolina is arts-and-crafts country, so it fitted in well. Beyond that, there is a certain character to the art of weaving that makes it especially suited to a life of prayer. It is creative and we kept it so, refusing to be tied down to a production of goods that would be the same thing all the time. There is a deep satisfaction in putting on a warp—a long business—and then throwing the shuttle back and forth endless times to form before your eyes, out of conflict and contrast, a pattern and a fabric never seen before. It turns out, as it were, that the material is a construction founded in contradiction, a reconciling of opposites, for the crossing of warp and woof, vertical and horizontal, repeated an infinite number of times, is at the heart of it. Without this cross there is no weaving, and the interplay, always maintained at proper tension and handled with profound respect, was fascinating to work with. Nor were the results predictable. Sometimes the components looked as though they might not blend, but nevertheless combined to create great loveliness.

We joined a craft guild in a neighboring city and took a loom to the annual craft fair where we enjoyed demonstrating. Though weaving in public borders on the irreverent, there was great interest and many visitors lingered to see it being done.

For a long time we kept goats for their milk and learned to respect their remarkable intuition. We kept peacocks and guinea hens for exotica and for taking care that wood ticks did not get too plentiful. A Dalmation taught us devotion.

To the rear of the monastery was an acre of tobacco, leased out, for we were not there long enough to learn how to farm it. And around us was a pine wood through which we cut wandering paths to the main road and mailbox a half mile away.

Usually we made our own bread for table and altar and were even able to get wine for Mass just a few miles away at a small, old-time winery. We ate no meat at the monastery, since this has long been a custom of monks to remind them of nonviolence. It also saved us money.

During our years in the Piedmont there was a great deal of anguish in the country over the war in Vietnam. Our concern was both with the lack of strong protest from the Catholic Church and the need to stress the monk as a person identified with peace. We felt that many monks were insensitive to the moral implications of genuine patriotism. A lot of discussion led to a small decision: to have the phone removed. We had learned that the phone tax was a specific war tax, and perhaps the only one. Though we could have refused to pay it, we decided to go a step further and dispense with the phone altogether. Doing so turned out to be a blessing. It was sometimes an inconvenience, but we had peace. A six-foot wall around the place would not have assured us more privacy.

We were not entirely shut off, although it is difficult to describe the situation. Large monasteries tend to attract hordes of visitors, and they come for all sorts of reasons. The curious come, as do travelers and people on vacation. They come because they've heard of your cheese or your bread or your farm. They want to hear your chant, participate in your liturgy. They are spiritually hungry. They are searching. They are faithful people who consider it a blessing to be in touch with a contemplative monastery. There are even those who would like to become monks and who come to see what their desire amounts to. Visitors are something of a problem to monasteries, yet, as St. Benedict noted in his Rule, you are always going to have them and the abbot should be hospitable.

But the little monastery in the Piedmont was another brand entirely. The liturgy was nothing to see, starkest simplicity, even rustic—a few figures in cowls, a psalter; it was clear that the cowls covered overalls; over the psalmody one heard the guineas and peacocks on the roof. We had no farm to show, no products save our modest venture in weaving, no great thing in Carolina. One does not go to a monastery to see goats and chickens. And the monks seemed no great species, nor the setting impressive.

Yet people came, from all over, all kinds. We had lots of young people from the universities. Professors came. Jews came. Sisters came. And Protestants. People of no faith at all. Young drifters. Priests came. People from the heart of New York, the woods of Wisconsin, a Swiss, a young man back from monks in India, local Baptists. A dear friend was a church history professor from a small Christian college some miles south; he came often with his students. Seminarians came, Dominicans, Jesuits, Divine Word missionaries, a bishop, a commune-dweller. Most stayed two or three days.

I do not know why they came. Often enough I was there alone, or perhaps with but one or two other monks. Most of the brethren who came there from Gethsemani or other monasteries found it difficult to adjust to the small place, the dominant lonely note, the rural quality of the life, and returned to their abbeys. In the end, after three years, Gethsemani passed the place on to monks of the order from another monastery [Saint Joseph's, Spencer, Massachusetts, ed.]. They are there at this writing and happy. But people did come. We did not advertise. True, the papers from nearby cities sent out writers and photographers to do feature stories, and we obliged. Our only condition was they were not to make our location definite, but to keep it vague, that they mention the horrible state of our road. They always kept their word. Sometimes the reporters came back to stay a few days with us. But we never suffered an avalanche after an item appeared; in fact, very few came because of a story in the paper.

Yet the word was passed around. One person told another. Much of the time, then, we had a guest or two with us; once in a while a larger number. We fit them into our life and continued as usual. We did not press anyone, but told them we got up at 3:00 A.M. and went directly to church. They always came. We put cowls on them and they took their turns at the psalms. When the hour was over, they did as we did and prepared themselves some coffee and toast and took it in silence. Then there was time to read or pray in one's cell, or the library, or the chapel. About six o'clock we rang the bell for lauds and Mass. After the thanksgiving there was a chance for a second cup of coffee, then we told them what work they could do if they wanted to help. They always did; some of them were very handy. At noon we all ate together, chatted, did the dishes. Then a short nap, after which someone went down with the dog to get the mail. The afternoon was free and quiet. No one bothered anyone else and it was a good time to study, to read, to pray, to work quietly if you wished, to take a walk. Around six we had psalms again and found something to eat afterward—something left over, or some soup or cereal—and the evening was ours, also in quiet. We were all asleep by 8:30 or 9:00. The owls and whippoorwills retired later.

The spirit was one of peace, of love. The place was friendly and warm. There was little tension, no fury. One did not get the feeling of aggression, violence, self-assertion. There was an aura of prayer. Yes, we made God evident; we erected a large wooden cross in the back field; there were shrines in the woods, icons on the walls, pictures, and mottos. But it was more than a pious place. The place was full of God. He was there before we were.

People loved it. We had little to do with it. God was there. Yet God is as much anywhere as he is there. Maybe people crowd him out. Drive him out, or drown his voice. Mostly in noise, in confusion, in din, in aggression and assertion. People seem to love fury and fight and angry words and contention. As do people of God. But God runs from such scenes.

Where there is quiet, there is God. And where peace is, and love. If God is dead, we killed him. And we killed him most of all with our noise, the noise of our fuming and agitation. We North Americans love violence and because it is directed against others, it does not lead to the kingdom. I don't think God can stand us when we are this way. He is afraid of us. He runs away. He hides.

There should be monasteries such as that in the Piedmont all over. Little communities of love. Small clusters of men, of women, of men and women who love peace, who cherish modesty. Small places, disposable places, dispensable—not expensive and impressive layouts. Places a peacock would enjoy, a dog, a dove, guinea hens, goats, sheep. Places where people pray—not elaborate, beautifully tailored prayer, but plain and simple, honest as the psalms.

For the life of me, I do not know why there are not many such centers.

There is but one necessary rule for small groups: adequate time to be alone. We all need space: temporal, psychological, geographical. Togetherness does not breed love. It tends rather to strengthen the notion that the problem is other people. Time to be alone guarantees commerce with God and one's heart; the former the source of all joy, the latter the source of all sorrow.

Monasteries are not out of touch. When people enter a monastery they take their hearts with them. In coming to know and understand one's own heart, in opening it to the Lord to reveal its ills, its poverty, its needs so that the Lord might heal it with his love, the monk is opening the heart of the world. What ails the monk ails everyone else. What ails humankind, ails the monk. Why is the person in monastic life any different? He or she comes from the same place. All the cloister does is open his or her heart to the mercy of God. And in coming to know his or her own heart, the person in monastic life comes to know the human heart of every person. If a human being is any kind of a monk, or nun, at all, he or she will be in touch with the times, not by virtue of *Time* and *Newsweek*, but through prayer. (Anyway, *The New Yorker* is better).

We all need contact with our hearts. Without that contact we are isolated from truth, divorced from reality. Quiet is certainly one of the ways to that contact. And peace. I suspect seriously that the single most effective weapon of Satan in our times is noise. I cannot think of a better way to alienation and loss of religion. Fill people day and night with noise, even beautiful noise. Allow them no time to think, to muse, to ponder, to wonder. Fill their air with sound, their ears with din. Their hearts will die soon enough. Now you have broken them. They can no longer love.

I conclude that it was the quiet peace of the Piedmont house that drew people to it, charmed them, filled them with joy. No one missed phone or radio or TV or stereo. We had a very good library, good papers and magazines, stimulating talks. And lots of quiet.

Once, in our concern for peace, and as a testimony of monastic concern for peace, I mentioned in passing to a peace-activist who was visiting the monastery that I had thought of making a pilgrimage on foot to Washington. I told her that the idea came to me from the custom of the local bishop, who, once each year, led his people on pilgrimages to the Virgin's shrine in that city. It seemed to me fitting that a monk should do the same, but on foot, for the cause of peace. Granted a monk should normally stay home, the gravity of the situation seemed to excuse something unusual, if a pilgrimage be considered unusual for a monk. At the time, peace people were very much discouraged, and she responded with such evident warmth that I could scarcely resist her pleading that I do it.

So I did. I left shortly after midnight on the sixth of August [1972, ed.], feast of the Transfiguration, anniversary of the atomic bombing of Japan. My plans were idealistic; I hoped to be able to walk by night and so avoid the heat, carrying a backpack with a small tent, sleeping bag, things for Mass, personal items. Perhaps I should have worn the Trappist habit—white robe and black scapular would have surely been visible—if I was so intent on giving witness, but I feared repercussions from superiors. The actual situation forced me to change things. Night walking turned out to be bad; it was either facing the glare of oncoming headlights or walking the rough shoulders in the dark. The backpack of forty-five pounds proved more than I could manage and after three days I gave that up; perhaps I might have been equal to it had my pace been more leisurely, but there was a distance of 250 miles to cover and I could not be gone too long. I slept a few nights in the tent, a few times in motels, in rectories of parish priests. I reached the outskirts of Washington in twelve days. I think it was a rather foolhardy idea. Highways, even old ones like Route 15, are no place for pedestrians, and the din of passing trucks was especially hard to take at close quarters. I had my Dalmation with me on a leash; she was good company all the way. The summer-sun was without mercy, so I had to dispense even with the short scapular I wore as a monk. At the end, a few reporters came out for a story and photos, a meeting arranged by my friend. When I was about half way, she had driven down to meet me to offer encouragement, just as a monk came up from the monastery to bring refreshments and a change of clothes. Once in the city I celebrated Mass in the National Shrine [now Basilica, ed.] of the Immaculate Conception with a group of Catholics in the peace movement. I had done a bit.

I was rather happy about having made the gesture, and somewhat pleased that I could still manage a good hike at the age of fifty-seven. Once the first two days were over, it was not at all difficult. The monks in other monasteries soon heard of it and were generally sympathetic, even if many had misgivings on how fitting it was for a cloistered monk. I shared their misgivings and understood when no one offered to accompany me when I invited them to do so.

Monastic life and peace go together. History makes clear that they have sometimes parted company, yet it grieves me that neither the Church nor monastic life is identified with peace, with nonviolence, especially in an age and a country as violent as our own.

The Piedmont was the kind of place that could permit such expressions of concern for peace. Larger monasteries, like institutions, have many aspects to consider, sometimes so many that the only solution to a question seems to be doing nothing at all. Perhaps the bishops as a group were ambiguous by trying too hard to be prudent, for beyond well-known exceptions, the Church's testimony for the Gospel of peace did not amount to much, and even that came late in the day. What action there was on the part of Catholics, and it was both vocal and sizeable, seems almost to have occurred in spite of the bishops.

There is now small point in warming over this history, except to indicate that the peace the monk knows in the heart, in community, is not some private garden. Christ builds it, and it is for those in monastic life to share in Christ's work of peace for all humankind. They cannot peer over the wall now and then and exclaim, "Oh, they're fighting again," and let it go at that, certainly not when the fighters assume that the blessing of the monks is with them. Yet, Thomas Merton, as an apostle of peace, was received among his brethren with about the same enthusiasm as by the People of God at large in our land.

It remains true. The monk's basic work for peace is in being a monk, in the pursuit of peace by the conquest of evil in one's own heart. There we touch the whole world. Peace is nowhere if not in the heart; it can take root in no other soil. By grounding one's own heart in Christ and peace, the monk, any person, anywhere, takes the fundamental stand, the basic one, the essential one. It is as such a peacemaker that the person is a joy to God and a blessing for the earth, a leaven in the whole mass.

Solstitial Ring

Five years after my original call to the solitary life, the abbot of Gethsemani resigned and we elected a new one. Not long after the latter took his seat, he asked me if I was still interested in becoming a solitary. I told him I was. We started talking about it, and a few months later he and his councilors agreed that I could go to New Guinea to live there alone. It was exactly twenty-five years since I had gone to New Guinea the first time.

Once it was clear to me that the way was open to a life of solitude, there remained only the matter of doing it. Yet, like most doings, this one too needed some symbolic expression which would at once say it and be it in ways both ambiguous and specific. I thought a ring was called for. I looked into the little jewelry shops in the local town and found a simple flat band: it was not silver as I wished, but white gold looked satisfactory and nothing else was available. An engraver inscribed it for me: *O Beata Solitudo* (O Blessed Solitude) on the outside; on the inside: Matthew Kelty—Gethsemani. The man who did the engraving smiled when he was done: "The name is familiar," he said, "I have some of your weaving on my living room wall. Your label is on it."

Then I asked the abbot if he would permit me to make a vow of solitude and put the ring on as testimony. He agreed. So, on June 24, feast of Saint John the Baptist, in the presence of the prior, I knelt before my father in Christ and spoke my vow, following a rite one of the monks put together for me. At the end I pronounced the words: "O Blessed Solitude, with this ring I do thee wed and plight to thee my troth." Then the abbot slipped the ring on my finger and it was done.

The date was fitting. I had made my first commitment to God in the same season thirty-two years earlier. On the very day, the feast of John the Baptist, I made my solemn profession as a monk of Gethsemani. Now, twelve years after that profession, made my pledge to the solitary life.

John the Baptist has always been a favorite of those in monastic life. His feast comes at the time when the sun first begins its journey down. We know this dying will lead to eventual life, and the monks see in the plunge into night their own way into the darkness of God. The inward journey has all the dressings of death, a decrease, which like death hides the truth of growth in life. John was prelude to Jesus also in this: there is no greater road.

Jesus in word and deed is almost violent in the call for death, for denial, for stripping, for abandoning, for letting go, for leaving all, for the journey up by going down. The monk, almost by instinct, looks to John, first in following after him on this new road. It is the way of contradiction, the endeavor to reconcile what cannot be reconciled. Yet, we all do it, all the time. There is no beat of the heart that does not attest by the very act, a trust that another will follow. Unless we are willing to release the air we hold in our lungs, there can never be a new breath or continued life. The tree must abandon its fruit, the farmers their seeds. Each night we lie down to die, sink into the depths with a hope of rising again. We could never let the sun set did we not believe it would reappear. This whole dialogue runs deep in us and all things. One could say, with complete honesty, that life is really no

than a series of heart-breaking good-byes, so full is it of
ng and letting go, of embracing and parting.

Love, then, is not merely clinging, but also releasing. The
womb must unbar its gates, the arms must relax, the fingers un-
bend. Yet, the faith that makes this possible is the faith that
makes life. God often leaves us because He loves us. The monk
knows that. John knew it. Jesus left his Mother many times over.
He left us all in the end. He does it all the time. Yet his leaving is
but the sun going down, the night coming on, the fruit falling
from the tree. For the sun will rise, day will return, the fruit
fallen and rotten will spring into life.

The ring on my finger bears witness: He will never leave
me, not really. And in the emptiness which is solitude, in the wild
night of the barren desert, he cannot hide from me. And even if
the sun should never rise and the night be without end, I will
still believe, even if I wait for all eternity. Though he never answer, I will yet knock, and knock again. He fools me not; I am
wise to him. I know him. I know he loves me, so I do not care
what he does. And in life without care, what joy of heart!

And in any case, in the tropics and south of the equator,
everything is something else again, for, come June 24, the sun begins to rise, not sink, it is on the way up, not down. Which is
what I have been saying all along.

Sea Route

*I*t seemed best not to make my journey to a hermitage in New
Guinea too hasty. Speed would not have been an appropriate
note with which to approach such a life, and I had no desire at
all to take a jet. It had to be by sea, but booking a passage was
not so simple as I had imagined. Freighters looked ideal; luxury
liners not. Yet the paucity of liners had made berths on freighters
very hard to find. It was by way of another's cancellation that I
sailed out of New York in November on a new container-cargo
vessel of the Farrell lines bound for Sydney via the Panama Ca-
nal.

It was a good trip on a good ship. Once under way, we
made but one stop, at Panama, twenty-two days in all. The Pacific is a mighty sea and we had ample time to attest to that. We
were twelve passengers, mostly retired people, lovers of the sea.

Ship life was quiet and restrained, the officers and crew friendly enough.

The ship was much like a monastery. There was good enclosure, better than the best of cloister walls. The captain made a worthy abbot, nor was a prior wanting, a subprior. Obedience was evident in practice, devotion to duty, to labor. The ship was no less on a journey than any monastery, and the presence of God was not subtle. True, there was no explicit praise of God, as one finds in every group of monks, yet his praise was there and I heard it. People of the sea live close to God.

As Saint Benedict notes in his Rule, guests were not lacking, and as the same Rule provides, we were hospitably received by the abbot; yet, like guests in any abbey, were something of a jarring note to officers and crew. We were alien and a distraction, full of silly questions; a disturbance, and a lot of work. I dare say they would sooner have had the ship to themselves, nor would I blame them. Over everything hung that same sense of unity that marks any monastic group, a being thrust together by some destiny that for a time made us one small world, one more solitary. We might just as well have been a lone mariner on a raft.

I caught myself calling the master an abbot, so close was the resemblance, nor was I far wide of the mark; he would have made a good one. Family life was wanting and, as in a community of monks, wives and children were not part of the scene, save among the guests—another factor that set the passengers apart.

Some think monasteries unusual and artificial. Rather, I find them as common and natural as a Greyhound bus crossing Kansas, or a subway crossing town, not to say a ship at sea.

There is no denying that the sea is a good metaphor of God. Its majesty and power stagger the mind of human beings. For the most part, this voyage was one of fair, mild weather, yet anyone who knows the Pacific knows its gift for violence and treachery. The sea can be cruel, relentless, without remorse or regret.

God is strangely like the sea. His ways are beyond fathoming, as was said long ago. Faith tells us of God's goodness and mercy; we believe. Yet, there is evil in the world; call it real, call it apparent. Nor is the world tidy. Innocent folk suffer much. Apart from death itself—no minor exception—there is much misery, most of it seemingly needless. There is no human being alive who cannot, from the brief span of his of her years and experience, relate an imposing number of tragedies that have touched those near, known to him or her. When one considers the world at large and its day-to-day story, one is stunned by the amount of suffering that exists. And even our own limited knowledge of history is one full of wretchedness for untold legions.

In the face of such a long-standing catastrophe one is hard pressed to sustain a faith in God's mercy and love. And most people have met individuals who have categorically rejected faith in God because of the very presence of so much evil about which he seems to do nothing.

It is always disturbing to meet fine people, blessed in mind and body and the goods of this earth, and after coming to know them more intimately, learn that sorrow and suffering have touched them, God's finger. One comes to realize, eventually, that all human life sometimes falls in his shadow, often dreadfully.

Spending hours looking out over the sea, I could not help telling her, "How beautiful you are! What a glory is yours! By day, by night, by moonlight, at sunrise and at sunset, what magnificence. But, ah, you treacherous one! I do not trust you. You would turn on me in a moment. You would gladly, happily devour me, and should the mood seize you, could so easily batter and beat this mighty vessel as to leave it a sinking shambles."

And yet the sea is like God. God is like the sea. Is it fair to say that? Proper? I do not know. I see God only as he comes to us. I realize in faith that God is supreme goodness and beauty. And I also realize that this is his world, that he sustains it and keeps it in being, that nothing happens without his knowledge and permission. I know his almighty will governs all things.

Yet, in the face of evil and the effects of evil, one is helpless. Only faith can sustain one.

Some priests stopped at the monastery one day and in the course of the conversation, the matter of evil, the devil, came up. They asked me if I believed in the devil, since I had already several times mentioned him. I said that I did, of course I did. It turned out that they did not, that they did not personalize evil, that they considered this an attitude of more primitive times, that they believed all evil came out of the heart of a person.

Perhaps. To be sure, all that fits more easily with our thinking, but it does not do much to answer the question of evil in the first place, and how it got into the heart of humankind. And one has to juggle Scripture very considerably to dismiss the devil, Satan.

For the moment I shall keep my belief in the devil. He is no great problem for me. His works are manifest. It is certainly just as easy, if not easier, to believe in the devil as in God. True enough, one needs grace to believe in God. We know Satan by his works, and they are all around us, in us.

The test of faith comes not so much in belief in God or belief in the devil as in God's toleration of evil. Why has he not banished evil from the earth? Or why has he not banished it from human hearts? I assume he does not will to because we do not want him to do so.

Evil does not float around in space. It is present only in our hearts. The evil that we experience in nature—in fire and wind and water—is a reaction to human hearts, a reflection of basic disorder and a desire to restore order. All things are tied together and when the human heart is not right, nothing is.

I have no doubt whatever that when the hearts of all people are renewed in Christ, the world itself will be renewed. But so long as evil abides in a human heart, evil is present on the earth and the earth will resist it.

Belief in Satan is not a projection outside myself, a convenient way of unloading my own guilt, my own evil. It is rather to postulate its source, the presence that my own heart shares insofar as it is allied to evil. The community of evil is some sort of union binding all who will to be so bound, affecting all hearts and the world we live in. Not to believe in this source and inspiration is simply to ignore the root because it is below the ground. It neither answers the problem nor disturbs it. It passes it by.

But faith also tells us that Christ has vanquished Satan and conquered hell and death. This means that despite the alarming impact that evil obviously has on the world and on me, its power is deceptive. Further, that the very pain, suffering, and death that we know, themselves become instruments of redemption for all humankind by virtue of Christ's undergoing them with us and for us. If Christ has known not merely human life and labor, human joy and happiness, but also human suffering and human death, then everything that Christ touched of life and labor, joy and happiness, suffering and death, has now been given a new character and a new quality.

The world has not changed much since Christ came. Things are pretty much the same. There are still earthquakes and cyclones and floods and famines. There is crime in high places and low. There is pain and death in every human family. The scene is not really all that different.

Yet, there is a difference. A total difference. Into that human maelstrom a divine life has been thrown which deprives evil of all its real power. What had led us to despair, to hatred of God, most especially to love of evil, now can lead us to salvation, own and that of the whole human family.

The Christian response to evil is thus dynamic. We do what we can to avoid it, but when it comes our way in whatever form, we are not overwhelmed by it, but rather overwhelm it in the grace of Christ, making of the very suffering the road to joy.

I rather feel that all people will be saved. It is at least possible that in the interval between life and death, before one steps into eternity, such light and grace may be given a person as to enable him or her to reject all evil, turn to God and goodness. I am particularly encouraged so to think in the face of so much suffering on the part of the innocent, of children.

The saints all embraced suffering, accepted it, bore it humbly for Christ and with him, in him. In so doing they aligned themselves with him in the salvation of humankind. Beyond the known saints, how many uncounted good men and women have borne pain for Christ's sake and so shared in his passion for humanity.

And beyond the end effect of participation in the ultimate triumph of good in the kingdom of heaven, the bearing of pain with Christ in this life is the greatest good we can do toward establishing the reign of Christ on earth, since such action removes the venom from suffering and turns it into a vessel of grace. It follows that the more hearts there are ennobled by grace, who enter on his way of pain to diminish the power of evil, the more quickly the end of evil on earth is brought about. It turns out, then, that union with Christ on his cross is the most fruitful means of hastening the coming of the kingdom. It is such a wisdom that led saints voluntarily to enter into suffering, pain, and death.

If evil is totally removed from the hearts of all, how could it be that nature would continue to revolt against the human race, and not instead reflect the goodness manifest there? We know from many legends of the holy men and women of God how animals responded to them with unwonted tenderness and affection, even animals otherwise violent. Such stories ought not to be dismissed too easily. Most of them are probably genuine.

Evil is a great mystery and manifests some great primeval conflict of which we know little save the results. We know, too, that through the ages the minds of men and women have struggled with this problem, a struggle that continues down to the simplest person on earth suddenly struck with catastrophe.

Job is a most excellent book, full of good food, pondering matter. The ancient problem of innocent suffering is there probed at length. We have the ultimate and most pertinent example of the innocent suffering in Christ, and know that in Christ's answer lies ours.

Our suffering, as often as not, has small relation to personal guilt. We are a guilty race and as such we suffer. Our guilt is communal, as is our suffering, and it is this very communal aspect that enables us to rise in faith to the awareness of our capacity to share in Christ's saving work for our brothers and sisters. We go to heaven together. Nothing is lost. Nothing wasted. The share that is ours does not, indeed, win heaven nor earn it, nor is it even necessary—anymore than Christ's passion and death were necessary. They were not. One word from Christ could have redeemed the world, but the Father's will was other. We can conclude that our suffering, too, is not necessary, but is in the Father's will. If we submit to the will of the Father, we submit to it in Christ and with Christ. Christ's agony in the garden was a complaint we may one day make our own if the Father's hand lies heavy on us and he permits Satan to buffet us. But in such submission we make possible our own share in glory, not ours merely, but a sharing by all.

There are not two principles in the world, one good and one evil. There are not two gods, one the Lord God, the other Satan. There is but one principle: good. There is but one God: the Lord. But the Lord God who is good is opposed, and this opposition is the existence of evil, personal evil. Further, this evil power was permitted to tempt human beings, and to this temptation we have succumbed. We have since suffered the consequences of that sin, in our own heart, in the hearts of all people, in the world around us.

Christ has entered into our human scene, become one of us, shared everything we have save evil, a gift we could not offer him nor he accept, since he is pure good. But he drives evil from our hearts if we will have him do so; he invites us to follow him in his bearing of suffering and death for others that the power of evil may be totally vanquished. The Christian is one who has received Christ into his or her heart and so is free of evil, possessed by the Good Spirit; one who freely takes on whatever suffering God's will presents, out of love for him and one's brothers and sisters throughout the world.

The many who suffer and die without awareness of Christ and his mercy do not suffer and die apart from him, we might k, but share in his work even if they are not aware of it. Certainly, the Christian so prays as an expression of his or her vocation in the world: a conscious participation in the redemption, a conscious entry into the conflict with evil, its conquest.

There is no question that evil is a great power and that suffering and death are most potent weapons in stimulating hatred for God, love of evil, despair. Further, we know that evil breeds evil, as violence breeds violence, crime breeds crime. Satan need never manifest himself, but simply permit the works of darkness to proliferate. Our enemy, then, is the evil one, to be driven first of all from our hearts, from the hearts of all, by Christ. The willing acceptance of suffering is, of all, most noble among the marks of the person of God, since it so perfectly relives Christ in his forebearance, nonviolence, nonresistance, patience, submission. The way of this world is flight from pain, refusal to bear wrong, rejection of suffering, hatred of death: a code of evil for evil, violence for violence; revenge, retaliation. The willing acceptance of voluntary deprivation and pain for the sake of the kingdom is the mark of the Christian.

The sea beats itself against a coral shore in New Guinea as it has been doing through countless ages. "Great sea, symbol of eternity on whose shores Christ stands and waits! Someday you will lose your cruel heart, you will be softened and made benevolent, no longer hostile to the human. Once our hearts are all renewed in Christ, you will be so rapt by their beauty that you will treat us all tenderly. On that day you will gladly support us when we walk on your waves. And should you become rough and unruly, one word from any of us will calm your waters, for you will willingly hear the sons and daughters of God."

The sea can wait, they tell us. Yes, and has been waiting, a long time.

Papua New Guinea

The bishop suggested a hilltop in Bogia as a site for my hermitage, the setting of the mission station before World War II. Since the missionaries' time on the hill had covered over forty years, it is likely to be well-equipped and attractive. The missionaries all remained when the Japanese forces overran the island and, although put under house arrest early enough, were decently treated until the tide of the war turned. Once that trend set in, brutality and cruelty became the rule and eventually they were either exposed to death or simply put to death. Over 150 of them were so to perish, including bishops, priests, Brothers, Sisters. And before all was over, little of the chain of mission stations along the coast, including the headquarters and cathedral near Madang, was left standing. The hilltop in Bogia was bombed bare.

When the missionaries returned after the disaster, they decided to settle on the shore at the edge of the coconut plantation, even though that meant giving up the splendid view, the breeze. The people had grumbled about the arduous climb.

A complete station was built down on the coast: church, rectory, guest house, convent, many classrooms, houses for teachers, store, workshop; a decent wharf, storage sheds, house for the plantation manager, garage. The total is no doubt more impressive than the former complex, though the old one was more conspicuous; the church tower was visible far out to sea.

My reaction to the bishop's suggestion was hearty; I liked the idea very much. For one thing, I was concerned about being assigned a bush station in a rather remote area that had become somewhat depopulated. There has been considerable movement of the people closer to the shore road and also to the towns. The road means access to stores, to work, to government centers, to the open market. Yet, the departure of many does not leave a village empty; the places are not abandoned, and former inhabitants return frequently to look after gardens and houses, to keep in touch. My being given a house in such a situation would thus involve me in mission work and, as a monk, I had not come for that. This had already been agreed to before I arrived, was a condition made essential by my abbot. It is true, I would not have objected to some modest involvement, but the dimensions that modesty suggests are not precise. It would be simpler to have no ministry at all.

This approach put my role in rather strong terms, and I was aware of that. On the other hand, I had made no effort to ascribe to my time in New Guinea any practical value. The monk, the monastery, has no evident use. The uses they do have and have had are not an essential aspect. If monks of past ages have been agents in the preservation or furthering of art and culture, a civilizing influence, this is not their prime role. True enough, guests of an abbey are generally impressed, but the impression is as likely as not to be a reflection of their own values. Monks are not too moved by praise of their skill in agriculture or art or manufacture or even liturgy; even, if the facts warrant it, for being people of peace and love. Those in monastic life live for God. Any appraisal of their life that is not referred directly to God is in some way impertinent. I suppose the ideal monk would be unknown to anyone and therefore not subject to human judgment.

To go to a mission land, then, where the life of the Church is evident in a vast ensemble of activities carried on by zealous workers for the kingdom of God, with nothing further in mind than prayer on a hilltop, some work in a garden or in the woods, some reading and study, hours of psalmody—all in a setting removed from day-to-day life—is bound to raise some serious questions. I see no way of avoiding that.

The monk's vocation is in the emphatic dedication to the praise of God, the study of God, the awareness of God. This is to deal with a set of values other than the works of mercy, though not to set them aside. No one ever said that the monk's life was total Christianity, nor the perfect following of Christ, nor the model for all. It is a misunderstanding to construe those in a monastic life as the ideal Christian or to endeavor to fit them into such a frame.

The monk gives body to one aspect of the Christian life, and that is prayer, particularly prayer in solitude. The monk is with Christ on the mountain alone at night, with Christ in the forty days in the desert, in the garden of Gethsemani, in the hidden years. But those in monastic life are not his companion in the ministry, in his preaching the word of God, in the healing, in his miracles, or even in his passion and death. The Christ at prayer is the monk's Christ and everything follows from that, though what follows may well include ministry, preaching, miracles, passion and death, should God so will.

No one can follow Christ in everything, but one can follow Christ with a particular attention to an aspect of his life. Without doubt, most Christians follow him in the hidden life, not the public one. Some are put to death with him and for him. Some preach his word. Some heal. Some minister. Most pray, at least at times. Practically all Christians, though, work for a living in the bosom of a family love, and follow Christ in those very years to which he gave most of his life.

It is true, we do not take Christ apart; that we follow him, not a portion of him. Christ is whole and cannot be divided. Yet, in our accompanying him we are with him sometimes visibly and sometimes not, most often not. For all that, we are with him incarnate, working, preaching, praying, healing, condemned, dying, rising, and ascending to glory. Very few, perhaps no one except the Mother of our Lord, knew him from the beginning to the end. Even those who were intimately associated with him were close to him only for a brief time, and even among them, some more briefly than others. Those who walked in his ways then, now, and all through the centuries have been beyond all counting, as have their manners of doing so.

The service of Christ cannot possibly be tied down to one or the other or several as more appropriate One does what one is called to. One does what one can. The basic call is to holiness, and holiness like Christianity, can be found anywhere, works anywhere. It had just better, for if we are going to wait until the world is fit to live in, we may be a long time waiting. It is better, it seems to me, to do what we can with what we have, and make the best of it. It is possible that our sanctification lies in precisely that, not in a better world that never arrives.

In being a monk, I assert my right to be myself and to do as I see fit. Or more aptly, to do as God wants me to do. Or more practically, to do the only thing I am able to do. Even if I choose to do nothing, who is to correct me? Anyone with eyes to see is aware that most human action has its element of corruption, that often what is done for the glory of God is heavy on glory and light on God. I fail to be unduly impressed with action and I use pragmatic norms in arriving at that impression; the results justify it. What goes on in the heart seems to me at least as important. Privately, I think it is more important.

Christ did nothing worthwhile for thirty years. One carpenter more or less in Nazareth could scarcely have mattered. For all practical purposes, they were wasted years. And it is precisely to that kind of waste most people are called. And even within the scope of his few public years, Christ was wont to waste further time by running off to the hills when there was work to be done. Even in the few years he did apostolic work, as we call it, he reached few, healed fewer, and in the end succeeded only in raising so much opposition and ill-will that they put him to death.

In all of that I see no justification whatever for the notion that work for God necessarily means a life of feverish action, back-breaking labor, constant tension and concern. This may lead only to mental, physical, and spiritual exhaustion. Neither the plan nor the result seems Christian. It may perhaps be no more than Western aggression and drive transferred to religion. It is more horrible to look at there than elsewhere.

Men and women of God are thus not necessarily all that concerned with God for reason of much bustle. They may be, but it is not the bustle that proves it. The lack of this bluster, then, can scarcely be said to be the issue, or the presence of it. Or, simply, what we do matters very little. It is not where the action really is.

God is still God. I have been on earth almost 60 years [now almost 80, ed.] and the majority of that time in his official service and I don't even know him. I've not begun to begin to understand him, to relate to him. I've spent half a lifetime doing what they told me to do, pouring myself out in a frenzied effort to produce, to deliver, to come up with results. The total result of all this seems, in terms of anything that can be measured, a zero. And in terms of my own inner fruit, the same: nothing.

Take your good works and be gone with them. I'll take my flute, the stars at night, my few books, the psalms. I'll manage somehow. And if I am forced to, I'll not hesitate to come beg an alms from you. In any case, I feel I was an arrogant monster full of ego, determined to provide salvation by dint of projects and programs of every sort. I've had enough for the simple reason that God was a diminishing factor in all of it. I am now headed in the opposite direction and have sworn to stay with it. I do not know whether I have found God, but I have found peace.

The bishop is all for it. He has given me this hilltop with the glorious view and has promised me a little house: two rooms, one a chapel, one to live in. Surely the most impressive feature is the water tank to hold the rain falling on the corrugated iron roof.

A sundial is on the way. We had one at the Carolina monastery, set up for a remembrance of the bishop's visit there two years prior. He blessed it during the rainy aftermath of a hurricane on the feast of Saint John the Baptist, summer solstice. I am hoping he will be able to come bless this house on the hill on the same feast this year, blessing the sundial too—our symbolic link with the cosmos. The day would be appropriate, for John the Baptist is a patron of monks.

Meanwhile I have a small cottage down here at the edge of the mission compound and manage well enough. I take my meals with the group, no monk's fare, but plain enough. For the rest, I have spent time on the hill, clearing it of jungle with the help of four local men from the area I used to work in years ago. The spot now looks ready. I follow the routine we had at the little monastery and find the psalms more apropos than ever in this new situation. The sea is at my door, the surf a persistent background, and around me lots of coconut palms, especially picturesque in these past nights of the paschal moon.

Each passing hour of the day is another kind of beauty, for the sun here is astonishingly bright and all colors most intense. Through the palms I see Manam, a volcanic island twelve miles to sea. Occasionally she spouts dark fumes from her depths, secrets from her heart that drift still unrevealed across the sky. The shoreline is a series of low hills, some wooded, some grassy, with palms along the beach. There is generally a soft mist in distant scenes, and rain clouds seem always to be gathering or scattering in some area of the sky. Now and then they come over, drench everything, and pass on to give the sun domain. The whole scene, in fact, is so moving that I wonder if I am not too handsomely set. And the top of the hill is still more of a spell.

I do not know what will come of it all. I really do not care one way or other. Possibly some of the people here will be interested; maybe not. It does not really matter. There are no other monks in New Guinea, though there are contemplative nuns up the coast at Aitape and also in Port Moresby. Their convents are impressive.

No one could know at this juncture, but it does strike me that coming alone may have been wiser than I thought. Had a group come, even a small one, they would have been more acceptable. In no time at all they would have built a respectable monastery, probably with library and guest house, and set up some form of income—industry, such as a cocoa or coffee plantation, a craft of one kind or other, a dairy herd for butter to sell— all bound to confirm everyone in the opinion that these monks had their feet on the ground and knew what they were doing. Which is to say, the whole thing would have made a bad beginning. One man, without resources, unable to throw weight because he has none, may be taken less seriously, but the emphasis on prayer and solitude will be there, and if that raises questions, the questions are at least relevant.

The primitives live in a world open to the spirit, and my suspicions are that monastic life will mean much to them— though a monastic life adapted to climate and culture, preferably lived in solitude. Solitude is not, I believe, a common element among them, nor even appreciated: the loner is often feared as one possibly endowed with superior magical powers; but a secluded community given to a life of prayer, simple labor, reading, might be a form of life they would find appealing. The Western Church has inadequate outlets for the mystical here too, so an opening in the way of the contemplative life appears called for. Perhaps it is too soon. That would not distress me. I feel God has called me here, so I shall simply live as a monk, and sowing that seed, let come of it what may, now or later. Personally, I have no desire whatever to lead a community, let alone found one, but if that is God's will, perhaps I could adjust to it until someone else comes along.

Out on a reach of the hill to the rear of my place is a small cemetery, almost completely invisible for overgrowth. We cleared it enough to be able to get to it and about in it. There are two priests, three Brothers, two Sisters buried there, going back to 1904. Three of them lasted but one year in New Guinea; in those days blackwater fever was a menace and many succumbed. I have company on the hill, thus, and find a certain comfort in their presence and in our assured relation in God.

I am not the first Cistercian in the area. Monks from an abbey in eastern Europe were here at the turn of the century with a view to founding a house. One of them was killed in neighboring New Britain in a native uprising and that seems to have been the end of the project. I would hope my venture comes to a different term, yet God leads us in odd ways, not loath to beckon us down blind alleys and up dead ends, but there is wisdom in his madness. A certain wry trust and bemused tolerance are called for in order to keep the heart light and the steps free. In the end, all will come out well, just as the lady Julian said in Norwich a long time ago.

One Way

Almost anything can be a way to prayer. Like a motorcycle. I am not sure this is one of the recommended methods, but it is for a person to learn for himself or herself what best leads him or her to God.

What is it about a motorcycle? Surely not the noise (they need not be used that noisily). Nor the power. Nor even the expense. It is more than a matter of gas economy and quick, easy transport. No, there is some mystic dimension that escapes no one. There is a fascination in a motorcycle that has deep roots. It surely has something to do with solitude. It is obviously related to the matter of journey, of pilgrimage. There is some quality of exposure, of risk, of total commitment that is evident to a remarkable degree in this medium.

It was a long time coming for me, for conditions made it altogether impossible. But one day everything fell together and I was mounted.

Is this a good way to make love? I do not know. I know only that for me it was. I have long tried to discover why it was so, and do not yet really understand. If I do not know myself, it would follow that I could not understand why I do the things I do. But there are things we do, even when we do not know why, that we feel to our depths are right. One knows when one is in love.

Not in love with a motorcycle, but in love. There is palpable poetry here, so evident that I am sure someone somewhere must have written of it. But I have never read of what I know.

What is it about leather? Again, I do not know. I managed not merely leather boots, but leather jeans (white) and shirt and jacket as well; and helmet and gloves. Is it wrong to feel they were vesture?

There are motorcyclists, I know, who never seem to go anywhere and do little more than roar around a certain neighborhood. And I know, too, there are unsavory groups who frequent highways in some locales. And there are those small bands who travel together, those who gather for racing or cross-country cycling of a hazardous nature as a form of sport or competition. But I am concerned with the lone cyclist one passes on the road now and then. I think this is the one closest to the secret of it all.

What is it about going down the road alone, open to wind and weather, up and down hills, around sweeping curves, so free, yet so much disciplined to a skill that makes the whole enterprise a magnificent form of play? The play that prayer is kin to. There can be little to compare with a lonely night in the rain, with lightning sometimes breaking the sky, distant thunder rumbling over the drone of your motor. Can anything equal the passage through mists in the mountains by night, riding into the chill dawn, the rising sun?

It is not that you see so much beauty—the sea, the dangerous bridges, the rolling country—but that you are part of it, share in it. You are not shielded from it, removed from its influence and impact. The wind pressing your clothes tight to your body, the life of the engine between your legs, the quivering meeting of the wheels and the road—all of it together releases some song of joy from the heart in a liturgy of thanks. Song on the way, thanksgiving for life.

For it is true, we journey. There is not one of us who is not on the way. We know when the trip began, we do not know when it will end. Nor do we know where it will lead us, what we will encounter on the way. We do know, in faith, whence we come, and, please God, where we go. We know that on the way his word and his sacrament sustain us, keep us going. We know that often the road is difficult, sometimes impossible, just as we know it is sometimes pleasant, happy. We know, too, that it is a communal journey, a community pilgrimage to some Holy City. We are all making it, we are all making it together. Even though I am all alone on the back of my machine, my solitude is shared by all. I am no more alone than anyone else, no one more lonely than I am.

What is that wholeness that makes a person one flesh? There are many forms of union, but the ultimate union is that totality of all that I am, that oneness of soul and body that is an image of the union to come, in which God and I are one. There is no earthly love that does not in some way describe the whole that everyone is called to, is not again symbolic of the nuptials to come in which God and I will be wed.

And that marriage will be the union of all humankind in God, a community of love in which we will both disappear and find ourselves. There is no love in which one would not gladly die, be totally submerged, no love in which I would not all the same be, and be forever.

The lone cyclist on the road is not alone at all. Instead it is a matter of one person of the community of the lone on their way to the King's City. This loneness is a seeming one, no more real than is the community created by a gathering of people in a coliseum. Love makes one whole and when one is whole, one is united to all. It is in the depths of the heart that we discover not only our own humanity, but all human nature and humankind.

There is some spouse within we must meet, and failing that, fail wholeness. It is not enough to be charitable, to be busy in the works of love, however splendid and generous. There is in the heart of us all some image of the Beloved we must not merely acknowledge, but know, love, embrace. Without this marriage there can be no real human life. The human being was not born to live alone.

But this is a mystic love, not a carnal one, a love born of poetry and music, nurtured by tenderness and compassion. Yet it is a love won only at terrifying cost and hard labor. There is an exploit involved here which is of greater import than any external act. Indeed, the external act can have small value unless it be transferred to the inner scene and made effective thus.

The meeting of the bride within is not had merely for the asking. Her hand must be won; love of her must be proven. Heroic effort is taken as a matter of course. She dwells beyond dark mountains and deep abysses, dangerous and difficult to cross.

Notwithstanding, many find her, and these are the people who have truly lived. It is these who know God and who will see his face because they know what love is. The mystery of life is in winning the beloved and union with her, for in their union one discovers God.

Why is it so difficult? Why should it be so heavy a labor to find God, know love?

I would suppose because we are so timid. We are fearful, fearful most of all of the truth. It is the truth that shall make us free, but at that price many would rather not be free.

We can be redeemed only if we want to be and no one will want redemption unless they know how much they need it. But we will never know this unless we are willing to look at our own face and into our own heart. And that is the reason we fear silence. And quiet. And solitude. For in that light we see light. And seeing it, take flight, sometimes excusing ourselves, often not.

And that is why you take the Gospels with you on your motorcycle, for in the Gospels we meet mercy. And it is Christ's mercy that encourages us to be unafraid of darkness, of rain, of storm, of mist and mountain. Or the face of evil.

No one looking into his or her own heart will do so long before confronting not merely evil, but the power of evil. No one knows his or her own truth unless he or she is fully aware that he or she is perfectly capable of any evil. The potency is in all. More than potency. Also the practice, the degree often enough being limited only by good fortune, good luck, and the grace of God.

One had best not enter into that wasteland without being armed with the Gospels. It is precisely in them that Christ is portrayed as mercy incarnate come to save human beings from their own hidden darkness.

You can learn a great deal on a motorcycle. For that matter, you can learn anywhere. Life is all mystical. There is another dimension to everything. All things can speak to us of God. That often enough they do not is because we do not permit them to. Do not want them to.

We complain about the darkness, yet will not light one candle lest we see what sort of creatures we are. We prefer illusion. Yet, to live with illusion is not to live at all. In any case, the truth we will not see within us will inevitably take shape before our eyes in the world around us. The chaos and disaster we refuse to acknowledge within will thus take revenge on us and become evident everywhere.

The Redeemer of the world walks unheeded our trafficked highways, unseen, unrecognized. No one needs a Redeemer. It's as simple as that. If they needed him, they would see him, for even the blind know his presence. They do not need him because they are not real and live in an unreal world, divorced from the truth. In an unreal world, reality does not exist.

So to live is not to live, for it is to live without love. The divine life within has never been known. The dark monsters that hide his presence are not faced, are not overcome. One lives in fear and dread of the truth, one is not free. In which case, never get on a motorcycle.

The Monastic Influence

*M*ost people do not think of seminaries as monasteries, but there are very real similarities, for monastic influence has made a deep impression on Catholic life. The prayer of the diocesan priesthood has long been similar to that of monks, if not identical, even though recited privately and not in choir. It was not long ago that parish churches had Vespers, and cathedrals often had a Divine Office similar to that of monks, sometimes sung by monks or the near equivalent. Perhaps the priest's cassock is derived from the cowl or robe.

The seminary in which I was educated for the missionary priesthood was in many ways like a monastery. In fact, when I entered Gethsemani, I found the similarity striking. In certain ways, in fact, the seminary was more of a monastery; there we had our own wheat fields, ground our own flour, made our own bread. We had a huge herd of milk cows and steers and hence our own butter and beef. We smoked our own sausage, bacon, ham. We had a large apiary and always had honey on the table. We had a large poultry farm and a set of shops for electrical, mechanical, and woodworking projects. If we did not have monastic enclosure, we had a reasonable facsimile. In my eight years there I was home for my father's funeral and my first Mass, seventy-two hours' leave in each case, and received one visit from my sister and one from my brother. We had our share of silence and seclusion. So there were similarities. The monks at Gethsemani had, in fact, long since given up their mill and their chickens, and their milk went for cheese.

Years later, when renewal [of religious life, prompted by Vatican II, ed.] came about, many seminarians were explicit in their desires to shed monastic influences, insisting quite rightly, I think, that they were not monks and were not meant to be. Neither are diocesan priests, though, like monks, they are celibate.

It is the questions of celibacy, monastic life, seminaries, that interest me. I rather suspect that a flaw in seminary life, as I knew it, was not that it was monastic, but that it was not monastic enough, or not monastic in the right way. I would say the same of diocesan seminaries.

It seems to me that seminaries have copied monastic observance and have suffered from the same omission as do monasteries: the lack of emphasis on solitude.

Certainly the measure of solitude to which some diocesan priests are exposed is a great deal more than the average monk knows. Many priests live alone. In the case of the missionary priest, he knows double solitude, since he not only often lives alone, but in a foreign land, an exile.

When seminaries did not pick up the solitary note in the monastic tradition, they perhaps missed what was most necessary, most useful. It is a difficult thing to live alone. One needs to be educated to it. I think few seminarians receive such help. Most priests seem to know little of the spiritual aspects of solitude, and I know that for missionaries, solitude is a very serious problem.

If the monastic life, especially through Merton, has recently begun to rediscover the values of solitude, perhaps seminaries ought to look into the matter as well. It is best to talk simply. If a young man has a passionate interest in women, he usually does not enter a seminary or a religious order. The idea does not enter his head. If the idea does come, we may assume that marriage does not strike him as essential to his happiness. All things are possible, so perhaps by reason of his milieu or his upbringing, the state of his mental health, or some romantic disaster, a man may venture into the celibate state with inadequate attitudes. It will be best for him if he is not accepted, or later discouraged from continuing, if he does not come to that conclusion himself. It would seem, though, that the usual candidate for the celibate state feels that for the love of God he could forego marriage.

This may perhaps mean that the presence of the anima within him is already so strongly manifest that he does not feel the need for an actual relationship with a woman in order to reach wholeness. There have always been such men, and I suppose there always will be. Often enough, it is among them that a culture will find its poets, its artists, its dreamers, its prophets, priests, seers. In a sense they are a breed apart, but in another sense they are a figure of the person to come, since they already have an initial grasp of an integrity that is humankind's destiny, that union of all forces in ourselves that makes us truly one. Every person is called to such an inner wedding, but to some it is a call to work out that union with Christ, not by physical love, but by mystical.

This is not an easy road to walk and it is full of dangers. Further, one needs counsel and inspiration in following it. Hermits learned early the wisdom of converse with a holy elder experienced in the ways of the heart, and monks soon joined one another in fraternal love the better to sustain the solitary endeavor. Yet, solitude remains the core experience, and one called to this state, no matter what the external circumstances, will always feel somehow as one apart and probably knows it has always been like that.

Yet in an age as opposed to the feminine as our own, such a person faces formidable difficulties. If we are the products of an environment that stresses reason, law, order, science, achievement, aggression, violence, self-assertion, organization, institution—there the anima is going to be driven deep and even beyond reach. What sort of person or what sort of culture this leads to we need not imagine, since we have only to look around us, but for the one called by God and apparently by nature to the inner union, the problems are real and immediate. The society that has small regard for woman is no help at all for man trying to come to terms with the feminine within himself.

By reason of an inner experience of the feminine, a man may sense no exceptional longing for physical union with a woman, and still be at a loss to know what to do with his own being. In a sensuous age he may simply drift into sexual union with his own kind, particularly if he is exposed to this before he has had adequate time to understand himself. It is no great grace to know too much too soon.

If the mystic dimension has all but vanished from our world, where are such people to turn? For it is to the mystic they are called. And the mystic has also nearly vanished from the church. The monastic life itself, nurturing ground for the mystical life, often turns to practical matters like education and missions, emphasizes prowess in farming or in marketing products, or expresses itself in arduous labor, grim discipline, or a difficult interpretation of the rule.

The scene is changing, to be sure. Merton certainly helped change it. There must needs be some rediscovery of the mystical, and solitude is a basic factor in that discovery. Yet one scarcely hears it given that much emphasis in monasteries, still less in the education of priests for congregations and societies or the dioceses of the Church. The figurative espousal of priest to Church is passed over.

Yet, it remains important, if difficult. Even in the contemplative life one senses that fresh attitudes and new approaches may fall wide of the mark and settle for more genial communities, less challenging demands, and a somewhat unconscious or instinctual avoidance of solitude. Fear of women is not unknown to men, and the contemporary prevalence of strong women is small help, for a consequent rise of gentle men will produce those who tend to lean on them rather than meet them and relate fruitfully to them. It is necessary to be a man to begin with, yet if man does not relate to woman he cannot develop. Man simply cannot live without woman.

Solitude is no easy answer, but it is a way to an inner dialogue that a man eventually must enter into if he is to become a person, one capable of great love.

Merton was pleased by the monks' moving into private cells built where the open dormitories used to be. They provide privacy, quiet. His overall impact on the monastery could likely be summed up in that: the place is quieter. It is true, the concept of silence is less rigid, there is dialogue and discussion, responsibility for material wealth, and a great deal less frenzy over work and production. Some concern for communal love is perhaps undeveloped, but there can be no doubt the monastery is a center of peace and of joy. With access to the woods and fields, with a scattering of little refuges and huts, there is ample scope for times of solitude, and Father Louis's former hermitage is regularly used for longer periods of retreat. All this is directly linked to interiority, and given time will manifest itself in a depth of charity and compassion, tolerance, and a spirit of prayer.

Once we have passed through our own inner darkness and moved on to the realm of the bride within, our sense of identity with the human family must be so intense that our very presence should convey it. To such a journey we are called, and called in particular are they who respond to the celibate life. These are the poets of the human family. They sing our love songs. What is more important than that a people have singers of songs, men and women gifted with magic words and mystic insights lest the rest of us famish along the way?

Some experiments are being conducted in new modes of both seminary study and seminary life. I know little of them, but there does seem a less intense community life, greater personal responsibility, genuine commitment to study. That the young are thrown much more on their own, must face issues and work out solutions, manage their lives—this is in the direction of solitude.

Bonhoeffer sometimes makes disparaging remarks about monasticism, yet when he was entrusted with the training of a group of seminarians, he gathered them in a small remote setting and established them at Finkenwalde in a community of prayer, work, and study that was very much a monastery. By reason of his influence on them and the quality of the life they lived, the period proved to be a rich spiritual experience for all concerned. These influences of meditation, silence, seclusion, in a framework of a community of love and worship, were as profound as in any real monastic community and remained with the participants all their lives. This experiment deserves attention and may indicate precisely what was originally intended in the modeling of seminary training in the Church on the monastic style of life, where monastic observance is not enough, or even required.

A few years ago I briefly visited the seminary where I had been educated; it was just prior to its transfer to a university campus and the students had been involved that season and some seasons previously with a form of controlled-environment encounter in which small groups tried to help one another discover his own truth.

At the time I could not help admiring their courage. As a monk I could understand what they were doing, though, as I told them, the method seemed harsh and perhaps dangerous, even if some profited much from it. The monk's method is slower, more gentle, but the end result is the same, at least at that stage. The monastic ascesis would lead one to a knowledge of the truth, the beginning of all growth in the spirit. Certainly the awareness these students had of the need to know their own truth, the price they were willing to pay for it, says a great deal.

One hopes they can continue further, not merely in finding new and effective ways to truth, but also into the mysteries of solitude and the life of prayer. Perhaps some students of Jung could help them. The question of celibacy is discussed often on too shallow a level, and surely so if the mystical level is dismissed. To do that is to reduce celibacy to an act of prowess which as likely as not can end only in ruining the person. Celibacy without a deep love affair is a disaster. It is not even celibacy. It's just not getting married. And the world has enough such people, married and otherwise.

Psalmody

*I*t is a great pity that psalmody has all but disappeared from the life of the Church. Beyond some monks and nuns who chant the psalms and the use of psalms in the prayer of priests, these prayers seem not much in use save for a certain role in the Eucharist. One could hope for a return to this form of prayer, if for no other reason than its special appropriateness for our own times. [Today, as a result of the reform and renewal set in motion by Vatican Council II, there is much more interest in and appreciation for the Liturgy of the Hours as the prayer of all Christians, ed.]

After the Our Father, we have no finer prayers. They are, to begin with, part of Scripture and therefore the word of God. Their use through Christian centuries and back into the days of the Old Law is a sort of perduring note that continues to be heard into our own time, even if more feebly. A return to the psalms is a return to deep prayer, scriptural prayer, human prayer.

The fright that people sometimes experience on picking up the psalter and uttering its words may perhaps express a kind of naive understanding of the human heart's mysteries. The psalms strike one with their frankness, their passion, their dipping into violence and wildness. Put side by side with what we think of as fitting forms of prayer, they appear primitive and extravagant, removed from the restraint and measure of the Our Father, the Hail Mary, the Magnificat, or the Benedictus.

Sometimes even monks are shocked at the language of the psalter and go so far as to delete what they feel to be inelegant verses, indeed, even to passing over whole psalms. They find the words out of place in their mouths. Many would join them in this attitude and prefer to think of the psalms as an interesting form of ancient religious poetry, but one ill-suited to contemporary people. Others dismiss them airily as simply not Christian and consequently not proper to our spiritual life as the followers of Christ. Yet, if the psalms are not Christian, it must be remembered that our hearts are not either, certainly not wholly. And granted even that our hearts be totally imbued with Christ and his spirit, it remains that the Lord himself used the psalms in prayer and commended us to look to them if we would learn of him.

I would suppose our lack of contact with the landscape of our own hearts leads us to assume that the psalms are not pertinent. Yet, if the world scene is so much one of chaos and fright, this scene is but a revelation of the human heart and its fruit.

If we listen to our dreams, if we remain still in the dark of night, if we are available to the evidence that rises from deep within us in moments of quiet, of pondering, not to say hours of anguish or sudden grief, we must conclude that any assumption that innocent tranquility is the character of the heart is unfounded.

In our own heart's depth we touch not merely a capacity for total good and total evil, but in some way, too, reach the whole heart of humankind and all that courses through it. It is perfectly true that all humankind lies hidden in the depths of every human being.

Yet this contact with total reality, our own and the human family's, is not something everyone is willing to make or to endure. It is understandable. Generally we have had enough to do with evil in our own lives to make us extremely wary about further evidence in that direction. Further, we may have so structured some sort of style, a set of things done and not done, that we are not able to risk this flimsy make-do in the face of what seems to be overpowering or even inimical forces. In fact, we may earnestly consider it our moral duty to avoid doing so.

The result of such living, however, may lead only to an artificial, brittle total that both we and others vaguely sense to be somehow unreal. And this sentiment may lead us to even more staunch efforts to hold our own.

This may be living, but it is not a way that makes real prayer a possibility. Prayer is rooted in reality. If we are screened from reality, our prayers are bound to be formulas. And since prayer is a form of love, it is not too much to say that in such a manner of life even love is inhibited and stifled, despite sentimental icing.

The peculiar lack of compassion and mercy that is often a quality of a good person may stem from this situation. If I do not know myself truly, then I take for my reality what I choose. The choice may be excellent and impressive, but it cannot possibly last, for it is but stage scenery.

When people given to living on a stage set are offered the psalms for personal prayer, their reaction can only be one of alarm, perhaps hidden by irritation or boredom, for a cagey instinct will warn them. The psalms walk backstage at once.

The psalms, prayed with Christ, can lead us to the truth and in the truth to freedom. The road to freedom is a good road, but it is not always pleasant going. It ends on the hill. There is true death in the act of becoming born free, just as there is true resurrection made possible in the rising of Christ. It is no small matter to look on as one's dreams and illusions are shattered, one's carefully erected setting demolished by an expert in a few deft moves. An empty stage and an empty theater become some great chasm full of the echoes of past make-believe. So seems our heart then.

Nor is that all. For the very theater which is our world is not merely empty and hollow, but its actual fabric begins to fall apart before our eyes, exposing us to the whole universe. We are totally overwhelmed by the outer darkness, nor is there any place to hide, for it is a darkness of penetrating light and insight. Our reaches are infinite, our capacities without limit. One stands nude before God, knowing God knows.

That is the reason we must always pray the psalms with Christ; or better, let him pray them in us. With him we can oppose the powers of darkness and evil, with him walk the way of God's will, with him pray to the Father for the triumph of good in my heart and every heart.

Until I have some hint of the inner scene, any exchange with my neighbor is bound to be shallow. I can reach only that depth in him that I can reach in my own spirit. If my self- perception is artful and hedgy, so will my hedginess approach his heart. It follows, too, that I will sense immediately when someone sees more deeply into me than I do, and will fly to my defense with vigor, a defense usually made effective by counterattack. Yet, once I come to accept the truth and join the human family, the futility of mutual sparring and jockeying becomes evident. It seems pointless to be determined to manifest superiority, to search out weakness, to take advantage of lapse and slip. Compassion is born only of my own passion, not another's. It is not to be had otherwise. Only those who have been ill can speak the healing word. If you do not know how it feels, this lack will be glaringly evident to one who does. And this has nothing to do with achievement, accomplishment, superb prowess. It is much more negative than that. Much more passive. It is something you let happen to you rather than do. It is a submission to truth.

It is precisely in this climate of truth and reality where we savor the poverty and frailty of humankind, our guilt, our capacity for evil, that we come to understand Christ as Redeemer and Savior. Christian life then begins.

It is good to pray the psalms. It is good to pray all of them, in order as they occur, for the moods of the psalms are more varied even than our own, come home more readily when we do not seek to match their tone to ours. In the small monastery in Carolina we used to read the psalms aloud, slowly, quietly. One read; the others sat still and listened. After a few minutes, another would continue with the next psalm, and so on. We read the whole psalter in the course of a week, one psalm after the other, dividing them roughly into three portions for each day; a generous one for the middle of the night, one at sunrise, one at sunset.

Dawn and dusk are obviously fitting times for prayer, marking the beginning and the end of creation, of time, of life. The night has long been favored as uniquely suited for prayer, for making love. And let not the place be too brightly lit, for one should be aware of the dark, the stars, and of the wind, mystery. Do not make a project of it. Perhaps it is better to let the psalms speak as they may; we should merely voice them. In time, we discover that we ourselves are speaking through these poems, or more aptly, that Christ is praying them with us, in us. Sometimes our heart is not quite in it. No matter, one keeps on. The heart will catch up later on.

At the monastery we used to add a portion of reading from the Scriptures; from the Old Testament at night, from the New during the day. Again, we took the books and Gospels and letters as they came, reading as much as seemed to make a coherent selection. It is good to hear Scripture read aloud, all of it, or to do it alone if one's prayer is solitary. And to understand the significance of our spiritual journey, nothing is better than going through the pages of the Old Testament, while as Christians, we cannot live without communion with Christ's word. It is especially the Gospels that explicate the psalms.

The earliest monks spent a great deal of time with the psalms. As monastic life flourished, as communities developed, so did styles of reading and chanting the psalter. Eventually, antiphonal singing of the psalms by facing choirs became customary, the psalms lending themselves without difficulty to this practice since they are poetry and often express their ideas in couplets. The quality of the accompanying chant was long known for its spirituality. With the passage of centuries, many elaborate additions were made, in music, attire, ritual, to produce a total action of impressive nobility, which for all its art may perhaps have somewhat muted the vigor of the basic ingredient: the psalms. Even when reduced to a barren reading done quietly and humbly, one wonders if the psalms do not strike home more directly. Let be. It is the psalms that matter, their use. Let contemporary art achieve, if it can, some manner of adapting the psalms to community use in one form or other. It would be a great service to the Church.

One could do worse than lead the people back to the psalter. We all need wisdom in the mysteries of the human heart; the very fact that the psalms have been so long with us indicates that they may have something to teach us. In the face of so much chaos, disruption, and confusion, perhaps people are beginning to suspect that most things happen first in the heart, have their source and font nowhere else. The psalms are nothing if not prayers of the heart, and thus the heart's salvation.

The Destroying Angel

*W*ho is this dark demon that pursues me? Who sent him? Why does he haunt me? Who can this enemy within be, and why has he chosen to destroy me?

I wish I knew. I know only that he has been around as long as I can remember. He sees deep into me and by his own mean insight determines with swift certainty just where and just when to strike.

Where would he lead me? Over what sudden precipice would he have me leap? Or slip? What is the scope of his designs, since he acts, be it secretly, or now that I am better acquainted with him, openly, for familiarity with him has given no indication whatever as to what his next tactic will be?

It is not so much that I fear him; he wears me down. He does not so much hurt me as hover over me like some wheeling vulture waiting his right moment.

What is it about us that turns us on ourselves? Where did I learn this black art? Somewhere, somehow, I discovered I was hateful and therefore that hate was called for. They loved me; I know that. Who then skilled me so? Perhaps I learned early that humankind is devious and far from God, that the good angel in me gave offense to the evil one.

As a child I used often to go sit in the woods on the little hill back of the house. The woods were birch and the quality of the leaves in spring, their scent, the play of sunlight on me, on them, the grass, the streaked white curls of bark—none of this has ever left me.

And do you know what I used to do there? (I do not remember seeing anyone do it, for my mother was no woman with a needle, but I must have observed it somewhere). I used to take a linen napkin from the buffet in the dining room, get colored thread and needle, and then trace in stitches the patterns embossed on the fabric or woven into it. The process fascinated me and I am sure I spent hours quietly tracing the whorls and whirls of the fanciful designs. It was a delight. And I remember consciously thinking, and I must have done so many times, that the world was very beautiful, but that people were not. I felt the world would have been so fine a place without them. I sometimes feel now that I was onto a truth, though I was yet to learn that I was people.

My father provided my sister and me with a tent mounted on a platform under a huge elm. We were not encouraged to play with other children in their yard, nor to have them come play with us. There were few children in the neighborhood anyway, so it did not much matter. Only later did we venture. But in those early years I spent much time by myself and have never lost the sense of charm that surrounded those days. Sometimes I would sit by myself in the tent, drawing or making a scrapbook of pictures scissored from magazines. Now and then my mother would come and get me, asking me to go to the store or telling me we were going for a ride, and I would drop everything and leave. Yet I always felt it a pity I had to, and sensed clearly enough that she was a little distressed at the way I was.

Once when I was very little, I was sitting on the floor of the porch with my back up against the wall. My mother was nearby. I began hitting the wall with the back of my head, not really hard, but hard enough to feel it and recognize that the wall was harder than my head. My mother looked at me as I kept it up and in a sort of pity, with alarm in her voice, told me to stop it. I clearly recall my reaction: she thinks there is something wrong with me, silly woman.

I liked being by myself; I always have. The early years were quiet and untroubled. When school days began, a whole new field opened up. I do not know whether we were actually taught it, whether I picked it up, whether it came from within, but I developed a quality of aggression, strife, contention that was ugly. From then on and for years I was streaked with something vicious. By myself, one sort of person; with others, often enough, quite another. I was dreadful.

Yet, I had friends who meant much to me and I knew deep affinities, though these too were marred with the same blight. Over the years a consciousness began to develop in me that I was different, that I felt things differently, responded differently. This was not accompanied by any feeling of inferiority, nor did I feel superior, but felt sure of myself, felt good in my own eyes.

I believe I was nearly in high school before I entertained any sense of inadequacy. There were some friends of the family with children the age of my sister and me with whom we sometimes exchanged visits. We all got on well. Once after my sister had come back from several days' visit with them, she told me that Mrs. H did not like me. Looking back, I sympathize with Mrs. H's point of view, but at the time it gave me a great shock that someone would not like me. I had always assumed everyone did and that they had some reason to. It bothered me for a long time.

The three aspects have lasted all through the years. I am now nearly 60 [now nearly 80, ed.] and sense just as keenly now as I did then, that there are no delights like the delights of solitude; all my life I have been contentious, full of strife, argument, sarcasm, ridicule; I have never really doubted that I had a destiny and that my gifts were real.

The only shift has come in the years since 1960 when I became a monk. I was 45 then. The fruit of my monastic experience has been a shedding of the love for contention. The whole shell of outer strife was exposed as a construct, and under the impact of grace, guidance, the monastic milieu, it simply disintegrated. Though it sometimes may still express itself, I know what is going on.

For one thing, I am not a natural fighter. Fight to me has always seemed silly and pointless. You were either right or you were wrong. Violence did nothing to change anything. Yet, I believe that in a society of competition, in a setting of achievement, striving, aggression, I either learned or was taught that fighting is part of the scene. So I learned, but in my own way. Since it was not natural to me, the results were disastrous.

The same applied to sports. I did not lack endurance, or courage, or ability to bear pain. I loved to ice-skate, to ski, to swim, to go sledding, to build tree houses; I enjoyed simple games, long hikes, bicycling. But the idea of organized play, with winning and losing and all that was involved, simply did not interest me. I saw no point in any of it. Even in going to motion pictures as a child, I used to be appalled at the wild exhibitions of glee or hatred for hero or enemy, which would burst from the audience with such intensity. I felt sure I grasped as much as did the others the impact of good and evil, but to lose one's self in such mass hysteria seemed something I neither wanted to do nor could do.

Sometimes I wished I were more like others. I am aware of a difference, some insight into things, some capacity for the poetic and the spiritual which, if not exceptional—and it is not—is still strong enough to set me off from others. Nor do I hesitate to say that this has some relationship to homosexuality, for though I have never practiced it, I am well aware of an orientation that is certainly as much in that direction as the other; further, that given the knowledge, the opportunity, the circumstances, I could as easily as not have gone in that direction. But people of my kind seem often so placed; the reason, as I have worked it out, being that they are more closely related to the anima than is usual and thus have far less need of the actual woman. What such people yearn for is solace in their solitude and an understanding of their fate, their destiny. I do not think a homosexual relation would be much of an answer. The man with a strong anima will always sense some inadequacy until he has come to terms with his inner spirit and established communion—no small achievement. Until then he cannot really act truly as a complete person, since he isn't one. He will thus be unable to relate in depth to others. The unhappy experience of many is that they cannot relate to others, not aware that the problem is their lack of communication with themselves. The blind comfort the blind, but they cannot open each other's eyes. True, a relation may release sexuality and in a sex-impressed context there may be no other way, just so one does not mistake one thing for something else. Perhaps a healthy culture would enable those so gifted by God or nature to realize their call and respond to it in fruitful ways. Our times seem not unusual for homosexuality; we are perhaps more self-conscious, have more contempt of the feminine, and have less reverence for the gift of insight than is good for us.

Yet, now that I have at last shed the veneer of acquired aggression, I have discovered a hidden monster I was not aware of before. Now he has turned his face on me. There is to the anima a companion sister who seems full of venom, spite, and the spirit of destruction. She is an evil woman who attacks the good anima with hell's fury, and for those endowed with a strong relation to the anima, this can mean only trouble.

It cannot have escaped anyone with even a casual knowledge of artists, poets, actors, writers, dreamers, and, I may add, men and women of religion, how their lives are often marked with and sometimes destroyed by disasters which often enough are of their own making. It does not make light reading, this study of the biographies of these gifted people that reveal so much suffering and sorrow, and, unaccountably, too often self-inflicted.

A destroying angel is near every poetic soul. Humble though my own gifts be, I am none the less more than conscious of a self-destructive urge that is active within me. I have repeatedly discovered myself having done things inevitably bound to bring rebuke, refusal, contempt, rejection. In a word, I ask for these things, unconsciously, unwittingly. I set things up that way. The only solace following the certain consequences is knowing that for a while, at least, the hunger of the destroyer is sated.

Why this is so, I do not know, but I know it is so. I do not think success for an artist would be any help. Indeed, it might lead only farther into the abyss, for the more his gift be praised, the stronger the enemy. Probably the only real answer lies in religion, in deep faith in God's love and mercy. But even deep faith does not necessarily solve all life's problems. Salvation, yes, but not necessarily happiness on earth. Yet, I do believe that faith is the greatest help against this demon.

If God has made a gift to me, there is no reason I should hate myself for being so gifted. Unless I happen to know I am unworthy; and then? Then you turn to Christ, aware that we are all unworthy, even of life itself; and acknowledging unworthiness and the forgiveness of all sin by his merciful death, we can resist the enemy.

It is good to think sometimes that if people who seem blessed with special gifts are yet unspeakably difficult, resentful, cantankerous, jealous—that this may be the only way they can release the venom of the evil angel within. Or, in more tragic situations, when an artist soul turns self-destructive, others should be compassionate. Great gifts attract demons.

Of late years contemplative monasteries are updating a lot of customs and traditions. In former days the abbot was simply head of the monastery and ran the place as he liked, more or less, according to the Rule of St. Benedict, the prescriptions of the Order, and an occasional rebuke or reminder through the authority of a visiting superior abbot. The beneficial side was that monks were spared administrative duties, meetings, boards, reports. Now that the atmosphere is gone very democratic, many more areas are open to the monks. This has led to interminable meetings, dialogues, discussions, and almost endless wrangling trying to come to a consensus or even a majority on some issues. Monks have long since expressed exasperation. Further, the sudden call from a life of silence to a life of exchange, of opinion expressed in public, of voting, of argument that sometimes becomes emotional or personal—all this has made evident the fact that monks are not exactly skilled in this sort of thing. The general assumption has been that having had nothing to say for so long, they simply lost the art of speaking. Monks find it difficult to express themselves, get angry, get upset. In the face of that, most agree more dialogue is called for, more discussion, until they get used to it, get good at it.

I wonder about that. In fact, I suspect it's all wrong. I'll venture a prophecy: that monks will return to the old way and let the abbot take care of most things, and submit only a few basic concerns to vote or discussion by the community—just about the way it used to be.

Because monks by and large are artists, poets. They are heavy with anima, sons of strong mothers. They are romantics, idealists, dreamers. They must be. If they were practical men of affairs they would have gone out and done something more useful than chant psalms in the night, spend a lifetime making cheese for Christ's sake.

If they are anima men, you can be sure they know the dark demon of destruction. And if they do, you can guess them generally hopeless in the give and take, the strife, contention, and controlled aggression that is essential to a good community discussion. I am sure most of them hate the whole business. They'd sooner suffer the whims of an abbot (they are all whimsical) than bear the venom of their own and another's abysmal spirit.

We'll see.

In monastic life, submission to the abbot is central, and for the kind of man called to the monastery, that form of discipline is superb, for he needs a firm hand. Not a hand that crushes him, but protects him from the forces that fight against him, his own self-destroying urges.

The same may be said of the monastery as a whole, for it forms an enclave of peace and of love in which elements that could only destroy are kept at bay. This means that the monastic enclosure does not keep the monk in; it rather keeps the enemy out, the evil one, the spirit of violence. When that is the situation, then the battle is centered where it should be, in the heart. External hostility is mere distraction for the monk, leads him away from his center, dissipates his energy in externals. His warfare is within, and, let it be noted, a more deadly combat than anything without.

It follows, then, that the introduction of fields for contention and provocation simply introduce an element that can do the monk no real good.

When the poet, the artist, the writer, must spend time fending, fighting off critics, earning a living, contending with any external forces, that can mean only the dissipation of a gift. A heaven of peace does not mean being spared conflict; it means the conflict is centered when the real enemy is met, not a stand-in.

The destroying angel that accompanies every person of the spirit is a real danger. Mere intellectual grasp of the concept will not do. Neither can will power avail. It is a matter mostly of prayer, a wrestling with demons with Christ and in his grace.

Not a few monks leave the monastery because of the destroying angel. He drives them out; I am quite certain of that. Not all of them, to be sure, for some should leave. But when a person approaches God, the enemy has a way of capitalizing on the utter unworthiness of the lover to the point that the lover cannot abide it. One needs a sort of compassion for poets and priests and artists. We do not realize what a precious gift they are to humanity. Or what a burden they bear.

When I began to experience the call to solitude, and to solitude away from the monastery, I was wary of the destroying angel and feared he might be deluding me. It was for that very reason I insisted that I would never leave without the abbot's blessing. When my abbot did refuse his blessing, it hurt me, but I had no great difficulty in accepting it. This was not virtue, but common sense. Monks get carried away with all kinds of ideas. Several years later a new abbot did give me his blessing. This confirmed me more strongly in my faith in obedience as the foundation of monastic discipline. It is this sort of death in the will of God that at once unites the monk with Christ before the Father and puts to flight the evil one. Yet, it is not always easy. They did not name the place Gethsemani for nothing.

The Virgin

Sad in the Church of our time is the weakening of devotion to the Virgin Mother of God. Does it indicate a disintegration of the faith? Is it a portent of chaos to come? Perhaps the only hope one can express is that in the loss of reverence for Our Lady in accustomed forms, new modes may develop from the depths of the Christian heart. Certainly not all devotion is genuine, nor its forms appropriate to every age.

I knew a bishop who prided himself on his love for the Virgin Mary, led pilgrimages, named every new parish in his diocese after one of her titles, yet, not withstanding, was rather cruel and hard-hearted. Precious little in him reflected the tenderness of Christ's Mother.

Perhaps loss of love for the Virgin is part of an overall rejection of woman that has been characteristic of this and recent centuries. A casual survey of the state of woman today gives one no great comfort. For all its forms, the movement for the liberation of woman may at least be taken as some sort of effort to restore her dignity.

We now know in full measure the fruit of long neglect of the human heart. In a world ridden with violence and turmoil, so accustomed to wars of unequaled scope and ferocity that we take them in our stride, we grow adjusted even to a life subject to global annihilation at any moment. In such a world to talk of the Virgin Mary is to be brave indeed.

Yet talk of her we must, and we must return to her somehow or other. The poverty of Protestantism in regard to our Lady is acknowledged by some, yet Roman Catholicism faces becoming an equally womanless faith. And, may it be said, a religion without woman is no religion at all.

No man is only male. The human race is not just male. How can we relate to God without reference to woman? God is as much female as male. And how can we come to know the whole Christ if we have no woman through whom to do so? And to assume that we can relate to the Church, our mother, Christ's spouse, without the model, his own holy Mother, is to imagine that mere formulas and concepts are realities.

Woman can mean very little to man if he has no contact with the feminine spirit within him. And woman herself, sensing this rejection and misunderstanding, will surely turn against herself. When woman means little to man, the Virgin Mary will also mean little, and a relationship to the church will have no real depth without her influence.

Carl Jung maintained that the most significant event of our times was the proclamation of the doctrine of the Assumption of the Virgin Mary. He saw it as such because it expressed the reality of the Virgin and the reality of woman's role in the plan of God in the face of a world that spurns the body, the Resurrection, and woman. He could think of nothing the world needed more and so rejoiced in it. So astute an observer of the human spirit deserves respect. Nor was he given to making statements lightly. He was convinced that because men were divorced from their own spirit, their own depths, all that they rejected would take revenge on them and confront them in wild fury from without. He does not seem far wrong. Spurned woman is lethal.

No man will have any serious affinity to the Virgin Mary who does not have a serious affinity to woman. One is impossible without the other. For a man of the Catholic tradition, one could almost judge his understanding of woman by his devotion to the Mother of God.

Sometimes we are annoyed at the forms devotion takes, the aesthetic quality of shrines, works of art, various practices. We could use some help. Yet, there are many lovely expressions to be had, and reproductions of the finest work in the world can be acquired easily enough. Nor are new works lacking. Even many old prayers are beautiful. The litany of Loretto is scarcely heard anymore, yet it is rich in imagery of a superior kind. The parish of my childhood was no more than a grubby basement-church utterly without presence. May devotions consisted of a layperson reciting the litany of Loretto while the priest was saying Mass. One could scarcely do less. Yet those melodious titles rolling out one after another have always remained vivid in my memory, even if the only bit of loveliness accompanying them was a ray of morning sun streaking color across the cool darkness.

Certainly the years in the seminary were marked by all kinds of devotional practices to Our Lady, some of them marked more by sentiment than by faith, yet saying something. An evening May procession with tapers to the Lourdes grotto was not lacking in picturesque qualities, nor have passing years substituted anything better. Yet, recalling past days and bemoaning the present serves small good. It must be confessed that a certain disenchantment, hard to shake, has settled on our spirits. Yet, if the faith lives, love of the Virgin will again flourish.

What a long time ago seems the gathering that overfilled Soldiers' Field in Chicago for the Marian year. It was a most effective work of organization, and I found it deeply moving. It was a cool summer evening with a light breeze off the lake, as I recall, and the great crowd was extraordinarily reverent, the thousands of candles burning in the dark stadium a sight not lacking in message.

Perhaps the day of such innocent pageantry and display is gone. Times are more bitter, the heart more grieved, and some great darkness has settled in on us, too dark, too somber, to bear the glimmer of little candles, since the darkness is touched with a despair we rather relish. One thinks of the power of darkness.

The National Shrine [now Basilica, ed.] of the Immaculate Conception in Washington is of that bygone era. It seems so prosperous, so happy, so sure. It does not reflect the mood of the times, since it glows with optimism in an unhappy city and an unhappy land. No matter. Give it time to make history. Let it live with us through these dark days and the days to come. Sorrow and suffering will soften its brilliance and warm its gold. Once it has shared our pain, it will come closer.

In our suffering, too, we shall grow closer to the Mother of God. Nothing softens the heart as does pain. We shall not resist her.

One night at Gethsemani the Brother I used to work with, taking care of the thoroughbreds we boarded then for local stables, came for me. A snowstorm had blown up and he thought we had better go take a look at the back pasture. Normally, these strikingly handsome animals were high-strung, skittish, excitable. In an open field they were not always easy to approach. "If they are in trouble," Brother said, "we'll be able to tell right away." They were in trouble. The wind was high; there was no refuge from it, with their coats already matted with snow and ice, they huddled together and looked most uncomfortable. When they saw us coming, you could sense their gratitude. With no difficulty we took the first two and led them off to the stables, the rest of them following in unusual docility. They were much tamed and sobered by their plight. "Nothing gentle as a horse hurting," Brother remarked quietly.

No one recommends trouble, but it comes, an uninvited guest for whom room must be made. Dorothy Day was once a deeply troubled woman. She had not long before entered the Church and had a burning desire to serve God and her brothers and sisters. She had repeatedly been frustrated in trying to find what work she was to do. She went to the shrine of the Mother of God—it was but a lower-level church then—and begged the help of the Virgin, then went back home to New York. Peter Maurin was waiting for her and out of that meeting was born The Catholic Worker, one of the great glories of the Church in this country. Such prayers, such answers, multiplied unending times, are what create a center of faith. Architecture has little to do with it.

Yet, for all our hoping and praying, it is probably to be admitted that our devotion to the Mother of God will be marked by the same attitudes we bear toward women on earth. When women are held in reverence, virginity reckoned beautiful, marriage and motherhood honorable, this will reflect itself in our relation to the Virgin Mother. We have a certain consistency.

A culture capable of combining contempt for women with the commercialized gush of Mother's Day is the same that is distressed by Christ's relation to his own Mother. The nobility of the few episodes passed on to us in Scripture manifests a respect of each for the other as a person that is profound, a complete lack of prettiness in form, revealing the love that makes candor not merely possible, but inevitable. They truly speak to one another.

That kind of exchange is so rare among us that we are shocked by it and hasten to explain that they really did love one another.

The very difficulty we have in sensing any common note in the attitude of bishop to diocese as a relation of husband to wife; or, for that matter, of pastor to parish, indicates that a great deal could be improved. Few relate to the Church as spouse, as bride, as mother in any evident way. Yet it is to be so. The Church is Christ's spouse. His bride. He gave himself to death for her. Mary, as Virgin and as Mother, is an image of that Church, virginal and maternal. It comes more easily to us to see the Church as institution and the bishops as presidents or constituting a board of directors. Or put the other way around, I feel considerable sympathy for the woman who is spouse of a bishop.

The age of abortion, divorce, sterilization, can scarcely be an age of reverence for women. Rather, it is barbarous in this as it is in its love for violence, massive wars, greed, oppression, contempt for human life and human rights. In such a nightmare, a call for devotion to Our Lady seems almost pointless. One might as well wring one's hands in the face of a tornado.

Yet she was there when we crucified her Lord. And heard him forgive us. And heard him commend us to her care.

The Company

The galaxies of spirits who surround God's throne and ours are as much a part of my life as wind and rain, dreams and daffodils. People who dispense with angels strike me as among the dullest; I find them no different from people who would as soon as not be deaf, would gladly go blind, cousins to dissolute youth who waste or destroy precious gifts, valuable property, in some false detachment or indifference. Humans cannot live without angels; when they do not have angels, they create them.

The fancy of a Disney or a Tolkien is not so much mere fruit of creative genius as an intuitive awareness of what grown-up children want most of all; something to believe in. The ability to provide it was theirs. They did very well, though reality is far more fanciful. An angel is no Snow White.

The trend is to cool the angels. [Contemporary interest in angels can be seen in the enormous success of the writings of Sophy Burnham on the angels (see Sermons 45 & 59), ed.] This is no great problem, since an age is entitled to its fads and styles. If yesterday's fashions seem ludicrous, yesterday's theological journals are as revealing as old Sears catalogs. We need not be too much disturbed. Scripture has a certain steadiness; it abounds in dreams and angels.

The glory of the celestial choirs is no more difficult to accept—is it difficult at all?—than one butterfly, one buttercup. Indeed, all creation declares the glory of the angels since with them it praises God and is in the same choir. But the created world, so far as we know, has no conscious voice. What voice the angels have is more glorious for their being conscious in a superior manner.

Creation has been wounded by sin and bears part of human guilt. It follows that humankind takes ambivalent attitudes toward the world, reflecting creation's attitudes toward us. The conflict see-saws through time. Plague, famine, flood, fire, earthquake, cyclone—all of them strike at us, now in devastating degree, now less so. We fight back. Our land is not what it was when we came. The seas and rivers and lakes have been abused. Great treasures have been torn from the earth's breast. The air is no longer pure. We are able to destroy the whole earth if we so want and feel free to do so if we choose.

Humankind and nature are at war, but not a total war. Much of creation is friendly. And not all people destroy; only some of them, and only more often. The Native American Indians lived here ever so much longer than we have; they seem to have been more kindly to creation. Perhaps they did not take their guilt out on nature as much as we do.

We relate to angels as creation relates to us. Most of our trouble comes from the angels, just as most of nature's trouble comes from us. In the original conflict between good and evil, that great moment of trial and crisis, some angels chose evil. When the human being's turn came for love's testing, it was the evil angels who were the agents. Human beings failed as did some of the angels. The human being, too, did not love.

It is true, at least in some way, therefore, that we are what we are because of the fallen angels. Had they not come, we would not have joined them in electing evil. But, truly, the fault is not theirs. Our time would have come in any case, fallen angels or not, and we would have chosen our option and taken the consequences. Even so, the angels were associated in what happened to us.

That may explain the particular compassion the good angels have toward us. Apparently there is a vast difference between our fallen state and that of the fallen angels. One gets an impression of something definitive in their fall; no one has said the Redeemer went to them as he came to us. One concludes that they knew better what they did than we, or that their superior qualities made a change of heart impossible. Maybe the story is not ended, more is to come. Yet, since we are redeemable, nature is also, and therefore we look forward not only to the new person, but to the new creation. The whole was redeemed, or better, is being redeemed.

Since the good angels turn to us in love, it seems only natural to respond. Christian tradition has known many ways of doing so, and like all customs, some of them are exceptionally apt, others less so. Our own age is perhaps unique in dismissing the whole lot.

Will a later age come up with a new understanding of Saint Michael, the archangel, and continue the imagery that surrounds him in icons, statuary, painting, architecture? The oddity of winged humans may or may not be to our taste, though Christian artists have handled the symbol so long and so well that we have long since made it a part of us: when we dream of angels they have wings. One need not, even so, picture angels embodied, or speaking, delivering messages, for as pure spirits they are beyond us.

Many things are. We are familiar with power, energy, influences, waves of various kinds. We do not fully understand them. If angels be conceived as centers of power or light or influence, whose nature is unknown to us, we have at least some point of focus, so long as we realize they are immeasurably superior to anything we know on earth. Their whole being is in the love and the glory of God. We cannot relate to them nor they to us save in those terms.

And those terms are good. We have achieved a great deal. The world abounds in great achievements of humankind. They give glory to the creative power of God. Yet love is a problem we find difficult to solve. Here we appear at a loss before the power of evil rising in our own hearts, visible in my life and the lives of others, reflected in the retaliation of a world wounded by our malice, our want of love.

Though we know well enough that all love is found in God, all redemption in Christ, and the total salvation of humanity and world achieved in him, provided we accept it—we need more.

We need the angels for the same reason we need the Mother of God and the saints—because we are human beings. As human beings we belong to a community. The "contemporary human person" is a concept. My neighbor is not. My brothers and sisters, my intimates, are real. And we need a wider community than that, for we are not only of this earth. Life is temporary, residence here limited. The trip is a short one, and then we move on to another world, one we have never seen, know little of, have rare reports from. I believe in its existence and my whole life's course is rooted in that, since heaven is the presence of God. In that presence dwell the angels, forever lost in the beauty which is God. Yet they know me and love me.

So, I have friends in the kingdom, people I know, people who know me. It is not a matter of having influential contacts in high places—unless you prefer it that way—but of being united with their love song, part of it. There is such a song and snatches of it were heard on earth the night Christ was born. Some day that music will be heard again on earth, the day when all will be consummated. Meanwhile we know it continues unending in heaven, the song of love which we are asked to sing with Christ.

Primal Water

Though a son of the Archer and linked to fire, it is to water that I have a more natural leaning. Water is always an invitation to immersion, an immersion with a quality of totality, since it would accept all of me, as I am. Some primal urge invites me to return whence I came.

At times I have done so. There is some special delight in simply walking into a stream, stepping into a lake. The child's delight in a puddle is my adult's in the sea. Come with me down a country road, round a bend to a pond in a meadow, and know the pleasure of turning the motorcycle aside to plunge into the pond with a certain delicious abandon. It is more practical on horseback, for one horse I had was a good swimmer and took to carrying me across deep streams and into cool waters with pleasure, the two of us merged in a common matrix.

No rain falls that I do not at once hear in the sound of the falling water an invitation to come to the wedding. It is rare that I do not answer. A walk in an evening rain in any setting is to walk in the midst of God's loving attention to his earth, and, like a baptism, is no simple washing, but a communication of life. When you hurry in out of the rain, I hurry out into it, for it is a sign that all is well, that God loves, that good is to follow. If suffering a doubt, I find myself looking to rain as a good omen. And in rain, I always hear singing, wordless chant rising and falling.

When rain turns to ice and snow I declare a holiday. I could as easily resist as stay at a desk with a parade going by in the street below. I cannot hide the delight that then possesses my heart. Only God could have surprised rain with such a change of dress as ice and snow. The pines in Carolina, covered with glitter after a night of freezing rain, were ravishing enough to make one overlook the damage, for the display would be costly in broken boughs and backs bent beyond straightening. In Gethsemani snow was rare, but it was not merely its rarity that brought the monks to the door and out into the yard, to stand there wide-eyed for all the white so softly laid. Monks are human. I remember one summer night we had a thunderstorm with splendid rain while we were at Compline. Afterward, it was customary then for us all to go to the dormitory; you did not go wandering about. It was evident, as we bowed in turn for the abbot's blessing, that the sun was at work behind the hills, filling the storm clouds above with light and color. I went to my cell and drew the curtain, wishing that I might go up on the roof and see what was going on. I waited a few moments until things were quiet, then slipped out and up the back stairs to the deck above. It was as I expected; the sky was all the fury of the storm turned into color. But I was not alone. There were half a dozen monks there ahead of me, silently taking it all in.

Most people love rain, water. Snow charms all young hearts. Only when you get older and bones begin to feel dampness, when snow becomes a traffic problem and a burden in the driveway, when wet means dirt—then the poetry takes flight and God's love play is not noted.

But I am still a child and have no desire to take on the ways of death. I shall continue to heed water's invitation, the call of the rain. We are in love and lovers are a little mad. The season of love is soon over; one is young but once. It seems a pity that one day I must leave this world, for if I forego rain, I forego much. One of the reasons it is easy for me to believe in a new world, a renewed creation, is that I can scarcely believe God could bring himself to destroy so much beauty. I believe there'll always be rain.

And dew. When I had that happy house beside the lake at Gethsemani, I had to walk through summer fields to reach it. Sometimes it was so rich an experience that I began to suspect it was sinful. The path crossed a small hill, descended through a wooded grove, then over the bottom of a long meadow. Mornings, the tall grass would be leaning over the path with dew, all sprinkled with truly thousands of diamonds so large you could see a rainbow in each. The wood to the left was blued with mist, and inside was cool darkness. I would be wet almost to the waist with such a freshness that I wondered if a shower of dew would not be a remarkable sort. Yet, by the time I would be heading back to the abbey, the sun would be up in the sky, the dew gone, the glass dry, the mist lifted, the woods patterned in sharp light and shadow. Then I would say to myself that I should not get so carried away with passing things.

Bright wintry mornings the temperature would sometimes drop to zero around Gethsemani. When there would be deep snow I would take off to the woods, if the chance came. The land went far in some directions and, even when it led onto neighbors' tracts, continued much a wilderness, deserted. I never met anyone. Sometimes I would go to a glen where I knew the pines were especially fine and not crowded close together. There were wide patches which in summer made quiet secluded havens, but in winter were deep in free-fallen snow. When it was really cold I used to strip quickly and roll in the snow for a bit. In no time the body would react, heat up almost instantly, and one would stand, looking at the brilliant blue above, steam rising from all over one's glistening flesh. One did not wait too long and push it beyond its time, but dress wet as fast as one could. It was a wintry baptism and good for the soul. The only difficulty was the soles of my feet; you could not stand long in the snow, for the heat soon melted it and the feet could not accept the icy water and snow. You had to stand on something else. Then I would head off again and be startled to see a deer dart through the pines. He'd been watching. Probably does the same thing himself, though he no doubt did not bother to kick the snow back over where he'd rolled, as I did.

This is all very droll. I do not go from one thing to another; it is more taking life as it comes. Yet, I must tell you that water is also deep. I have lived close to water all my life and been in and out of it all the time. I have a good relationship with it, but a relationship based on an appreciation of the truth. The pull of water is also a pull backward into that abyss from which we were thrust by a creative force strong enough to prevail. If we are to maintain that creative act, we must not merely abide it, but further it, otherwise life does not catch and we drift back into mother and are absorbed by her, now a devouring primal power, not a life-giving one.

Our touch with water must always take this into account. There is some need to enter her and to unite with her, but if it becomes an absorption, then we have surrendered more than is ours to give and we are lost. Then what poses as love reveals itself as longing for death. This longing has to be renounced and we must face the prospect of being alone, on our own, away from mother.

The same woman who bore me will entice me back, and do so deliberately, happy at once to fail and to succeed; if she fails, a person is born; if she succeeds, she has the pleasure of prevailing. Dominance is the dark side of water.

Drinking alcohol means little to me except in terms of delirium. I do not need the stimulus from day to day; life itself is so full of spirit that more seems too much of a good thing. Transport is something else. Inebriation appeals to me in any form, for it is what I am born for, what I live for. Any water that will convey me to a sharing in another life I will gladly drink.

Yet it is clear that not every rapture is a preview of heaven or a preparation for it, and then it is a lie. We are called to ecstasy, but in responding we must take note of who is calling. We can be deceived, easily.

No matter how ravenously hungry we be, not everything that passes for good can be eaten. No matter how thirsty, some drink is poisonous. Our spiritual hunger and thirst are more real than bodily; our desires for eternal union in love more powerful than anything temporal. We are deceived when we forget that we are immortal and that our basic longings are infinite.

So life cannot be abandon. One cannot jump in every river, nor dive into every pond. Nor roll in any field. Nor taste every joy. Yet we are tempted to do so, because the calls within us are so very pressing.

I believe I could easily have become an alcoholic. It would require no basic alteration of my shape to lead me that way; I have a perfect disposition for it. I could adjust to it easily, since I have all that longing for primal water, for delirium, for surrender, for rapture. Yet I am aware that I would be walking in the direction of heaven and hell at one time, for I would insist I was seeking the eternal feminine and the divine union even while I knew she was a devouring monster leading to the embrace of extinction.

I am just as aware that I could have moved into a sexual relation with my own kind. It attracts me. I like the idea. It comes naturally. Yet in doing so I would know quite well that it would be a betrayal of that solitude that is basic to my being human, for I would be aware that I needed company in my loneliness, some companion to stand by my side, to assure me he knew how it felt, willing to testify to that by giving me all I had to give him. Yes, and leave me quite as I was before, not one whit less lone.

From early years I knew I had been called by God to priesthood and the celibate life. I sensed the reality and permanence of this vocation as the very being of my life and could not see departure from it as anything less than self-destruction. Christian tradition has been clear in its view on homosexual union: it is to be avoided. Virginal, celibate life by its nature means a union in love which is solitary and does not express itself in sexual commerce; it rejects that mode outright, totally.

There is considerable discussion in this field. I relate it to a basic attitude to the feminine. If I reject the woman within, I simply succumb to the pressure of a common contempt and under its pressure abandon my call to mystical love. On the other hand, as I see divorce and abortion as sins against woman, so also contraception. Though this teaching of the Church is both opposed and ignored, so long as it be her teaching, I accept it, compassionate toward any with problems of conscience in its regard. But to be logical, I do not see that if the sexual act in marriage can be effectively separated from its generative power and used only as an expression of love, why the same act could not be used for love between two of a kind where generation is also not involved. In both cases, a sexual act is used to express love between humans in which generation is or has been rendered impossible. It would appear to me, then, that if one sees birth control licit, one must also concede liberty to homosexual love.

Yet, even if the Church in virtue of new light or fresh insight in the Spirit, declare both of these moral, I would nonetheless continue my chosen path, for it is God's call to me. My road is to be walked alone. My life is within. Virginal love and sexual love are contrary ways.

It is perhaps worth noting, since one at times hears opposite views expressed by those assessing seminary or religious life from the outside and without experience of them, that I found neither in seminary nor monastery anything to foment or express any same sex tendencies. Quite the contrary. If the men following such a state of life are typically, in my view, strongly marked with anima, few of them seem to be positively or obviously drawn to overt sexual engagement. Further, the life style itself served to slough off into the life stream whatever such tendencies they might have had, as it certainly did in my own case, in a way that not only weakened them, but disposed of them. The ideals of fraternity, love of Christ and the Virgin, dedication to the service of God and one's neighbor, coupled with a life of work and worship, with a strong ascetical emphasis, all combined to create a group of happy men. If I had tendencies that were sexual, in whatever direction, they were absorbed into a love-life of another kind to the point that I was scarcely aware of them in the seminary and less in the monastery. It was rather in the intervening years when there was a less intense communal life, a weakening in prayer and asceticism, together with a not wholly satisfying ministry, that I came to experience a pull I had not formerly been explicitly aware of. For all that, such conditions normally would give stronger voice to sexual desire.

Further, it was only in my late fifties, be it noted, while living a much more solitary life, that I came at last to recognize that my trend is real and powerful, and this in a context both spiritually vigorous and dynamically rewarding. In other words, exposure to solitude has given me total truth. I can only conclude that the way of life of monks, or religious, is not only a good one, but an excellent one so long as its tone is good, that is, marked by intensity in the mystical, ascetical, communal—solitary aspects. And let only those move on into solitude who are certain God calls them to it, for only then can it be an experience ultimately good. I shall myself continue in it as long as it seems so to me; if I cannot manage, I shall happily return to my abbey. [Matthew Kelty returned to Gethsemani in 1982, ed.].

But I must make clear that I consider religious life, and particularly monastic life as I have known it, an exceptionally fruitful form of life for those called to it. My belief and my hope is that in coming years monastic life, especially of the contemplative kind, will flourish, in that many will find in it a perfect expression of everything they desire. Yet, it is a life of faith and, unhappily, it is precisely faith that is weakening. Without faith monastic life appears weird, and in a sensuous age without faith, even more so. With no such faith, the numbers of men and women who will not find in monasteries lives of deep meaning and satisfaction will be large enough to be tragic.

Yet there can be no pretending that monastic life is easy. It demands exceptional generosity and a genuine asceticism for Christ's sake, a total acceptance of the virginal, celibate state—the fundamental solitude—with an abandonment of sexual love. Love for the community, love for silence, for work and reading, for prayer, for quiet seclusion and peace—all this against a background of unrelenting determination to follow Christ to the end. Christ is no cheap love or easy grace. Though he is mercy incarnate, in obedience to his Father's will he is merciless; that will must be accepted wholly, no matter what it leads to. Sensuality is really not the test of the monk. Obedience is. This obedience leads to death, yet it is a death which in Christ's case, as in ours, is the price of life for us all, the ultimate love.

Since my life has had a quality of journey, perhaps some lingering trace of the wandering Celtic monks of ages past—I have come to live the solitary life in New Guinea, the mission world I knew many years ago. Here at my feet is the sea, beating tirelessly against the shore. If we understand one another, the sea and I, it is not an understanding I have always had. I now relive my past in many ways. When I was young and told my mother I was going to study for the priesthood, the reactions were mixed. There was consternation, disappointment, confusion, reluctant acceptance. At no point was there anything like an enthusiastic or encouraging gesture. Nor was there any for many years. I am grateful to her. It was for the best.

I suppose a priest, like a monk, like a prophet, a poet, a dreamer, a solitary, is a jarring note, a disturbing nonconformist voice. Possibly he frightens people. I have been frightened myself. Perhaps if I am too acceptable, to myself or others, I am no help at all.

Easter Sunrise

*H*oly Week comes to an end, almost entirely spent in noting these reflections, and I come to realize that much of what I have said is not the truth.

It turns out that my elaborate endeavors to detail a pursuit of solitude against opposing elements were no more than an advance disguising a retreat. Flight from woman has been my sin, too. I am a man of my times.

For I have resisted her wooing, have feared her charms, played off her sweet invitations. Now it is clear that it was I who spurned her while making a show of winning her love. The fire I would steal was refused as a gift. I know that now. The elemental truth comes home to me and I see it as it is, yet without regret.

I begin to tell her as we sit on the hill looking out over the sea. She says nothing at all. She smiles softly, takes up my flute and plays a quiet tune, and across the pipe looks into my eyes. She knows. I know. The struggle is over and I surrender.

So long a love affair, and yet it could not have been otherwise. If I had to do it over again, it would be no different, for I would do the same thing in the same way. My history is mine and no one else's. Given a fresh sheet I would write exactly what I wrote the first time.

I listen to my own song rising from her breath, from my flute held in her hands. With the rising music the sun begins to rise out of the sea at her back and there are no longer two of us. Its light catches the white-gold ring on my finger.

Talks and Sermons

1
If I Had My Life to Live Over
A talk given to monks in Chapter, Abbey of Gethsemani.

There used to be a song in the old days, "If I had my life to live over, I'd do the same thing again." We think of a few sentences given in Scripture, "Depart from me, Lord, for I am sinful; leave me, Lord, for I am a sinner." Think of a couple who gradually grow old together. The children are grown up and gone and, suddenly, they are on their own again. The couple face one another across the table as they once did long ago—just themselves. In a marriage that is one of deep love, they begin to fall in love all over again but ever so much more deeply. He is the same. And she is the same. But yet they are not the same two people at all; they are very different, and that is what gives poignant beauty to their falling in love. They are different and yet the same. It is not hard to see the analogy in the religious life.

After a decade or two, one is no longer the same; one is and yet one isn't. The person of 40 is not the person of 20. What was done at 20 may seem long ago. The person may seem hardly to have known what he or she was doing. After all, to a person of 20 the world looks inviting. At 40 we know better, but it is at 20 that God speaks and that one's vocation is normally settled. [This is much less true in the mid-1990s. Young people may not "settle" until their late 20s or early 30s, sometimes later, ed.] It is precisely in the time when one's delusions are strongest that one must make one's choice. That is part of the beauty of the choice. Indeed, what one gives up may be no more than a delusion, but the delusion seemed at the time very real.

You have heard husbands say of their wives, "If I knew then what I know now, I would never have married her." He may even say it to her, throw it in her face—there's something monstrous in that. Or worse yet, "You talked me into marrying you." This coming from an adult is surely the shameless expression of childishness—of a person who never grew up. And yet we hear these things. Your word is your word. I think it good to dwell with these ideas and reckon with our need for love. It is only the husband who loves his wife every day who will find in his old age that he loves her dearly. You do not play fast and loose with her all your life and then in maturity settle down into the quiet haven of true joy. It doesn't work out that way.

In our own life, from day to day, we must love and grow in love. And each day to live for love. And each day to love a little more. This does not exclude failures and weakness and sin, but it does involve a use of the heart. I fear a land of little love and of betrayed love. And our land may have many men and women who do not love. Who never have loved. And who literally do not know how to love, and yet they bring children into a loveless world. Children who grow up with a dreadful wound in their depths. Children who have not known love. Will they ever be healed?

And yet we cannot despair, we must believe in love. And as people of God in our world, people who share all the weakness and the frailties of our own day. Persons also wounded and hurt by the loveless world that is ours. We must continually return to the sources that answer our need—to Christ and to faith in Christ. This faith is a gift, and we have only to open our arms and to receive it and to accept it. Original sin you did not accept—you had no choice in the matter—but Christ you do accept. This is a matter of choice, though we perhaps discover that we really have no faith in Christ. But to discover as much is a great grace. We may have had great notions of ourselves. We may have thought we amounted to something: in mind, in body or in spirit. And the day may come in the silence and seclusion of the monastery that we discover that this is our greatest delusion. We may discover that we are poor indeed, and it is then we must turn to Christ. Hence happiness does not lie in smug contentment with a life well-lived, but rather with the deep awareness of the goodness of God and that everything turns out for the good for those who love God. There is a sense in which we must truly be able to say with full meaning, "If I had my life to live over, I'd do the same thing again."

There is, of course, one sense in which we could not say this—in the sense of our sins. We could not deliberately hold on to them and the evil will which made them possible. We could not think of living over again and wishing to sin once more. But there is one sense in which this saying is very true, and from two points of view: first, we shall not be given life to live over. This is simply not granted. We shall not pass this way again. We are born. We are young. We grow old and we die and move on. That is for sure. We know that any notion that we will live over again in the life on earth is delusion. The other point of view is that sooner or later we are going to have to accept our lives in their totality. Someday our whole life will be laid out before us, in all its aspects—every detail as it truly was—nothing hidden, nothing kept quiet. And all the real, though muffled, motives and intentions will be manifest. And we are going to be asked to put our name to it, to sign it. And this will be utterly impossible unless we have accepted the mercy of God.

I believe that the major part and pain of purgatory will be the fire that awakens in us faith in the mercy of God. To have no faith in love is a great sin. Not to believe in love. And that is why it can be said, "If I had my life to live over I'd do the same thing again," because my life is me. My response to the reality which is God in the world. I cannot be separated from my life. And my good and my evil are all part and parcel of it. My sins are just as much involved as my good acts. I cannot be separated from the world I have known, from the words I have spoken, from the deeds I have done any more than I can be separated from the graces I have received. From the time I first drew breath until the last, there is a time and space complex that is part of me. Either I accept my life or I don't. It is all of it or none. I cannot be responsible only for what was upright and noble and beautiful. I am author also of much that is shabby and disreputable and regrettable. I cannot possibly say to the one side, "That is me," and to the other, "That is not." But the only possible way I can accept it all is in the mercy of God—who has pardoned my guilt, who has forgiven my wrongs—indeed, who did so even before I committed them. Who loved me even before I was and created me in love even though he knew I would turn against him.

To accept all, then, is not only what we are called upon to do, are suggested to do—this is what we must do. To take the full responsibility for my life, even to the point that I can say, "If I had my life to live over, I'd do the same thing again," because God's love for me is woven into the whole of my life. It is he who brought goodness out of evil. Who showed mercy and had compassion. Who turned everything to good account. I will not be given my life to live over. What is done is done and cannot be undone. There is not a moment of your life that is not history, recorded history. It will, all of it, live forever. The day of your birth, the mother who bore you. The father from whose seed you sprung. Where you lived—what you did—who you knew. This is all history, in some sense eternal, and it is only when in faith we believe that every bit of it is engulfed in the mercy of God that we can undertake to accept it all. I do not say "understand," I say "accept," for we cannot understand nor do we need to. But we must believe in love. And unless you can say, "If I had my life to live over, I'd do the same thing again," can you then say that you really have accepted it—your history, your story. We can see, then, the tremendous seriousness of our life. Every day we live we write in the book of life, and sometimes how stupidly, how hastily, how heedlessly, how thoughtlessly. What is written is written and can never be erased. And some day the book will be handed back to us and we will be told to read it aloud.

I have shed many tears for my sins, and I am sure I will shed many more before my life is over. And looking to the future: While I surely have no desire to offend God, who can reckon with human frailty? Who can live without hope in God? I do not mean these thoughts to be gloomy, but I do mean them to be serious.

A man told me of a divorce action he had to take against his wife who abandoned him and went to live with another man. In order to protect the rights of his child, he had to take action by force of law. And he saw that he would have no way to handle it except by hiring a private detective. And so, for a week or two, a team followed this unfortunate couple around, never once letting them out of their sight. Every blessed move was recorded. Now they went here, now they went there. Now, at such-and-such a time, they stopped at the drugstore and bought a pack of cigarettes. Now they went to this dance together. Then they went to have something to eat. Now they went to this place to have something to drink. Someday in court it will all be read out loud. What a business.

God is not some private detective following us around. But he is our judge, our Lord, our Creator to whom we shall answer for all we have done. That is certain. And it is a wholesome thought. But we must couple this awareness to a deep faith in the mercy of God, else we shall go mad. For God loves us more than we can possibly imagine to be true. And on the other side, our love for him is so dear to him that we could not possibly believe that either, did we know. This, then, is our task: to live in love, to accept God's love for us, to give him our love, and day by day to live under the eye of God, true to my inmost being. True to the self God created me to be. And that self is attainable at any moment. At any moment: you need go nowhere, you need do nothing, you have only to accept God's love and accept yourself, which is the object of God's love. You will never know how beautiful is his love until you sense how unworthy of it you are. People spend their whole lives running away from the love of God. They refuse to believe it because they know what they are. So they shut their eyes to their own reality and keep on running, trying to make life liveable somehow or other. But a monk is a person who has stopped running, who asks, "What am I running for? Why am I running away from God?" The monk stops and, like some frightened deer, he awaits the approaching hound of heaven.

A person can do this anytime. But sometimes even monks may be a long time getting there. So we must be patient. You cannot rush it. You cannot tell monks what to do. They know what to do better than you. Give them time, give them the grace of God. Above all, give them love. It could be that the bit of undeserved love that you give them may be all they need to make the final step into believing that it is really true that they are the beloved children of God.

If I had my life to live over, I'd do the same thing again.

Gethsemani
Circa 1970

2
Blessing Fields
Homily delivered during outdoor Mass
for blessing of the fields

*A*lthough the Great Society, as ours has sometimes been called, has some favorable aspects, it must also be admitted that the American way of life is not without its failures. One area of grave fault is that of cruelty.

We are in many ways a cruel people. And one of the objects of our cruelty is God's created world. And if good people have for years been pointing this out—one of our own among them—it has only lately come home to us that we have reduced the place God gave us to live on to such a state of squalor, debauch and waste that it is an open question whether or not we can ever make it all good again. The land, the rivers, the lakes, the seas, the air we breathe, and outer space itself are all of them polluted by noxious debris, filthy greed and noise. And the horror continues.

That being so, it is good that we gather on this hill in prayer to God. To ask pardon for our sins against his creation. And in thanks. Despite our wretched abuse of what God gave us, we express at least our desire to be grateful. In petition also, that he would help us in our need, that sin and darkness might not be so strong in us, that we may be less cruel to one another, that we may be less cruel also—since all our actions flow from our heart—to field and forest, to hill and valley, to every presence of our sister water and the sweet spirit which is the air we breathe.

When we wound others, when we kill others, it is ourselves we wound, ourselves we kill. And when a person is cruel to anything God created, he or she ultimately is cruel only to one's self. And this cannot be. For if we cannot lay a cruel hand on our brother or sister, neither can we on wind, on water or on the earth. Nor indeed on one's self. Hatred is not Christian. Cruelty is not the law. Love is. For God. For our neighbor. For one's self. And for all that God has made.

Our gathering here today is testimony of this, witness to these truths and our determination to live by them. That being so, let us bless the bread and the wine, and eat and drink them together in Christ's holy love, on this lovely afternoon on this lovely hill, in sight of the surrounding lovely countryside and in the shadow of his cross.

Amen.

Gethsemani
May, 1970

3

Dreams and Visions and Voices
To missionaries in Papua New Guinea

*P*erhaps we are starting off with the right foot in our relations with the people of Papua New Guinea if we—I speak as a European, at least as one whose roots are ultimately in Europe, the case with most foreigners here, though surely not all—if we acknowledge that we stand to benefit the most by the exchange. I am sometimes a bit miffed at both the local people and expatriates who take it for granted that any encounter has benefits in only one direction. For my part, I make it plain that in coming to this country this time—I was here 25 years ago for a while—I have my own good in mind, first of all, and I do not mean that in any particularly material sense. Quite the contrary.

It may clarify the air some if I state blandly that as far as I see it, European culture is very sick. I am not the only one to make this observation. The sickness, to describe it simplistically and in one way, is that Westerners are almost totally divorced from their unconscious: their whole life is in the conscious world. This development has been going on for some centuries, and in our own time has come to a head. "Development" is scarcely the appropriate word since the end-product is disastrous. Many are aware of the situation and have analyzed it with care and precision; indeed, the awareness has been with us for a long time. It is the remedy, however, that is hard come by. How does one reestablish relationship with the unconscious? The question is no longer academic, for the spurned unconscious now erupts all around us in terrifying form; we literally witness the collapse of a culture.

Having short memories, we forget that we ourselves only lately emerged from primitive life. A major factor in that emergence was the role of the Church in its sweep across Europe. That sweep was not so much an imposition (something foreign) as something gladly received, for in the faith all the hungers of the heart were answered, the riddles of life given a clue. Further, in creed and code and cult the great forces of the unconscious were both controlled and held in check, given scope but held in line. This made possible the evolving of the whole person, a real people.

In the passage of time, new forces entered the scene, the unity and authority of the Church was broken, the rational side of the human person given total emphasis, the unconscious side degraded and ignored. This one-sided growth led to the most astonishing achievements in the material order, achievements which continue in our own day to stagger the mind for their breadth and power. But along with this record has been an accompanying sense of misgiving that has now become extremely serious, a major source of doubt and anguish.

Meanwhile, the vanquished unconscious, so long restless and stewing beneath the surface, furious at being permitted no voice, no outlet, has finally rebelled and broken forth. It is not too much to say that diabolical forces currently roam the world without let. Despair, disillusionment and fear fill the human mind.

When people from such a setting come to a place like Papua New Guinea, most of them equipped with skill and competence in some area or other, one wonders how profound a grasp they have of their own background, for that same awareness will measure their grasp of the local picture. People who do not know what is going on in their own environment will not usually see with any depth into someone else's. We enter only as deeply into another as we do into ourselves.

This people, living on this island for centuries uncounted, has developed in that time some sort of life that had things by and large in hand. It had serious drawbacks, but it worked with some measure of success. If consciousness has but lately emerged, it must also be said that adequate curbs had been placed on the unconscious to prevent uncontrollable emergence. At least the endeavor in that direction. Some sort of balance was achieved.

Now the crunch. If Westerners come here, share all their secrets in terms of material progress, they set the people on the very same path that they have trod. Many coming think they could do nothing better than that. But if that way is wholly rational, is all in the practical order, if mystic dimension is given no attention, then it can be predicted that the seeds of disaster so sown will one day sprout, no matter how impressive the ostensible material progress. The proof of that is in Europe and America today.

I do not see too much evidence that Europeans as a group are aware of these implications, still less among the people here. Papua New Guinea buys the West as is. The major concern is that they be allowed to run things themselves, that their land and their people be not used merely to profit others. The techniques, the methods, the skills, progress and development—the more, the better.

For which reason I privately maintain that the only important thing going on here is the Church. I do not feel any consensus on that view. Development is good, but unless that development is of the whole person, it will not work, not for long. If attention is not given to the spirit, to the immaterial, the unconscious if you will, the development will be schizoid, split. The frustrated area will eventually erupt. In Papua New Guinea this is even more at issue since consciousness is but lately emerged, is not tough and strong: the powers of the unconscious are just about under control and not much more than that—not even that at times. In the face of that, it will be objected that the obvious need is precisely in the growth of rationality; that all this business of mysticism should be allowed to drop since the people in the past were all wrapped up in this, and to no good. In this view, a program of hard work, enterprise, solid education in needed areas of commerce, medicine, agriculture, administration is what is essential. All truck with spirits and this sort of thing is nonsense.

I am not so sure. The powers of the unconscious are stupendous. They do not go away just because you tell them to, or ignore them. They rumble underground far more dangerously than any volcano. Unless these powers are given carefully-programmed release, they will come forth. The Europeans were able to hold off the explosion because their conscious ego was strong and tough through long exercise. That is not so here.

In any case, even the tough ego broke. A carefully-programmed release means some way that the unconscious can express itself. When the Church moved up into Europe, she brought the rich life of the work of redemption acted out in the liturgy day by day, season by season, year by year. In that world of faith, embracing creation, the people of God, the Exodus, the entrance into the Promised Land, the infidelity of Israel, the coming Redeemer and the whole myth of his birth, life, teaching, death, resurrection, ascension, the sending of the Spirit, the birth of the Church, the writing of the Scriptures—all these marvelous mythic-historic doings entered into the very heart and life of the people. An entering into the heart, no mere appendage, some veneer on the surface. It was deep precisely because all these truths responded to primeval myths that rose from human depths and took various shapes and forms among various peoples. Christianity did not crush these myths: it answered them, fulfilled them, supplanted them with something richer and more complete. That is why the Europeans accepted the faith with such ease; in that way they were no different than the people here receiving the word of God: it was very good news indeed. They were glad to hear. It was what they were looking for.

But to bridge the gap between the old myth and its fulfillment, there is need to make evident how the one is the answer to the other. Thus one knows the old myths. If one does not, there is the risk that the new myth will not be truly or wholly absorbed, but mingled with, merged with, or simply tagged on to the original. Or, in the interval between the passing of the one and the assimilation of the other, there may be a blank period which is at loose ends. The Church, then, ideally has a rich liturgical life with a full complement of feast and season, with varieties of indigenous rite and ritual, all celebrated with as much awareness as possible. The word of God is thus not merely read or even heard, but is acted out, lived, participated in. But the connection must be there, the living contact of spirit with Spirit. If this is not so, the whole will not come off. The life of the Church will be merely external, not ring in the heart. When such contact is not there, even if the externals are kept up—and there is not much hope for that if the inner response is wanting—the old life will go underground or be carried on in some other way, along with, independent of, or counter to the life of faith.

It would seem that two major keys in contacting the life of the Spirit would be dreams and what might be called prophecy: visions and voices. Western people do not take dreams very seriously: people here do. Although it is said here that "we no longer dream since you have come," it may be assumed that this is said because it is obvious that dreams mean little or nothing to us. A dream must be interpreted: that dreams be interpreted in the light of God's truth is rather important if the people are to integrate the faith into their being. I do not think that usually the local Christian would associate the Church and dream interpretation. I doubt if many think of the resident priest as master of the spiritual life and one to consult in matters of dreams. It would seem to me, however, that some facility in the interpretation of dreams would be appropriate. Dreams are the voice of the unconscious and their message is important, certainly in what might be called serious dreams. If there is no one to help dreamers interpret, they are left to their own devices to handle as best they can, or they may consult others, or simply ignore it: this may not be a healthy situation. None of which is to say that we make a cult of dreams, cultivate them. This is as dangerous as ignoring them. The primitive mind fears dreams in the same sense that we fear God: a voice from the unknown. At least a healthy respect is essential.

Through the dream we enter into the unconscious and, as it were, christianize it. For Carl Jung, Europeans' use of Eastern techniques in the realm of the spirit would never work because the European unconscious is Christian, Catholic actually. Most Europeans, if they go back far enough, contact the Catholic substratum. And all carry this in their depths. Any method that is concerned with our deeper realism must reckon with this: our techniques, then, according to Jung, must be Christian. Even Catholic.

On the other hand, the same Jung maintains that missionary efforts with primitives in various lands are futile, since the imposition of a foreign element onto the native unconscious will not work. Jung was a great mind and a splendid scholar, but there seems something amiss here. After all, Europeans, too, were once primitives, and they accepted and absorbed Christianity. Through centuries of Christian experience, our unconscious became in some sense Christian.

It is in this sense that Christianity does not destroy a native culture but fulfills it. Even if aspects of a local style perish in contact with the faith, the better and richer elements are purified and given noble expression. The myths that people evolve to give them some understanding and interpretation of the great mysteries which surround them spring from our depths, even if their particular form is our own doing. These myths spelled out in ceremonial become a form of sharing them, participating in greater realities. The quest of the human spirit is something common, something all experience, indicated by the great similarities noted among the primal myths of the world. They prepare, as it were, the coming of the Lord and the great myth of redemption.

Since we of the West are out of touch with our dreams and, indeed, with the whole of the unconscious, it follows that we would not be at our ease in the handling of dreams. Possibly with some instruction and guidance one could establish better communion with oneself, and thus be able to make fruitful use of dreams. This is one good that can come of contact with a people more open to the whole of the human personality than we are. One would think, moreover, that young men being prepared for the priesthood in this country ought to be led to some skill in this direction. Even if they have lost touch with their own heritage, as is likely, they are in a position to renew it; and well-grounded in the faith, gifted with imagination and insight, they should be able to make such interpretations of dreams as would be of great benefit to themselves and to the dreamer. Even if many dreams are trivial and of no moment, there are other dreams that appear in times of crisis or difficulty: intelligent understanding of their message is a worthy work. It would be a pity if our own particular lack in this area would be picked up and carried over into an era when the work of the Church here will be wholly localized: it would not be the best thing to leave behind.

This role of interpretation is a share in the Church's governance in the Spirit, a communal function in that the Church is one in Christ, subject to the Spirit. Every spirit must be tested, all interpretation. Authority here is genuine. We are with the Church if we are Christian; we are community in the Spirit: communal enterprise, not private; submission to the Spirit, not inflation by it; a deeper entrance into unity, not alienation.

The same interest might be directed to visions and voices. It would not surprise me if there were more of this than we suppose. If misuse and misapplication of such phenomena is a likely source of mischief, prudent handling of them would bear good fruit. One thinks of the cargo cult and the frequent appearances it made (or makes) through some party either somewhat unbalanced to begin with or else endowed with more than average contact with the unconscious. If such is the case, it is a happy thought to picture such people coming to the Church for a correct view of what is at work in them. This seems a matter of some significance. We might view the cargo cult, after all, not so much a matter of cargo which, though certainly involved, need not be the major focus: it might just as well be some subtle method for emphasis on the role of the Spirit in human affairs, an endeavor to maintain some semblance of power of a spiritual order to compensate for the obvious impact of material functions and products. If that be so, due respect for such manifestations of the Spirit is not inimical to religion but partial to it. If, however, such visions or voices are either disregarded or made light of or even condemned, the activity is not thereby thwarted. It is merely driven underground. We then have a counterpart life of the spirit running along with the life of the faith. This counterpart may be far from pure, even contrary.

We cannot dismiss voices and visions out of hand. Neither need we see them as the work of God or of the evil one. If we ourselves were more open to other aspects of reality than the mind and senses, we would ourselves have more awareness of things of this sort. Dreams we dismiss rather easily; voices and visions and such we treat more sternly, seeing them as either indicative of mental illness or of high sanctity. We forget that priests and monks and nuns wandered through the earth in times past, working wonders. We pass much of this off as legendary, the work of pious writers. Maybe. Yet many of these wonders may have been natural enough, in the natural order, as we say. We know that miracles do not prove holiness. They witness to it, but do not prove it. There have been more real miracle-workers than saints. Perhaps many of the saints of times past were really not all that holy: good people, but perhaps more whole than holy.

Their wonders came from wholeness more than holiness. This is not to disparage, but to indicate that our "unwhole" state vastly inhibits human action. Our faith is real enough, but it is all in the head. I do not doubt that today we might find among the people here what might well be called "miracles." What are we to say of them? For that matter it may very well be rather much a mystery to the typical person here, some vague unexpressed wonder how it is that in the people of the spirit of the West so little of the Spirit is evident. We work no miracles. The charge comes up now and then: you are hiding something from us. True enough. We hide it also from ourselves.

Much of the old culture has gone. Some might think it too late. Many of the younger people, for example, know little or nothing of all their rich past. There are no doubt many in Papua New Guinea today, living in towns, active in business, government and education who are totally removed from any style of life which would involve communion with the world of the spirit. They may not only dress Western, talk Western and so on . . . they may *be* Western also in their outlook. With or without Christianity.

One considers the violence and unrest in such places as Port Moresby. It is possible and very likely that it stems from nothing more than what we observe elsewhere: undisciplined youth, lazy good-for-nothings who want all they want for nothing, fed with a certain amount of resentment, envy, greed. And bad example. On the other hand, it may go deeper. Much deeper. What comes if you have a generation of people with everything they want but who are empty inside?

The noted alcoholism of the American Indian and the Australian aborigine ought to suggest something. If a people is removed from its mystical heritage by contact with another culture, and nothing supplants what they lost, nothing enriches it or ennobles it, then such a people will be overcome with sadness, a sense of death, a gnawing hunger: oblivion, immersion in alcohol is one way out. Not only is this a false mysticism, it is a lethal one. I venture to say these people are apt for this sort of thing. For all that, I am rather hurt at heart when some local people have a sing-sing and get royally drunk in combination with it in order to get anything out of it. That can only mean that the sing-sing has died: it has no significance. No meaning. Beer keeps it going. This is not common, but it is around.

Nor will merely keeping up old traditions matter much if the heart is gone out of them. They may become commercially useful and draw tourists, but in terms of real culture this is a travesty, almost a sacrilege. The culture is not kept alive by such tactics. Even art will die. The old patterns may be repeated and the old items reproduced, but if the spirit dies, the art dies with it. Art is nothing if not an expression of the spirit: that is what produced it in the first place.

But when you have a widespread malaise, the same lack of meaning that undermines the West, there will be a seething undercurrent of pent-up forces that set the stage for upheaval. It can come in any form, on the slightest provocation, and may take a most savage turn, for the unconscious is not merely good but also evil. When the unconscious takes revenge, it is frightful. Cast a quick glance over Europe in the last years—say from the beginning of this century. No one in their right mind would have ever believed that a people claiming to be civilized should come to this. Nor have we seen the end. Nor need I add that when I say Europe, I do not exclude the United States.

It follows, then, that the cultivation of the spirit is of great importance in Papua New Guinea. Of prime importance, I would say. Yet the Church—the factor most concerned—has formidable opposition. For one thing, Christianity itself is a divided house. This grave scandal is not our doing: we inherited it. And many very fine people are caught in it, willy-nilly. Yet the truth remains: it cannot please God. For another, there is the gross impact of an almost totally-materialist West on this land. In the face of it, a voice on behalf of the spirit is scarcely heard. Finally, we ourselves. For we, too, come from an unhealthy climate; we, too, suffer the disease of the time, and thus our own faith, our own Christianity suffers for that. These are not small hurdles.

I am still full of hope. The grace of God is almighty. Even if we judge that the forces of hell are loose in our day and working most dreadful evils, we know that Christ has conquered the evil one and subdued him. Further, we know that a great surge of the Holy Spirit of God moves through Church and people today. And the Spirit goes very deep. The "problem" of meeting our unconscious grows daily more simple: we are confronted with it. We begin to see what we really are. In the ensuing darkness, fright, despair, our fluttering faith can spring to life and assert itself. To be sure, the darkness and catastrophe will still be there, but it will be filled with a presence of God that will be working, bringing into being a new people, a new world. We may yet live to see what God can do once we fall to our knees. Meanwhile, any effort here to give scope to the life of the spirit, to integrate the age-old longings of Papua New Guinea with the fulfillment that comes in Jesus Christ can only bear good fruit. If we can show how every myth and legend has its blossoming in Christ, every dream its answer, every voice and vision its true source—better, if we can share a life that is a participation in the great drama of God in relation to humanity through all history, through our own time, through my own life, we cannot have lived for nothing.

There never has been a perfect time. There never was a messenger of the Word who was not saddled with a peculiar poverty. Yet it is not the perfection of the time nor of the minister that qualifies the power of God and his grace. It has its own inner power. We simply do the best we can. That is our share. If we have made mistakes, and we have, we acknowledge that. And perhaps ask those who come after us to express their forgiveness by not repeating them. They will make mistakes; let them at least be their own, not ours. There is nothing perfect in this world, not even one perfect leaf, one perfect tree. For all that, God's beauty is everywhere manifest. And his grace is at work in the midst of human imperfection.

The dream is to build a Christian community which has all the flavor and tonality of these people, a new being which integrates the initial work of God here with his coming among us in the Church. The dream of community means at once a rejection of a materialist, individualist, aggressive West, as well as a rejection of the community-myth which was the dream of Communism, in favor of a human family united with Christ and one another in a preliminary version of the kingdom which is to come. That preliminary version must be Papua New Guinea, because that is where it began: the Christ who comes to them is a Christ responding to a spirit that God sowed in these hearts a long time ago. Such a Christianity is no more foreign than humanity is. In the depths of the unconscious, God was at work. And still is.

Papua New Guinea
Circa 1975

4
Knock Your Socks Off Christianity
Seventh Sunday of the Year
Matthew 5: 38-48

*A*t the reading of this passage this morning, the hearing of it, one can only think: how they must have loved that man! The boldness of it. The nerve of it. "You have learned how it was said . . . but I say to you."

"—*the achieve of, the mastery of the thing!*" *(Gerard Manley Hopkins)*

And they resented him, too. Were angry at him. No one likes being unsettled, really. No one likes having solid positions challenged, assured verities questioned. You and I, too. We are famous for loving peace, that is, for your leaving us be, for your not upsetting us, your not disturbing our tranquility . . . monastic tranquility. I think the Gospel reminds us that if we are not now and then quite shaken to our roots by the word of the Lord and his action on us, among us, in us, then it can be assumed that we are out of touch, no longer with it, no longer among the living. So the first question is: how long since you have been rattled by the Lord? (Or, in the words of an ad I read at Christmastime, "How long since you had your socks knocked off?")

I came to this monastery for the first time in November 1959. It seems only yesterday. I was a middle-years' priest then and at odds with things, as one often is at that period of life. I fell in love with the place at once. A number of things were involved, but there was one in particular. And that one thing was this: it was the first group of celibate men I had known who were able to be tender and gentle, who were not afraid to be as they liked.

They are more gentle today than they were then. And still not afraid to be as they like, to take their cue from a Spirit that is not of the world around them. I was completely at a loss to account for it. As individuals they were not and are not all that exceptional. The place as such has not that much going for it, then or now. One ecclesiastic of position, at his first look, said it was the ugliest religious house he knew—a travelled European he. I later came to the conclusion that it was the wall, that symbolic gesture that tells the rest of the world: inside is ours and we do as we like, when we like, if we like.

In other words, this was the first place I ever was in where you could be free. A house of freedom. Freedom from the awful tyranny the world imposes.

And what tyranny most of all? That macho culture which imposes aggression and competition and assertion and strife and contention and says this is the way to live, this is natural, normal, human, and above all, manly. I have news for you. It is nothing of the sort. It is a diseased form of living. It is a sick society that lives by such ideals. It is as weird and as queer a kind of living as humankind has ever known. And it pervades everything. Even song and dance and drama and the cult of the noblest gifts is permeated with this way. Ask anyone in law school, in art school, in medical school, in music school, what it is like. They will tell you what it is like: a vicious jungle.

And it is this spirit which breeds war. Cultivates it and blesses it, ennobles it and sanctifies it. And humanity dedicates to that horror the totality of its gifts, its resources, the brilliance of its best minds, the talents of its most highly-endowed. Science is in the service of war. Further, war is the biggest business we have. We the biggest country in the world. And business is good. I do not think it possible to be a Christian and be committed to such a world. So I came here to a world within a world where ordinary people can become ordinary Christians and not have to apologize for it. We believe in love and in patience and in tolerance and forbearance. We believe in littleness and forgiveness. This is not a house of self-assertion and self-aggrandizement. We do not cultivate contention nor reward pushy go-getters. We praise service. And humility. Gentleness and dedication and the love of beauty. Pretty clothes and pretty music and pretty ceremony. Song and dance in the night. Bells ringing for joy, for sorrow. Incense making the air blue with fragrance, and flowers cluttering up our ways.

This house of counterrevolution. This center of rebellion. This nay-saying stronghold that knows another way. Sings another song. Not only listens to a different drum but beats it for all who can hear. A world away from that hideous scene called the pursuit of excellence.

But we are still much in the world, one with it, but one with the world of the troubled and trod upon, those untold millions who make up the poor suckers of the capitalist kingdom, those currently rejected from the working scene, those left by the way for incompetence. The inept, the unable, the old, the stupid, and above all the poor, the poor who don't make it.

In his book *Origins*, Richard Leakey—I assume he is a capable anthropologist, as was his father—says of early humans that cooperation was their characteristic. And not for centuries, not for millennia, but literally for millions of years. That this is by far the basic story of human beings in relation to others: cooperation—and that competition and strife are something new. Hence the old saw that has aggression in our genes, native to us, is gross blunder and neat convenience. And the teaching of Jesus, then, far from being something out of this world and impractical and mythical, is something within the reach of us, the more so in his grace. It is as natural to us as the supernatural.

The news, then, is not that you are special but that you are common, the normal. Not the freakish, but the ordinary. And in following Jesus and his way we are not only close to God but close to our true neighbor. To be like Jesus, that is the ideal. As tough, as gentle. As rooted in love.

The other day I was over to Nazareth Motherhouse (near Bardstown, KY, several miles from Gethsemani) to buy some books for a New Guinea nun. I visited the graves of the Sisters there. 1500 graves. Think of that. What a sight. What a moving sight! Whole fields sown with love. What a vision. Women have served Jesus so well and in such numbers. And men so poorly.

It is the oddest thing, is it not? The teaching of Jesus that sounds in our world so far out, so wild, so extravagant, is really not that at all. It is the worldly world around us that is far out, that is weird, crazy. Like in New Guinea. Making Christians of them was nothing at all. The Good News was good news to them. They took to it, loved it. But making capitalists of them? That was something else. Too alien in spirit. And so the foreigner wakes up and realizes that the Christian veneer over capitalism is deception and fraud. Nothing betrays religion like religion.

"You hear it said . . . but I say to you."

Say on, Good Lord.

Gethsemani
February 19, 1984

5
The Hidden Ground of Love
This rare book review by Matthew Kelty
is instructive because of what it says of Thomas Merton
by a monastic confrere who knew him quite well.

The Hidden Ground of Love: The Letters of Thomas Merton on Religious Experience and Social Concern, selected by William H. Shannon, New York: Farrar-Straus-Giroux, 1985.

Some years ago, a young man who had been a semi-professional dancer and actor entered the monastery at Gethsemani. He did not continue at the abbey and later he told me why. "I was always on stage," he said. "You know, since I was a small child I have always been called on to sing some song, to do a little dance, or some such thing, and that continued all my life. I developed early an awareness of people watching me, applauding me, making much of me. Now it seems part of me. And so here at the abbey. All the more with its liturgy, ritual, costume and other dramatic aspects. I could not shake myself of an audience, real or imagined. Try as I would, it stayed with me and ruined the place, the life for me. And so I had to leave. Being a monk is a lot more than an act."

There is a photo of Thomas Merton as a preschool child sitting at home at a little desk his mother had gotten him, a book in his hands, I think, and though not looking at the camera, very much saying with emphasis, "See me at my little desk and note that I can read and write already, so small a child." Merton had then, and had all through his life, an enormous self-awareness, an idea that what he said and what he thought and how he looked all mattered very much. And he pulled it off.

I think this is very much an achievement. Eminence in anything, from holiness to art, to learning, to dancing, requires an engagement which is all-consuming. It is taking one's self utterly seriously. And getting away with it. That is to say, so managing it that the self is lost in the self's assertion. Holiness, it seems to me, means a commitment that is so overpowering that it literally burns up everything in its being achieved. I think Thomas Merton had that sort of engagement in the search for the love of God and neighbor. And there is, to the average person, or to put it more modestly, to me, something shocking in it.

This volume of letters, first of a projected series of four [now that four volumes have appeared, there is a projected fifth, ed.] makes this clear, I think. Each collection of letters covers a certain area: this one, religious experience and social concern. They are arranged chronologically under the name of each correspondent. Thus one follows a certain series to the same person and in the same general interest. This makes for a certain seesawing through Merton's life, but is in the end not confusing. The range of persons is extraordinary; so, too, the subjects.

A monk reading this volume will not be very far along when the question will arise, "Where did the man get the time?" For a monk will know what a monk's life is, knows what it was like in Merton's time. Merton fitted letters into the day somehow or other, had the ability to seize a few moments and sit down and bat out a few words to a friend, words often enough running into an essay full of sound thought and comment. Another monk in the same time might be standing and looking out the window a while before the next bell, checking the bulletin board. Merton had enormous energy, great discipline, and, of course, brilliance. Carried off, be it noted, with a certain cool style. He did not give the impression of being extraordinarily busy, rushing from this to that, harried and pursued. The opposite. He would look casual, but it was only a look. If there were others in the monastery who took pains to appear in workclothes as much as possible, it was he who perhaps did more real work than anyone else in the place. He used time well.

But the puzzling thing to me is how it was possible for this man to sit down and share some thoughts with a friend, knowing the while that the carbon copy would be filed away (he kept orderly files, if sloppy in other ways), would some day, without much doubt, see itself in print. Just as when he made entries in his journals, many of them private and semi-private, he was able to write as if he did not know that every line would one day show up in a book, or at least be edited for a book. Apparently the self-awareness did not bother him. Or, to see it so, he was so totally given to his calling that everything entered into that with a purity of heart that dazzles one.

Put in worldly terms, he was very ambitious, very shrewd, quick to capitalize on anything, even anyone who would further his cause. Not his own cause, of course, but what he stood for. For he took himself with a most amazing seriousness. And this is what makes the difference: his love for God. He was as determined to advance his career as any striving artist. But the determination was inspired.

I remember once going up to his hermitage with him and a group of guests to discuss some spiritual subject which I have quite forgotten. He wasted no time in getting up there—or perhaps he was already there waiting us—but what struck me forcibly at the time was this: that once in the room and seated, he at once launched into a prepared lecture from notes. Not a minute spent in small talk, warming up, the exchanges that can make a gathering rather delightful. And I thought: how serious this man is. How important what he says seems to him. So I remain convinced that holiness involves some such driving passion.

Here is a brief sample of some of the people he wrote to (only the correspondence from him is given—not the other party's): Thich Nhat Hanh, Erich Fromm, Dorothy Day, Paul Tillich, Jacqueline Kennedy, Pope Paul VI, Bernard Häring, John C.H. Wu, Cardinal Wright.

The man is fascinating and so are his letters. He can be wry, sarcastic, charming, impatient, frustrated, frustrating, impetuous, timid, determined. And lots else. And it is all there to see. The tone he took, for example, in writing to the Pope was so reverent, respectful, that I was amused for it being so out of character. Yet I am sure it was all in childlike faith. When I was a novice in the first part of the 1960s, Pope John XXIII sent him a stole as a personal memento. Merton was almost in tears when he received it, so great was his delight. He used to wear it on special days of prayer we have every month. Yet the stole was no work of art, rather garish, tasteless. That did not bother him at all, and he could be so cutting in comment on Church art he did not like.

The letters are edited by Monsignor William Shannon, professor emeritus of theology at Nazareth College, Rochester, NY, and author of *Thomas Merton's Dark Path*. He has done some "prudent editing of some of the letters" to keep them within length. I doubt if we have missed anything, and one has no sense of being cheated.

Next time you write a letter, have in mind that it will be in print some day for the world to read.

Gethsemani
Circa. 1985

6
No Poison, This Mercy
Third Sunday of Lent
Luke 13:1-9

Some people arrived and told Him about the Galileans whose blood Pilate had mingled with that of their sacrifices. At this He told them: "Do you suppose these Galileans who suffered like that were greater sinners than any other Galileans? They were not, I tell you. No; but unless you repent, you will all perish as they did. Or those 18 on whom the tower at Siloam fell and killed them? Do you suppose that they were more guilty than all the other people living in Jerusalem? They were not, I tell you. No; but unless you repent you will all perish as they did."

An unexpected death among some primitives I have heard about, especially of a younger man or woman, always has a reason. And the reason is always "poison." I'd say, "But are you sure? In olden times, maybe. But today? More likely malaria or pneumonia, maybe." They would look at you in sympathy, or even pity. The matter was not debatable. It was too obvious. It was poison. And after several of such experiences, it occurs to you that "poison" served as an adequate explanation for an implausible event. It satisfied and gave them peace. They knew why he or she died.

We, when we hear that someone has died, usually ask, "And what did they die of?" As if it mattered a whit. Rare disease or common, accident or simply old age, incompetent doctors or incompetent cooks—what does it matter, really? But we derive some comfort from a fact that gives us a hold on the mystery of death.

Linking death, suffering, disease, misfortune with God's displeasure is perhaps back of it all. If we can make it clear that a punitive God was not at work, but can name a culprit, then we escape a dreadful situation. It is not rare to link misfortune with God's anger. Or for that matter, good fortune with God's good pleasure. In us.

So when a plane crashes, ships collide, hotels burn, a shuttle does not launch, then we do the necessary: we appoint a commission to find out what happened, why, who was responsible. It gives us a hold on history.

Like the weather: we can do nothing about tornadoes and hurricanes and earthquakes, but predicting them is a help. And keeps God at a distance.

Death always means God. And the question always is, "Is he angry? Did he do it on purpose?" And the suspicion always is, "Yes, he is. And he did." And so we try very hard to get something between that worry and ourselves. Something we can hang death on.

It does not work, of course. Naming the cause, knowing it, does not remove death. And yet death comes anyway. It sure does. And why does it come? Because of sin.

So Jesus took his disciples to task on their error: the Galileans were not more guilty than others. Nor the victims of the Siloam tower. You are *all* sinners.

Monks do not have many tragic deaths. But sometimes we do. Brother Michael was known to be reckless and rather careless. But he died because he was a human being. All of whom die. Father Louis (Thomas Merton) was known to be inept with devices and tools and equipment. But he did not die because of that. He died as a member of a sinful race.

So if we are to deal with death, it is not enough to deal with superficial circumstances. We must go ever so much deeper. In healing humans of what ails them, we can sometimes help them by going back in years to past history, to childhood, to confront the event from which stems so many aches and problems. They can then deal with this material so long hidden, repressed, yet hurting them. Sometimes even that is not enough and we go all the way back to the womb. And there unravel the knots that have them all tied up.

But if you want to be healed wholly, and wholly indeed, then we go back to the original scene. And that is what we do now at this table. It is seasonable this decade or two to make much of the Eucharist as food and drink, as a divine meal, as our common gathering around a common table to share the one bread and one cup in one love for the one Lord and for one another. Who would gainsay? Yet there is more.

It is also sacrifice. There is altar. There is priest. There is victim. And immolation. And only after that, communion.

And we are not watching something. We are doing something. We are going back to our primordial past to the day we put Christ to death. And by that fact learned to die. Death entered the world by sin. Also ours. The old legend is neat. When they dug the hole for the Cross, they found the skull of Adam; our history is one piece. But the mystery we enter into is also a mystery of mercy. He has forgiven us. And the proof is in the eating and the drinking of his Body and Blood.

So we do not have to ask about someone, "What did they die of?" They died of sin. Along with the Galileans and those by the tower in Siloam. Along with Michael and Louis and absolutely everyone else. And because we do this today and everyday, we do not fear death. Nor the God who brings us death. Nor the reason for it all. Here at the altar, we face the issues and live reality. If we put Christ to death, that ought to end it: no need now to put myself to death, or others. No need for violence against myself or others. No need to punish, to bring to heel, to take to task, to shape up or bring into line this mess that is life because I hate it and everyone in it. No need for the war we love, communal, familial, national. We've done all that, seen all that - *deja vu*. It is, rather, time to breathe fresh air and see wide views, and know a warm sun rising in the east. Because mercy has become the climate in which we live. Which is to say, we know what it means to repent: it means to accept mercy. Otherwise, we perish.
Amen.

Gethsemani
March 2, 1986

7
Of Word and Symbol
Fifth Sunday of Easter
John 13:31-33a, 34-35

*I*n the beginning God created. So does Scripture open. Creation is by speech, indeed, is a kind of speech: "Let there be light." That is why the Son of the Father is spoken of as the Divine Word. In the beginning was the Word. Speech is creativity and creation is a work of God, a sharing in it. In the highest and most perfect sense, the Word is God.

Can it be a surprise that when God made a human, God should at once teach speech? God showed Adam and Eve all the world and bade them name everything. God spoke and so made man and woman: they speak and so create with God, for by their work they make the named thing part of themselves. The nature of the created becomes a creature of the mind. And by way of that word, the mind carries creation a step further and adds word to word in reasoning sequence. So are human beings God-like in having the nature of things in themselves and by thought creating a new idea. The world would be incomplete without the human to name it, to contemplate it, to fructify it, to love it.

God taught the secret of the universe in speech, for it is by speech that we learn that all is symbol and sign. The world is God saying: I am beauty, I am goodness, I am love and light and wisdom. It is the word that reveals this, for with God we create symbol just as he did. And through the word share the mind of God.

When we read of the congenital deaf who can move easily into the realms of the mind through sign language, we are brought face-to-face with the fact that we are naturally symbolic . . . taught so, made so, by God. We do not make love with concepts, but words, with deeds. What is in the mind remains there until I say it or play it or act it or do it or mime it. Nothing leaves the mind but by symbol. Nothing enters the mind but by the same route. How splendid! You smile at the little infant in your arms and the little infant smiles back. A shattering experience.

The whole world is symbol, all telling us something. All the time. So it is necessary to learn sign language, to learn speech, to learn symbol. Then we can read God. All the time.

The monastery teaches us that, much as God taught Adam and Eve. It is all symbol. That is why we meet in this handsome church. After all, a barn would do, a hall, an auditorium, an aula. We wear symbolic clothes, do symbolic actions, our song is symbolic, our gestures. Not to say the words themselves.

We do not have a corridor or a hallway. No, a cloister. Our refectory is a place where monks eat. It is not a lunchroom or a cafeteria or restaurant or buffet or even a dining room. It is the refectory. We gather in chapter: it is no board room, no conference room, no community room. As chapter it is a very special symbol. Our scriptorium is no lounge or living room or sitting room or reading room. It is a symbol of its own.

So monastery says "monk" to the monk all day. It is what he is, what he should be, what he wants to be. That is the symbol he is, the word he utters unceasingly. All the neighborhood knows this: for miles around we are known not as the abbey, not as the monastery, not as Gethsemani, but directly—we are the monks.

The futility of saying, "What good is it? What use? Who needs it? Who needs incense? Who needs bells? Can't you get yourself a watch? Who needs cowls and choir stalls and cloister and abbot?" No one, really, if that is your approach. Who needs daffodils? Or blue skies? Or whippoorwills? Who needs song and dance? Who needs processions and icons and candles? Candles? All these lights on—39 of them, 12,000 watts—and you light candles. You are mad.

Yes. The way God is mad. God made the world for the joy of it, not the need of it. It is full of his glory. Still. Despite what we have done to it. Kentucky was once magnificent forest of mighty trees, giants rising from a clean floor. Look at it now. Skimpy woods full of undergrowth. Yet, for all that, it is glorious with God still. The symbols may not be all they were, but they still speak loud and clear. Even the deaf hear them. And they reply, they whom God loves more than miles of woods.

My brothers, my sisters, how splendid is God in creation. Infinite wisdom in the smallest insect, in the remotest planet. Yet, most magnificent of all, in the human. For he can do, she can do, what nothing else of earth can do: make the world their own. By word the human creates anew in the marvel of symbol-making. We are like God.

We are not always conscious of all that. As if that matters. We may use few words in a day. But we use symbols all day and all night. And every one of them is of God; they are God speaking. And since only a modest part of our mind is conscious and a massive part unconscious, it is this unconscious part, which is still mind, that feeds us, nourishes us, sustains us. It would be difficult to live as monks in the Holiday Inn down the road. Not because the inn is ugly or sinful or plastic. It could provide all we need, but it speaks the wrong words, that's all. It is not a monastic symbol. And the word the inn is would be at work on us all the time, unconsciously unsaying what we are trying to say. Even though this, too, is an inn. And we the passing guests here but a while. And then gone to another country. It may not be as comfortable as the inn down the road, but you get more for your money. God is explicit in the night at this inn.

We are each and all a symbol: we are saying something all the time. All of us preach. Spread a cause. Take a stand. All the time. Everywhere. The world God created is full of God and his glory. We aim, each of us, to be just like that: Godlike, Godly, radiant in his glory. After God had fashioned you and finished you, he stood you up, smiled at you, touched you lightly and said, "Speak! Tell me that you love me."

Gethsemani
April 27, 1986

8
Saint Benedict's Day
Feast of St. Benedict

*W*e are comfortable with the awareness that out of the Church came tradition and out of the Church and tradition came Scripture. We are not comfortable with the notion that all stems from Scripture. The appropriateness of our comfortable view is seen in a comparison with Benedictines and the Rule of St. Benedict. It is not hard to recognize that the monastic life came first, then tradition, then the Rule. Even though we like to give priority to the Rule, we know that the Rule was lived before it was written, and it was written in the context of praxis, that is, tradition. What is puzzling in the matter of monks, tradition and Rule is precisely what puzzles in the triad of Church, tradition and Scripture. Thus: how is it that tradition is not explicitly supported by Scripture in some areas? Strictly speaking, Catholics and Scripture seem at odds at times. We might say the same of Benedictines.

If we run through the Rule in an effort to catch some basic themes, I do not think we would need to run through it many times before we would sense that a major melodic permanent is the idea of relation, dialogue, communion, exchange, consensus through sharing, discussion leading to solution. The opening word of the Rule, *ausculta* (listen), suggests that assertion must be coupled with reception, giving with being given. The last page of the Rule notes that the proficient are still but beginners, and that returning to the sources will lead to further growth, going back to the beginnings.

Given contemporary distress at failures in dialogue in family life, social life, economic and international life, it can be of interest to us to see how the stress that St. Benedict laid on relation is deep in the Rule, deeper still and more dramatically in tradition.

Any monastery anywhere, anytime, will be recognizable without a monk in sight by the shape of the structure. The church will be choral and the chapter nearby will be choral and the refectory on the third side will be choral. Choral, that is, the two choirs across from one another, not only in church where the choir is functional but also in the chapter where it is not, as it is also not in the refectory. This must be so because the choral form is more than a setting for antiphonal psalmody. That would explain church but not chapter, let alone refectory.

If we examine what goes on in chapter, we see the need for choral setting. When the abbot calls the brethren for counsel, he listens to them, hears them out, monks talking to monks. Every monk is heard from and in communal context. And each gives his view with deference to a sought truth, not in a stubborn clinging to notions. A monk does not go to chapter with his mind made up, though he may know what he is going to say. His saying his say will be his contribution to the whole. His listening to what all the others say will help him to reshape, rethink, reformulate his own mind, change it or confirm it or modify it. When the pure of heart exchange in such wise, the truth will emerge, a consensus will not be too long coming. The abbot has then been well-served. He takes it all to heart and, in the end, returns his conclusion.

This is better than democratic rule by majority, for majorities can be tyrannous, foment pressure groups and lobby; further, majorities can be wrong. This is better than autocracy for an autocrat is not beholden to other light than his or her own. It is a superb mode of governing. And, I might add, this dialogical way is something we find very difficult. You and I. We come, all of us, from a highly competitive society in which self-assertion, aggression, drive and the private pursuit of excellence are much-touted virtues. This is not to condemn competition. It is only to say that it is a world away from the world of the cloister. And so we tend by our background to turn dialogue into assertion, relation into put-down and shut up, exchange into a vigorous defense of personal views. Some communities never dialogue because they do not know how. Culture lag.

Modern religious societies and congregations dropped choir service and, consequently, choral forms. Interesting to note that their government, too, became more authoritarian, less communal, more organized and much more efficient. Monks are not beyond a certain partiality to this style as one closer to our own culture than the monastic way, a more time consuming one, if nothing else.

An odd thing is that when it comes to the fabric of the monastery, of the choir form, St. Benedict has not a word. He took it all for granted. The tradition was already there, and in the tradition he wrote his Rule. This is something at least vaguely like the Church being present before the Scriptures were written, the tradition a living thing before a word was recorded. No surprise, then, that not everything traditional is explicit in the written word.

And yet the monastic tradition and the Rule of St. Benedict on relation is more than a manner of governing communities, great though that be. It is rather more than that, being, I think, a way of life or an approach to life which is basically dialogical. The monks deal with abbot and with one another in frank, open exchange, barren of passion, violence, pride or duplicity. It is candid and kind because it can afford to be, being in the service of truth, the search for God's will.

And this dialogue takes shape first in choir where the monks chant the psalms to God in one another. They are not chanting before altar or tabernacle, but to God present in the brethren. We face one another, we are *koinonia*, community, the brethren, where God resides. And the abbot presides over the community. God resides in all. Hence, when a brother speaks, he can speak only of what of God there is in him. But that much he must share so that his portion of the truth be added to that of the brethren, so that the whole truth emerge and be recognized as such by the father.

We gather at table in the same choral manner, one choir, as it were, facing the other, breaking the bread that sustains us in service and in love. I do not eat alone but in communion. There may be duality even in the two handles on my cup [until recently, monks of Gethsemani and in other Cistercian houses drank from two-fisted mugs, ed.], like the two handles on the chalice of grace I drink, gracefully integrated.

We are in living dialogue with the brethren at all times. And that again is a picture of my dialogue with God. One does not deal with God as competitor, aggressor, in self-assertion, in search for the first place, the top. God does not understand that language. We dialogue with God. We share with one another in candor and warmth, God and I. I can learn to talk to God in monastic choral living.

And there is finally that inner dialogue of all those choirs within me, those dualities that face one another and make up my inner architecture, sometimes my inner contradiction. My head and my heart, my reason and my intuition, my memory and my imagination, my male and my female, my past and my future, my mortality and my immortality. How learn the subtle language of this profound discourse but by the monks' dialogue in choir and in chapter and in refectory? No better school, surely.

Until the end of time. Then we will gather not in open-ended choirs opposed to one another, but as now in a great circle around the throne of the infinite God. For the choirs of heaven are great circles of completion and wholeness. That great cosmic dance we begin round this altar, to break the bread of eternal life and drink the cup of joy we share with Christ, that slain brother Abel we would not face across the choir, across the chapter, across the refectory, but with whom we are now reconciled.

Amen.

Gethsemani
July 11, 1986

9
Funeral for Father Peter

We are gathered here this afternoon to pay, as the phrase goes, our last respects to Father Peter. Better say: to celebrate his triumph, for a triumph it is. In the first place, it is better to refer to him as Father Mary Peter. The tradition of the Cistercians was to use the name of Mary as the first part of every monk's name, but out of deference to human sensibilities, only the initial was used, not the name, as in M. Matthew. Not so for Father Peter, no great one to bother with popular taste. He was Father Mary Peter and you could like it or lump it. And so now we write the last page of this man's story, and perhaps delve a little into the mysteries of this parable; for is not everyone's life a parable of some sort?

The facts are simple enough. He was born in Philadelphia, June 21, 1898. It is worth noting that he was baptized in the Nativity of the Blessed Virgin Church on July 10, 1898. Some 50 years later, at the same font, were baptized two infants who were to become monks of Gethsemani: Brother Malachy Samanns and

Father Francis Kline. Father Peter entered the Congregation of the Holy Ghost, a missionary order, and was ordained the 29th of August, 1925. He entered Gethsemani July 11, 1938 and was solemnly professed on All Saints' Day, 1940. He died August 1, 1986. Thus he was 88 years old, 60 years a priest, and 45 years a monk.

If the facts thus spelled out are simple enough, the story is not. He was sent to Sierra Leone in West Africa as a newly-ordained missionary and was there a few years. He returned and was engaged in various ministries in this country, and then began to think of the monastic life. He tried the life at Our Lady of the Valley, forerunner of Spencer [St. Joseph's Abbey in Massachusetts, ed.], but did not stay long. Some years later, he tried the life at the Abbey of New Melleray in Iowa and stayed a few years. Later on, he came here and was received, and here he remained until his death.

In the early years of his priesthood, something went wrong. Perhaps the experience in Africa triggered something. That happens now and then to missionaries, for not everyone adjusts to the enormous cultural change involved in leaving this country and living in another of quite a different kind. It has nothing to do with strength of character or depth of spirituality. Something hidden in the depths of the person emerges under the stress or strain of the adaptation, something usually quite unpredictable.

In any case, Father Peter was assaulted by the demons of darkness, of doubt, of despair, and they haunted him the rest of his life. At that time, little was known about these things, let alone any cure, and so he had to make do as best he could. By the time knowledge and remedies were at hand, it was much too late, of course.

The experience of the enormous power of this assault took great toll. His whole personality was affected, the strength of his ego weakened, and he had constantly to cope with guilt, with helplessness, with an awareness that he was like someone struck by God. Can you imagine what it must be like to be smothered with such an onslaught of doom and damnation?

All this was perhaps already begun when he sought admission to the monastic life, for some shrewd insight told him that a life of regularity and order, of intense spiritual quality, and a life identified with penitence and penance would be good for him. Though much an extrovert and perhaps not eminently suited to this sort of life, there must have been something in him that he realized and the superiors realized, and so he became a monk.

Very much like some Fathers of the Desert, he spent the rest of his life dealing with the demons that seemed to possess him. He was a man of superior intelligence and of many gifts. Those of you who heard him preach attest that he was an excellent preacher of the word years ago. And even under the stress of his lot, he managed to be of service in many areas, even if, as is usual with those so afflicted, one thing would follow another and nothing last too long. But birds did. He was a permanent lover of birds, and had an amazing affinity for them. Older monks will recall the trained turkeys that followed him around. Almost to the end he had a bird in his room, the last of them now with Brother Paul and dying, it would seem, for missing Father Peter so. He was into typewriters and their maintenance, into clocks the same way. He was an excellent rosary maker and made thousands, very beautiful ones. He was into guitars, too, and the finest guitar in the house was his, a gift to him from the maker in Spain. And he was into recording and tapes, and recorded little talks which he passed on to innumerable friends who loved him. And there was fishing. It was not too long ago that he was out in his boat when he should have been in his bed. I am sure there were other interests, but these come to mind. Meaning: he did not quit on life.

At one stage, for a year or two, I heard his confession every day. Not that he was such a sinner, but the sacrament helped him deal with guilt and darkness. I do not think most of us have any idea what this can be like. And yet he kept his faith shining bright, never gave up. And he did that mostly through the Mass. No priest in the abbey loves the Mass more than he did; even if his theology as well as his piety were dated, his love was not. And I am sure it was through the Divine Sacrifice, as he loved to call it, that he made his way.

If you are aware that we deal with mystery here, you are on the right track, I think. Is it not clear that this was the man's ministry, his apostolate? God knows there is darkness in our times. God knows the powers of evil thrive. God knows many succumb to despair. I need not go into that. And here is this monk entering deep into all this, willy-nilly, and answering it with faith and hope and love. Those of us who find it hard sometimes to deal with trial and trouble can only be awed at the dimensions of this man's trials, the intensity of his suffering in darkness.

If it was a stressful life for him, and it was, I guess the same could be said for those who lived with him, for he was up and down, was not always well-balanced, and could make demands.

People so tried, you know, need so much to be loved, and yet they find it so hard to believe in that love. So they test it and test it again to make sure it is real.

The things he would do! Like write his name all over everything he had, like a man making desperate efforts to keep an ego alive, to believe he was. And mutilating or spoiling things to individualize or personalize them one way or other, so making a mess of them, as if acting out what he must have felt God had done to him. And so be able to deal with it.

If you talk of heroic sanctity, has it occurred to you that maybe we have something of that here? The courage of the man!

I think this is the parable of the monk who has lived out his life in our midst: that no matter what happens, there is a God, and God is good, and he loves us. He stuck by that to the end. And yet even on his deathbed, he was still plagued by those demons of darkness. And won out over them. That is why this is a day of triumph. Why we can all rejoice. For all his ups and downs, for all his love of wandering, of change, for all his desires to escape his lot by going someplace else, a merciful Providence guided him to the end and he remained faithful. God be praised. God be thanked. A person could do worse.

And for those of you monks who did not know him too well, may I say something? He loved you. He was grateful beyond telling for the monks and the life here. He told me that time and again: "How good they have been to me." Maybe you should rejoice in that, too. I suppose that is why so many loved him. The wounded healer. You know there is something uncanny about those whom life has wounded: they have great compassion. I suppose even the birds knew it.

Rest in peace, Peter, man of God. Rest in peace. It is all over now.

Gethsemani
August 2, 1986

10
Two Men Went Up to the Temple to Pray
Thirtieth Sunday of the Year
Luke 18:9-14

Sunday morning in chapter. Or maybe Saturday night. At least that's what it seemed to be. And it was time for questions. So one of the monks, one of the anxious kind, rose and put a question. Not to the abbot, for the abbot was gone and his seat was occupied by Jesus. And so Jesus said, "Yes, Brother. And what is your question?" And the Brother said, "I'd like to know about us. Are we all going to be saved?" There was just a flicker of disturbance in the Lord's face, then a long pause. At length he said, "Yes, Brother, you will all be saved. Save one. There is some doubt about him. I doubt that he will make it." The monks were all quiet, then started to look at each other. And would you believe it, after a moment or two, it was clear they were all looking at one man, the one, surely, about whom Jesus was speaking. There was no malice or forethought in this. It simply followed from the nature of things. And then one of the old monks got up, far up on the line, close to the end. He would remind you of Father Edward. Strong in the chin. "Lord," he said, "all my life I have listened to you, served you, obeyed you. But I cannot go along with this. If our brother will not be with us in the Kingdom, you will have to excuse me." And the old monk bowed gravely and left the assembly. The silence that followed was very loud. And do you know, a moment or two later, on the other side of chapter, a second old monk rose and, saying nothing, left the room with a bow of reverence first made. And then, one by one, on the abbot's side, the prior's side, this one, that one, took their leave in quiet dignity.

And so it happened that after some moments' time, there were only two in chapter: the Lord and this Brother. But the Brother by now was in tears. In fact he could hardly control his feelings, heaving with the sobs of the deeply-afflicted. And then, noting that they were alone, he came forward, this Brother, and he said to Jesus, over and over: "I never knew they loved me so. I never knew. I never knew."

And Jesus said in a soft voice: "I know. I know. It is the usual story. Dry your tears. Go out and get them and bring them back."

And so I did.

The Gospel is telling the same story, the familiar one: the righteous and the unrighteous in the Temple. And the blessings are changed and the one takes the grace of the other.

The usual lesson follows: that you and I are both these men in the Temple. And that we must somehow reconcile both in Jesus. For if we think that Christianity does not involve sacrifice and service, we are mistaken. Mere standing in the back of church, on the fringe of the group, beating your breast, is not the Christian ideal. If we love God, we will have to show it. I want to see it in the soup you cook, the way you wrap cheese, how you clean a lavatory. Pious talk, pious gesture is no substitute for religion.

And yet service is not the sum and substance. In fact, it isn't it at all. That is why Jesus and the Gospel are so baffling. All our standards are shaken off their foundations.

Once on the hill by the sea in Bogia [Papua New Guinea, ed.], an old nun came to me. She wanted to see in her 80s the place where she began 50 years before. She visited the grave of her first superior in the mission when she was a young nun, with a lifetime of heroic service before her. And she cried a little. This beautiful woman had been through decades of hard service, including a war and all that means, and came out a radiant, lovely person of deep spirit. And she came in and sat down:

"Father, give me a good word."

"A good word, Sister? You ask a good word of me?"

"Yes, Father. You live alone on a mountain and can surely give me a word."

"Very well, Sister, here is a word. You are an old lady now, old in the service of God, soon to meet the One you love. The word is: do not make too much of what you have borne, what you have done."

She looked at me and, almost forgiving me, said, "Father, it was nothing. It was nothing."

"Sister," I said, "go in peace. You know the secret."

Sweet brothers, go easy when it comes to bragging on serving God many years, so many decades a priest, so long a monk, tried and true, loyal, faithful. That's all well and good. But it is not Christianity. It is only your side of the story. Your end of the dialogue. Your dance as his partner. Do not forget what he did in giving it to you.

As an old man, Father Francis Markert, S.V.D., used to have German friends from German parishes of Chicago come to visit him summer afternoons at the seminary. And he would stroll with them around the pond, sit in the lovely park, take some refreshment, and then cap the visit with a tour of the printing plant he had built and managed so many years, now in the hands of a new manager full of vision and enterprise. He was so proud of his work and that it continued to be blessed. It gave so much meaning to his declining years. And one wintry night, in a couple of hours, it burned to the ground. Only the front door was left with *Ora et Labora* inscribed above it in concrete. *"Jahveh nathan, Jahveh laquak, Y'hey shem Jahveh m'borak,"* said the rector the next morning at breakfast. The words of Job: "The Lord has given, the Lord has taken; Blessed be the name of the Lord." And so Father Markert went to God with nothing in his hands to show him.

So we are all on occasion at one end of the Temple or the other. Now is the soul rejoicing in God's gifts and blessings, work well-done, years of service gladly given. And on other days beating our breasts, realizing that we are not all that much, that what we have done is nothing. That only the love he has for us is our saving.

It is the usual story. We want so hard to earn that love, and in the end find we had it all along and did not know it. It is joy even then to discover it, for your discovery of it is in some way the salvation of your brother or sister, too.

A priest, a monk, a nun, a married couple, a good family are great gifts of God. That we must not forget. Gifts we probably have no right to. So is a monastery a great gift of God, a magnificent one. It is not just a human achievement. Yet all these gifts need the gift of response, the sacrifice, the staying power, the love that puts ideals into practice.

Yet that is still not enough. We must move beyond into purity of heart. Then is our gift the sweetest music, the totally-selfless song of joy. That is what the Gospel parable is all about. Sometimes we achieve purity of heart only through failure. So the man at the back of the Temple. Much better the good life of total service grown into total gift born of detachment, the music played not for gain or name but straight from a pure heart in free joy.

God will give us also the gift of the pure heart if we let him. And the response that this takes is the greatest love there is. The

saints glorious in achieving great things for God all went to God empty-handed, stripped clean, dazzling in beauty from within, great in the awareness that they were nothing, God everything. Love is all that matters. We are good Protestants: we are not justified by works. We would like to be good Christians who love a Lord who loved us first, loves us last, and always. How sad to discover too late that we were dearly loved and had not faith enough to believe it. We are all of us saved by that love.
Amen.

*Gethsemani
October 26, 1986*

11
Expectations Overturned
Third Sunday of Advent
Matthew 11:2-11

*B*uddy Ballard used to work at the alfalfa complex on the hill. We called it the de-hy for the dehydrating process in making pellets from alfalfa. And Buddy had a red convertible, a Ford, I think, with top down all summer: very smart, very sporty for the mid-60s. I used to work up there with Brother Gerlac. One day, things were a mess, and in the midst of it, Brother asked me if I would run down to the post office and see if the spare part had come. "Sure. Buddy, why don't I use your convertible?" "OK. Go ahead." So I zoomed down the hill and up the front avenue with work scapular blowing in the wind. I came to a dramatic stop at the gatehouse. Standing there, just come, were three impressive ladies looking like queen mothers, big-bosomed dowagers. They gave me a haughty going-over, obviously distressed at this display. I ran in to the post office, got the package, ran out. They were still standing there with long faces, like El Greco. I waved to them, pointed to the red convertible and said, "Pretty nice, huh?" They were not amused: "We thought you'd be in your cloister." I had no time and scooted off, leaving total disillusionment behind me. I had not measured up to their notions of a monk of Gethsemani in 1965. And they were very vexed.

I frequently had occasion years ago to be in on it when Fr. Louis (Thomas Merton) would meet someone or other, usually in connection with vocation work. It was interesting to note how many were frankly disappointed with the real Merton. Not all, but many. They had their own idea what he must be like. But when confronted with his person, they were at a loss to adjust to the reality. He was so bland.

Indeed, at his very last appearance, as it were, when he gave that last conference at Bangkok, two monks who heard him to the end were not impressed. In the blunt way of scholars, one said to the other, "Well, that wasn't much." Maybe it wasn't in terms of what the monks expected: no doubt some dazzling performance that would leave all breathless and on their feet with applause. He had not measured up to expectations. It happens all the time. To me. To you.

This morning to Jesus. The Baptist sent a delegation: "Are you He who is to come or do we look for another?" Possibly John had his doubts. Far more likely is it that the questions were put for the benefit of the hesitant, the perplexed. And Jesus answered them by showing how the Scriptures described the person of God who was to come: "The blind see, the deaf hear, the lame walk, the dead are raised to life, and the poor have the good news preached to them." They could draw their own conclusions.

And presumably they did. And we know from history that the majority concluded that he did not measure up to expectations. They rejected him. They had their own ideas of what made a Messiah, and it was up to any Messiah to conform. His problem, not theirs.

Strong stands like that are dangerous. They have great power. And they are so likely to lead to action. They led to the death of Jesus.

A sure sign that you or I am engaging in the same dynamics of trying to adjust reality to fantasy is anger. Anger is the give-away, the tell-tale. Especially hidden anger. Resentment.

I think it is something we all know in the course of a life. We have all been disappointed. Men often marry an illusion. Only later do they meet their wife, hopefully come to know her and love her. The man she marries may not exist save in her dreams. It can be difficult learning to love reality.

How many of you found here what you expected? The older you are and the longer here, the easier it is to say with certainty: not one of you knew what you were getting into. How could you have? No one could have guessed ahead of time what happened here the last 20 years. Or any 20 years. And in any life. Ask one of the neighbors, "Has life been as you expected?"

So, of necessity, somewhere along the line you dropped fantasy and began to love reality. For your notions of monastic life were all in your head, written in a book you read. They had no contact with the real. And if you did not abandon your fantasies and enter into loving union with reality, well, it is no great insight to say you are an unhappy person, an angry one.

For you have been disappointed. The reality did not measure up to your expectations. You are like the dowagers in the avenue who were indignant at a monk who did not behave as they thought he ought. In a way, they did not deserve an explanation or get one: that it was not my convertible, or even the monastery's, that we worked outside the cloister as well as in.

Thomas Merton was a constant annoyance to many in and out of the monastery because he catered to no one's pious delusions. Even now it is amusing to ask someone how soon they think Merton will be canonized, with the 10th of December his feastday. It is not the merit of the case which is the issue: the very idea strikes them as ridiculous, their faces cloud in distress at the very idea. Their notion of sanctity and Merton have nothing in common.

I take the matter seriously. Not Merton and the Bangkok conference, nor me and the visiting ladies, but you and me and Jesus. If we are not willing and able to give all away in our relationship to God, to God's service, to the Kingdom of heaven, we are in very dangerous waters. We shall never know freedom nor the joy this Sunday celebrates. We may program our Jesus and expect him to conform to our program, but he will honor it only by ignoring it.

The dearest thing to me in the monastic life I came to was the Latin office. I make no bones about it. It had everything. And one morning, I woke to find that it was gone. And they did not even bother to ask me first. What we have in its place is something else, but a poor thing to what it replaces, for all its beauty. The lesson was a good one for me: the love of God and his service is beyond anything you can lay claim to. You meet God as he comes, and he comes as he pleases. When he pleases. If you are not willing to meet him on those terms, you will never meet him. And then you will have to be content with the fantasy Jesus you have made for yourself. Who is not real. In whom there is no salvation.

Art thou He who is to come or shall we look for another?
I was such a disappointment to the ladies.

Merton was such a disappointment to those who met him, who heard him talk.

Jesus was such a disappointment to those who waited for the Messiah.

The Church is such a disappointment to so many.

The monastic life . . . my marriage . . . is such a disappointment . . . my children . . .

And so on . . .

Art thou He who is to come?

Thou art.

Come, Lord Jesus. Save us from the bogs of narcissism, for our being also such a disappointment to ourselves.

Come, Lord Jesus. Come any way you like. Any time. Anyhow. You are the one. You are the fulfillment of every dream, the God our illusions tried to hide.

Amen.

Gethsemani
December 14, 1986

12
Week of Prayer for Christian Unity

A lady named Fanny Monroe from up in Connecticut writes for Masses now and then. Come Christmastime, she sent a gift for the monks and wrote me that Christmas is the worst time of the year for her. They are a big family, and every Christmas they get together and, she says, "We do nothing but fight. I am always glad when it is over."

An Australian friend, John Humphrey, says they are an early family in the country, came first to the USA and then moved on to Australia. "And there are two branches to our family," he told me. "And we have no relation with one another. We do not even talk to each other. Something went wrong a long time ago, and we no longer know what it was. But the tradition remains: we do not speak to one another."

During the days of January before the feast of St. Paul's conversion on the 25th, we have the Octave for Church Unity. It was begun by a former Anglican community on the Hudson in New York, early in the 1900s. They became the Catholic Society of the

Atonement at Graymoor. Similar efforts were made in Europe—
prayer for unity was the way it began. Since only prayer can
help.

The thrust of the movement for church unity was born in
the missions when both Catholics and Protestants saw in a fresh
light what a disaster a disintegrated church is, what a spectacle
to the non-Christian world for Christians trying to teach others
the rule of love when they do not love one another, when they
cannot maintain the unity in faith and love that Christ taught.
Their own house is not in order, and they set out to tell others
how to live. Here at home we grow up with this situation and are
used to it. But when you go abroad to a non-Christian land, it
strikes you very hard and very clear: What a scandal it is! And so
a great movement is taking place among the followers of Christ
toward the slow, arduous work of doing God's will in being one
in faith and love, as Christ insisted we must be.

And arduous work it is. Who does not know how difficult it
can be to keep a family at peace? How easy it is for feuds to
arise, for wounds to be made, feelings hurt so that rifts appear,
differences that can settle into permanent breaks. You try and put
such a group together again and you have some sense of what we
are about in seeking Christian unity. That is why from the first
awakening of concern in this, prayer was seen as basic. This is
more than we can handle alone. And prayer, of course, does help.
It is not a gesture of futility. It does set free the power of the
grace of God among us all. And so things happen that never happened before.

A good way of looking at it is to see the religious orders of
the Church, the Franciscans, the Jesuits, the Dominicans, the
Benedictines, the Passionists, and the infinite varieties of Sister-
hoods devoted to as many kinds of work and interests. So many
gifts to God's people, God's Church—so many manifestations of
the Spirit, charisms for the glory of God and the good of all.
What if each founder had gone off with his/her gift and broken
from the Church, founded a new, separate faith? That way, the
whole body of the Church is deprived of something very beautiful. And yet each denomination, each form of Christian witness
has some special gift, some particular feature meant to enrich all.
The point is to preserve those gifts in the unity of the faith.

The tragedy is, of course, that we *are* all one. The fact that a
family quarrels, falls apart, each section going its own way without reference to the other, does not mean that they are no longer
one family. They are. You can repudiate father or mother, you can

change your name, move to another state—that changes nothing. You are who you are for all eternity. So is the Church. It is one. And only one. Always was and always will be. Cannot be other. You are baptized real and, consequently, you belong to Christ, you belong to his Church. Christ is not divided. Nor is his Church. There is no power on earth, or above or below, that can divide Christ's body. It is we who are divided. People. Like members of the same family who snub one another, do not speak, do not relate.

What we want then is to make that unity visible and evident and complete. Each with his or her own gift from God, all united in the one Lord, one faith, one baptism. It is God's will that this be so. We pray, then, that God's will be done.

Gethsemani
January, 1987

13

Sts. Robert, Alberic, Stephen
Holy Founders of the Cisterians

*B*rother Wilfrid had an older brother named, happily enough, Jack Spratt. Jack Spratt was a priest. He died some years ago. On one of his last visits here he told me, with considerable satisfaction, that never once in the course of his long priesthood had he eaten a meal in a private home. He seemed somehow to connect that style with being a good priest. And good priest he was, for one of the monks told me so: that he was much loved by the people. He taught this monk as a boy how to serve Mass; he was his parish priest.

The point is, modalities change, ways of doing things. Yesterday's seem bizarre to us, just as ours to the generation that will follow us.

On this day commemorating our Cistercian founding fathers, it may be fitting to reaffirm our commitment to our monastic tradition, to the character of which tradition Saints Robert, Alberic, and Stephen gave particular form. A major point would be, I assume, to have clear in our minds the conviction of a need for certain norms or modes of living, an awareness of how variable these can be over the centuries, or even decades, and, finally, how necessary to see them for what they are, namely, means and not ends. There is a constant witness in history that such a patrimony often withers. That is so in any enterprise, but perhaps even more than usual in religion. For custom and tradition become vague in those who follow them, or become rigid and frozen forms, and then have a tendency to become ends instead of being the means they are. No one opposed Jesus more and more successfully than the professionally-religious people of his own time and place.

Not too many years ago, when the abbey produced more printed material than now (calendars, holy cards, verse cards and the like), there was one particular scene that was very popular. It pictured a monk, vested for choir in robe and scapular and cowl, hood up, standing demurely with book in hand, face hidden, at the shore of a little pond called Alban's Lake, back into our woods at the foot of the knobs. Wholly unreal, yet it seemed to express the popular understanding of what a contemplative monk looks like, what he does. Yet no monk in his right mind would be wandering around the woods in his cowl.

Romanticized notions of what monastic life is are bad enough in people not monks, and disastrous in monks. I was not a novice very long when I happened to see from a front upper window of the monastery a cluster of monks in a hidden corner having a gleeful and, at that time, forbidden conversation among themselves. And I remember being miffed and annoyed: so here is this famous Trappist silence I hear so much crowing about. And later, after a fire in a rear building, we began to tear the monastery apart in a long-expected total renovation. It was the beginning of a decade of mayhem, dirt, dust and hard work against a background of air compressors, pneumatic drills, tile saws and other noisy equipment. In the midst of that, I happened on a brochure from Snowmass, that lovely Cistercian monastery hidden in a valley of the Rocky Mountains, lost in peace and solitude. I went to Father Louis (Merton) and said, "I am sure Snowmass is where God wants me to be." And he was just as sure it wasn't. And one of the priests here served as a second opinion. With some native shrewdness he heard me out, and in heavy compassion carefully repeated after me every sentence of my list of frustrations and desires. By the time I was done, the sound of my own absurdity coming back to me was more than I could stomach. So that finished that. In the context I was stuck in at the time, Snowmass would have been just as disappointing for the simple reason that the monks there, too, are human, not to say the hordes of skiers and art people from Aspen who over-whelmed the place.

All our sacred traditions and holy customs derive from hu-man beings, are interpreted by them, and lived by them. They are therefore, all of them, for all their profundity and beauty, made real only in the living. No monastery exists in which the ideals of the Order are not defended, expounded and espoused with sin-cere love. And no monastery exists in which the reality is any-where near the ideal.

And even if by some freak of history a house would be per-fect, we are still not talking about monastic life, for the reason that the life is not the mere living of it. The encounter with God, the love of God, the love of neighbor, the entry into the mystery of God in time and eternity rest upon the fabric of the life, the day-to-day practice of what we call exercises. But to think we came here to practice monastic exercises is as quaint as to think their perfection is the measure of the monk. God is what we are here for.

In the post-World War II rebuilding of the Church in New Guinea, there was much difficulty because of the shortage of help, especially Brothers. The former combination of Fathers, Brothers and Sisters, and their dedication to the development of Church and country, was a marvel. Now that was impossible. We saw the Lutherans with young volunteers from Iowa and Kansas and Minnesota doing great work, and wondered why we couldn't get volunteers: builders, truck drivers, pilots, mechanics to serve a few years for love. And so lay missionaries were born, a new venture in modern mission work. But it went down hard. We did not like outsiders getting so close. They'd see too much, know too much. And all their romantic notions of priests, Brothers, and Sisters in the missions would be shattered. Which is exactly what happened . . . to some of them. They may have never been near a priest before, let alone a Brother or Sister. All their knowledge of missions came from mission magazines and maybe a text or two of cultural anthropology. And the reality was nothing like their idealized dream. And so they turned around and went back home...some of them. Most of them adjusted, adapted, matured and did good work. They went home when their term was fin-ished, enriched, deepened, and with something to talk about the rest of their lives. And some decided to stay on permanently and become part of the mission. And a few became priests or Brothers or Sisters. And the missionaries? They, too, adjusted, became more comfortable with their own humanity, less given to illusion, more given to trust in God's grace and mercy. For they were a wonderful group of people. But they were human beings. And their humanity showed.

Yours shows, too. And mine. All our practices, however perfectly executed, will never hide our humanity. Nor should. We do these things in order to move on into the love of God. We get as good at them as we can, then forget them and do them as a matter of course, easily, free to give attention to what matters.

Brother Meinrad wrote to the Joan Baez he admired, "I want to sing and play like you. What are some of the secrets of your technique?" Her mother wrote back to Meinrad, "There are no secrets. You learn the skills and from then on it is you. Joan's singing and playing is Joan. Yours should be you, not an imitation of someone else."

We had a Norwegian weaver come to us in Oxford [North Carolina, a small, experimental Cistercian community, ed.]. We were self-taught and wondered if we had it right. We did. She said we were doing very well. I asked her one day, seated with her on the bench before the loom, "Are there some tips, some tricks you could show me?" She looked at me, exasperated, "There are no tricks. You learn to weave, get good at it, and then take off. You do your own thing. That is what art is."

The traditions Sts. Robert, Alberic, and Stephen handed on to us come to us through human beings. They are constantly being changed, adapted, corrected, perfected, renewed. And yet remain the same. We do the best we can by them, for they are essential to our life. Without them, there is no monastic life. And yet they are not the monastic life at all. God is. Love is. So we get as good as we can at what must be done and as soon as we can. And then we get on with it and get with God.

Jack Spratt was not a good priest and a much-loved priest because he never sat down to a meal in a private home. He was a good priest because he loved God and his people. Hopefully, in the steps of Robert, Alberic, and Stephen we can do as much. Even if we give the credit for it to rising at three every morning, wearing white robes and staying single.

Amen.

Gethsemani
January 26, 1987

14
Lazarus Raised
Fifth Sunday of Lent
John 11: 1-45

few weeks ago, a Brother asked me to go with him to Conway's in Bardstown to pick up a car. In the showroom was a 1926 Model T Ford Roadster, wholly restored, just like new. The 1926 price was just under $500.00. I do not know what that Ford would fetch today. Maybe even enough for a current model. It reminded me of the Resurrection. Is not all renewal, restoration, rehabilitation of the old and worn—so popular today—the more so when it is a perfect return to the original? Is not all this in some way testimony to the complete re-creation that Christians believe in?

The drama of Chapter 11 of St. John is still powerful, still at once frightening and inspiring. A sudden death is a traumatic event to witness and seriously affects us, may numb us, put us in shock. Can we think that a return from the dead would not do the same? Jesus had to tell the sisters to release their brother. Do you not suppose that the fingers that wound the embalming bands around the dead body of their brother were not shaking with fear and joy as those same hands unwound a body now alive, breathing?

And yet this resurrection is not our own resurrection, but a symbol of it, a sign of it. Here is rather re-animation, the soul returning to the body. Even so, a great wonder, testimony to the power of divine love. And given not to dazzle so much as to prepare for suffering and death. For right soon Christ will be done to death, and His shamed body wrapped in linen and placed in a tomb: someone else's. This was a prospect the disciples could not abide. And yet had to face. The return of Lazarus would help them. And help us. Suffering, death is the lot of all. Wrapped in linen or not, our flesh will return to the earth common to us all. And before that, it will know suffering. We are human.

And as we may have wondered in reading the classics of the spiritual life: how can we be human of spirit who have not entered into the darkness of the soul, the realms of personal and generic sin and evil? And confront them not with posturing but with the mercy of a redeeming God who heals because he loves. We return with Jesus to our desolate landscape and our fire-stormed cities, to the devastation and death which are the harvest of sin. And acknowledge this as our country. And so in Jesus we know healing. Jesus desolate in our desolation, dead in our death.

There is no way to eternal life save the human way. And we are not the realized human save as Christian. For Christ has touched all human suffering, every human death. We know that, we declare that, we witness to that. And in so doing, we enter into Christ's redemptive work, make articulate what is mute, speak the unspoken, shout the good news while there is yet time. Like Lazarus, we leave the land of the dead and are alive because of Christ's powerful love, attest to it to a dead-in-sleep world, tired of living and scared of dying.

How else explain the torpor of a generation in the face of enormous evils, nuclear war only the worst among many, save that it rises from a contempt of humankind, a refusal to believe in our own significance, a rejection of glory, a love for our own deserved destruction? This in the face of all that Jesus is.

The resurrection to come will not be a mere restoration job, good enough as far as it goes. We will rise into a new world and a new creation, and with bodies glorious because immortal, for an eternal life in a Kingdom we can describe only by hints and hunches. Our own bodies, truly, for we will be recognized. Complete and perfect. Impassible, as the word goes: that is, never to know pain, wholly subtle and agile and of clarity. Terms to describe a body we have never seen, at once spiritual and material, local and yet not bound to space, visible and yet radiant as light. Such a body had the Resurrected Christ.

The end of a song, the death of a child, to go deaf and blind, being brought down with some hideous disease - what can try our faith more than these? Then are we forsaken by God in a garden of our own Gethsemani.

Lazarus is then a prelude, a foretaste. Not the real thing, but an indication of it. By him Christ fortifies us to encounter suffering and death. We in turn by the gift of faith become an instrument of peace and a source of comforting for our day's passion and death. One could do worse than live such a life, die such a death. Given the Resurrection.

Your faith needs a little stimulus, a hint of encouragement? Mr. Hurst says he will give you a ride in his Model T anytime (mint condition!). Fresh as the day it came off the assembly line.

Gethsemani
April 5, 1987

15
On Dom James
Easter Monday

James Fox was abbot of Gethsemani from 1948-1967.
He died on Good Friday, April 17, 1987.
Matthew Kelty circulated these reflections
to friends of the monastic community.

*I*t is a bit bold to try and say something about a man of the stature of Dom James in a few paragraphs, but I want to put some thoughts on paper under the impact of his passing, in the interval between his dying and his burial. He is at the moment laid out in the choir, with monks at his side praying the psalms for him.

The man was totally given to his life as monk, as priest, as abbot; every inch of him given to God and the Church. He took himself seriously, had an awareness of the significance of his life, knew his position, knew his power and authority and used them with vigor, with love. He literally enjoyed being what he was. And it was all pure, unselfish. He was proud of Gethsemani and had a grasp of its place in the Church and in the world that was profound.

I think of him as a great leader of men, a shrewd analyst of character. He would pick outstanding men and do what many leaders do not do: give them room to use their gifts for God, the Church, the Order, the monastery. He was blessed with fine men and made superb use of them. Just to mention a few who come to mind: there was Father Louis (Thomas Merton) first of all, as best known. Their relationship was a very special kind, often strained, always warm. Merton literally flourished under the man and candidly recognized the fact that he was truly blessed in him. Another was Brother Clement, responsible for an amazing development of the economic side of the abbey and making it possible for the monks to earn their own living. Even if many areas have since been curtailed because we do not have the numbers we once had, the basic industries of fruitcake and cheese continue to flourish, keeping the place going. Father John Eudes was a doctor and psychiatrist and did much to improve the physical and mental health of the house, besides being responsible, with Father Herbert and Father Flavian, for the formation of a whole generation of monks. Then add Father Chrysogonus and his creation of a new liturgy that made possible a worship of great beauty not only for this abbey, but many other houses in the Order who used his material. One wonders what the prayer life of the monastery would be had God not provided us with this monk's gifts. It was Dom James who recognized the talents and competence of these men and made full use of them, giving them ample room to be creative. In other words, if the man loved authority, he also loved to share it and did so. That is surely the mark of greatness. There were, of course, many others, not to say a whole monastery of monks who entered into all this. And that in a time of enormous change in the monastic life. Add to that the fact that the monastery buildings themselves were totally renovated within the same two decades (he was abbot from 1948 to 1967), plus three new foundations made (New York, California, South Carolina) and a house adopted in Chile, not to say the development of two foundations already made by Dom Frederic, and one begins to appreciate the amazing amount of work this one man did and supervised.

A final note must be made: that Dom James was open to new ideas, new ways, even if they were alien to his own. He truly admired someone who would stand up to him, not with arrogance, for he could not stomach that, but with sincere conviction, and defend a cause. And if the person could prove the point, Dom James would accept it. One case was the matter of the eremitical life. Dom James was personally interested in it, but thought it was not in line with the tradition of the Order. Father Louis, through his study of the sources, was able to show that, on the contrary, the hermit life was in our tradition. It was Dom James in General Chapter who persuaded the abbots of the Order to legislate in favor of eremitism. And later, after resigning, he lived himself for some 12 years as solitary. This was a turnaround from his first stand.

He was, then, a man of absolute dedication, a genuine leader, one who could share authority and leadership with others, a man open to the Spirit and responsive. That adds up to greatness of high order. We are much indebted to God that in his Providence such a man was where he was needed, at a time he was needed. The history of Gethsemani for the years to come will be in great measure profoundly influenced by this wonderful man.

Praise God!

Gethsemani
April 20, 1987

16
Peter's Confession
Twenty-first Sunday of the Year
Matthew 16:13-20

*A*s a seminarian in the early 1940s, I was, with my confreres, much taken with the trends that were in the air. These trends were, to us, sometimes quite bold, quite daring. And when we wanted to sound far out, far left, we would take to expounding on them. Matters like: a revived diaconate, a vernacular Mass, the Office in English, concelebrated Eucharist. All these questions seemed to us to be at once so desirable and so unlikely that they were an unending source of debate. And the debate was both safe and dangerous.

I do not know why Peter was the only one in this Gospel who knew who Jesus was. What did he have that the others lacked? They too were with him day and night, talked with him, heard him out, saw what he did. And yet could not say what Peter said. Why? It would seem that Christ himself gives us the answer: "Flesh and blood have not revealed this to you, but my Heavenly Father." Very well. Then why did the Heavenly Father reveal it to Peter? We do not know. There is a logistics in divine things that we do not understand. It may be related to freedom, to human dignity, to divine reverence. If that be so, then much may depend on us and our response to reality.

Years after, our heated exchanges over what ought to be done was actually being done in the Church. It was as if someone had overheard us and did everything we suggested. And then, of course, we had second thoughts. Doubts emerged. These doubting thoughts became more powerful as time went on and we began to see the actual shape of all that we had so urgently insisted on. So Peter in the first flush of an insight that moved him profoundly had no choice but to reveal it, share it, take responsibility for it. So he did. It was something dangerous and safe. The regrets came later. The doubts. Finally, the denials.

First insights are often best, the initial intuitive grasp perfect. It is the later doubts that are at fault. The later thoughts that say: Where was I coming from when I vowed my vows, swore my oath, pledged my service? How could I have known then what I know now? How could I have foreseen the consequences of so radical a stance?

Brave youths were we, talking off the tops of our heads about what the Church should do. Brave Peter he was, and so spoke a profundity no mind on earth can grasp, no theology adequately express, explain. A man made God/God made human. It was spoken in a moment of madness. And yet the brave youths spoke well. The brave Peter's words are inscribed in massive letters around the mighty dome of St. Peter's. We are sometimes in touch with our own truth, and these are our best times.

It was such a disappointment to me that after all the dust had settled after the upheavals here in the 60s, we did not end up with a community one and united in choir, in Eucharist, at table, at work. Instead we took off in several directions and settled, some for this, some for that. For I assumed all were like me, and I love choir, a common Eucharist, communal meals. Though perhaps I do not love work, I know the joy of communal enterprise. But people differ. Even among us. Some pray another way, see life differently, feel things differently, respond to reality in their own manner. I see that now. You and I look at the same flowers, and yet the colors we see are not the same. I eat the same soup you eat, eat the same portion. What disappoints me delights you. If this be true of banalities, what of the eternal?

And so the lesson follows: be true in everything. Be true to the light you have, the gift given. If you are true, the divine will follow, for untruth will not bar the way nor the fog of delusion deceive. The Father revealed to Peter because Peter was true to Peter.

Purity of heart is not easily come by. We are born deceivers and may well die that way if God's grace does not intervene. And what truth we do grasp we are not loyal to. We are traitors to our best moments, our moments of truth. Dwell with Peter and his sublime confession. May it inspire us who have also made a similar sublime confession. And we are one with Peter in having gone back on our own truth. But we can also be one with him in a return to the youthful heart that was so right, so rash. There is joy in it.

Gethsemani
August 23, 1987

17
All Souls

*P*eople still send in offerings for Masses to be applied to their intentions. I would say that a majority of them are for the dead, sometimes specific people, often enough for all the dead, the "Poor Souls," as tradition has it. After all, there is little you can do for the dead beyond praying for them. And certainly some involvement with the mystery of the Eucharist is deeply satisfying. One could bring the priest some bread, some wine, some candles, something for the poor—anything—just to do something tangible, to be involved: hence the offering. Fixing up the grave is common enough, putting some flowers there. And above all, to remember. To remember and to be remembered seem so much to so many. And makes one pause. Is Lincoln better for our remembrance of him in that splendid memorial in Washington? Are we? The Vietnam Wall there with the names of all the dead is so simple a thing, yet so powerful. Have you ever seen a military cemetery? USA has them scattered over Europe. Why do we remember? Why Memorial Day? Why did Jesus say: "Remember Me. Do this in memory of Me."

Do we not touch the eternal in all this? What can being remembered serve anyone unless they be somewhere to know they are remembered? How can I ask anyone to remember me unless I am to know it?

I go to the airport in Louisville or Boston or anywhere else and note the crowds. I do not advert to the fact that it was also crowded yesterday and the day before, for that means little to me. Memory is not just a recall of the past, but a participation in some union. There were monks here yesterday, 10 years ago, 50 years ago, 100 years ago. And Cistercians before there was a USA, a Protestant, or the English language. We are part of Cîteaux [the monastery at which the Cistercian life began, ed.].

There is this world just beyond us, so much a part of us and we so much a part of it. And this visible, tangible world is but the surface, the appearance. The cult of the imaginary addresses a need. When we do not have another world, we imagine one. And even when we know we do, we can imagine. There is a communion of saints, there is the Mystical Body of Christ. There is a divine life that flows through people.

I looked around the house to see if I could find anything of Brother Sebastian. A wall he painted. A chair he made. A song he wrote. There is nothing. He has disappeared. Left nothing behind him. And yet he is here. Here far more than the music he once made on the choir organ and now gone forever. Someday your name will be on a cross in the cemetery at the door. The years will pass, as years do, and fewer and fewer will know who you were, will remember you. And yet you will always be here because this is your place, where you lived. You are here forever. And your heaven will have its roots here, else it will not be heaven. And the holier you are, the more so, for you will be deeper into God, into heaven, into Gethsemani. Lincoln haunts this land because he loved it, died for it. In heroic love.

I think today is a good time to renew heroic love. Plausible love is acceptable. It gets by. Plausible solutions, plausible answers are okay. But I have a hunch that the day of the plausible is passing. The world is in too much of a mess to be helped by plausibility. I hear a call to the heroic.

"Do this in memory of Me." Do what, Jesus? "Put me to death again as you did long ago, that your sins may be forgiven. And then die with me for the world I love and die for. They are all your brothers and sisters and mine. The dead must live and the living must die. Then they will put a name on your cross as they did on Mine."

I posted the story of the gays in Washington and the huge quilt they made with the names—the names—of nearly 2000 men and women dead of AIDS, representative of more than 20,000 such. A quilt yet. A blanket of mercy. Of love and remembrance. With a name on each. Two acres of memory on the mall.

You might think on that if you would think of heroic love. They look to us. And you know what they do? They smile. Sadly. For we are celibates, we priests and nuns and monks and brothers. We religious, as we call ourselves. Committed to the celibate life. Forever. Maybe. And maybe gay folk mock us because we cannot handle it. And we tell them, "We are free to be celibate if we want. But you must be so because of the law of God. You have no choice." And they answer, "You are celibate for the cause of love. But if love wears out, you drop it. And yet if you had to, you could do it. You expect us to. Your love is not a very noble love, you who are so carefully chosen and nurtured. You are formed in a tradition from the ages, and given to the most sublime cause on earth. And still you are not up to it. So many thousands?"

Maybe the time for the plausible is done. It may be time for heroes. For death is revealing. In the face of death, things are different. A Brother changes once he is dead. And we change, too, in regard to him. It may be the lesson of this day. Lest the beautiful things we do slip from our hands. . . . Sweet brothers, you may be more heroic than you know. God help you so.

Amen.

Gethsemani
November 2, 1987

18

Houses and Homes
Christmas Midnight Mass
"Transeamus usque Bethlehem
et videamus hoc verbum quod factum est . . ."
"Let us go over to Bethlehem
and see this thing that has happened."

A generation ago, it was considered neat to begin a sermon with a Scripture quotation in Latin, the more so on a more solemn occasion. Today, this is passé, old-fashioned. But it is old-fashioned things we dwell on this night. Old-fashioned things like "home."

Who knows what particular design was at work in Jesus' being born in such pathetic circumstances? Born, to be sure, in his ancestral village. But born nonetheless as one homeless. Maybe it is not inappropriate, then, to pause this night to ponder the wretched situation of so many people this very night. How humiliating for this great country that a foreign visitor upbraids us, we so eager to give instruction to the rest of the world, for the neglect of the thousands of homeless. Not to say the whole dismal housing scene, with costs so high that for too many to dream of owning a home is to commit one's self to a lifelong burden of payment for both house and money.

Home. Home is a word so rich in association. I say *home* and I dearly hope there is raised in each of you a host of happy memories. Yet human happiness is a very fragile thing, perhaps not as common as we think. Nor is home always what it could be. It is no small matter to build a home, over and above having a house. Things go wrong. There is sickness. There is death. There is separation. There is heartache of every sort. I need not tell you. Yet if any of us have known what this can be like, it must be a school of compassion for us, a means to grow in mercy for others. When you know how hard it is to build a home, raise a family, then one is more apt to have some understanding when things do not work out for others.

And this night, this holy night, is a call to say it again, to commit ourselves again to the struggle, the endeavor to know, to do, to live love. For what is the point of building a house for your family, painting it blue, with a red front door, maybe—what is the point but to make it a center of peace, of love, or permanence? And why is this so important? It is important because it is an act of religion. It is a service of God, a preparation for the Kingdom, indeed a building of the Kingdom. For when you know peace, when you know love, when you know something of stability, then it is easy, easy to believe in God, in his love, in his peace, in an eternal home that awaits us.

The tragic thing about the homeless—and note that we call them homeless, not houseless—is not just no roof over their heads, no place to sit down and eat together, no place to lie down at night. These are bad enough, the Lord God knows. But this hideous plight shatters faith in God. How can religion, religious people, mean anything when you live on the street?

It is not that I berate you for a national disgrace, as if it were your fault. It is rather to stress compassion, that if God has been good to you, if you have a good home, a good family, if you know warm love and peace and the tranquility of order, then be grateful. And continue to work for all this. And go easy in faulting those who have not done as well as you, often enough through no fault of their own.

We had a lovely home across from the church on Adams Street [in Milton, MA, ed.]. Across from St. Agatha's Church: eight rooms, stucco, with a beautiful garden out back. Hard times came in the early 30s and the bottom fell out of everything for millions. One day a handful of men came, stuck a red flag in the lightpole out front, and auctioned off the house so the bank could get its money. I watched from my room upstairs, kneeling at the window. In five minutes, my home became someone else's house. So I know how it feels.

But we are monks. Do we have a home? Is this our home? Sort of. Most homes do not have a huge refectory where you can seat 100 with ease, nor a large chapter room where they discuss things, not to say a chapel. Is this, then, our family? Sort of. Yet not really. A family is father, mother, children. How much time did we spend wondering what to get the kids for Christmas? How many nights do we lie awake worried about where our young son is, what he is doing? But it *is* community. Ah, yes! That it is. A community. Of love. Of peace. Of permanence. Yes, that it is.

So that is what we have in common with the families around us: we are a community, as is each family. And if community, are we not then Church? We are indeed. And this is the gist of it. Each family is a little church, this community is a little church. Both are symbols of the great community which is the Church at large, the Kingdom of God on earth. Not only symbols, but truly Church, the community of faith and hope and love in miniature.

And so we come to the heart of it: it is the Church that is our home. And this is what we celebrate this night, this silent night, this holy night. Christ has come and dwells among us. He is in the midst of our Church, our community, our home. This is the joy of it. *"Et verbum caro factum est et habitavit in nobis!"* God Almighty has become human flesh and made his habitation among us, dwells among us, lives among us.

And this makes all the difference in the world. Then the measure of things is not our success, but our faith. We can try and we can fail, despite noble efforts, good intentions. But faith must not, cannot fail. This is the witness we seek: to have such a family, such a community, such a Church, that it is easy to believe in God, in an eternal home, in abiding love.

There is great power for good in such a commitment. We had a Brother among us many years ago who served the community very effectively. Before he entered the monastery, he and some friends had organized a company to build affordable housing for the poor, for average people, people who wanted a home but did not have a fortune. In coming here, it was not as if his concern was abandoned. His life here was rather a witness to the same truth he had once done in another way. To live love, to live peace, to abide in them is an influence in grace. And grace is the most effective presence in the world, for it is God alive.

Jesus, we thank You for coming. You are well come. We are glad to have You. And with Your help, we will live in love, in peace, for now and until we come home to an eternal now with You.

Amen.

Gethsemani
December 25, 1987

19
Losers Get Prizes, Too
Fifth Sunday in Ordinary Time
Mark 1:29-39

A French abbot visiting us, back before we had our renovated church, said to us, "I cannot help thinking, knowing a little history, of another day for you. Now you are prosperous: a big novitiate, a full house, a thriving business, writer monks who spread your name over all the world, your cheese served at White House state dinners . . . All impressive and, unhappily, subject to change. For how can I help but think of another day when your numbers are down, your novitiate slim, your old many and your young few? What then? What then?"

Good question, Reverend Father. At the time, of course, we thought, "He is just a European abbot, a bit jealous, maybe, because over there so many houses limp along, barely making it in choir and out of it, happy if they have a novice every year or two, having to borrow money if they build a chicken coop." Even so, we listened and we wondered. Winners are always in fashion. Losers not.

I just read about a university north of us: they tell how they handle a new class. There were 8000 applicants for 1800 openings for the freshman class of 1988. How do they handle that? Easy. They take the best only. The winners. You want in? Are you head of the class scholastically? Do you dance, are you into music, do you act, take art? Are you into some ministry? Have you a varsity letter? Are you leadership class? Have you got the $65,000 it will cost you for four years here? You have these qualifications, you are in. They want winners, this school. And you know what they teach them, once they have them? They teach them how to lose. For you will never be a winner unless you know how to lose. It is, after all, a Christian school.

Obviously, only a few are Number One. What of the many? Do they count? Jesus rather thought they did. He had an eye for losers: the halt, the deaf, the dumb, the blind, the leper. He had a feeling for sinners and the reprobate. He had small bias for winners, the successful. Died between thieves. Lived among sinners. Taught a Gospel that was as far removed from competitive capitalism as his day from ours. Thank you, Jesus. But we are not a nation of losers and do not intend to be. Let us see.

Last summer at the same Notre Dame, you know what they had? They had the Summer Special Olympic Games. Five thousand youngish men and women, boys and girls, and their coaches from 70 nations and 20 states competing in a variety of games under Olympic standards. Who? The handicapped, the retarded, those with Down's Syndrome, the halt, the lame, the deaf and the mute. With their coaches and 20,000 volunteers to take good care of them. Plus a host of stars from sports and song and film to host them. What was the point? To teach them how to win. For they divided them according to levels of competence and then set them against one another for the prize. And so taught losers how to lose. Back of this enormous enterprise that filled a stadium and left a dear memory on all present was one family in particular: the Kennedy's. As you may know, they are a family of winners who know how to lose.

For you are no winner if you cannot lose. Poor losers are undeveloped, unfulfilled people, who mistake fantasy for reality, who will not play unless they can win. Consumed with envy and jealousy, ambition and lust for power, greedy for place and prestige. Raw capitalists who have not tempered endeavor by absorbing Christianity into the blood.

Losing is as much part of life as winning. Who is spared suffering, sickness and failure? Who in the end will not lose all of life in death? At the moment, in the tailor shop we are busy filling an order from Father Felix, the infirmarian. He told us he wanted 24 of those white canvas pallets on which we lay the dead, with the six long bands for the bearers to lower the body into the grave. "Twenty-four?," I said, with some alarm. "Are you expecting a plague?" And he answered in that matter-of-fact way of his, "Well, you'd be surprised how fast they go! And in any case, they're all going. That is for sure . . ." So I told Brother Octavius, "Do a nice job while you're at it. One of them is for you and, no doubt, one for me too!"

Dying is as much a part of life as living, and it is not morbidity to live with that awareness. The cross is elemental to

Christianity, and the only winners are they who attain to eternal life in Jesus. Losing is part of that winning. The ability to take what comes for God's sake. To be, as it were, one with hands extended, open palms up: "Everything I have I give to You, Everything You give to me I accept." So goes love. With vigor. With enthusiasm. And with perdurance.

For Jesus was at pains to make the message clear. He went about touching now him, now her whom the world had written off as losers, declaring with finality that everyone matters, those at the top and near it, those in the majority's middle, those who hover toward bottom. The rules of this game are something else again by the world's standards. Dazzling in their daring. Formidable in forthrightness. And relevant to every human without exception.

How superb your style when you achieve in God significant love. This is excellence that will wear. This is a race of aristocrats of whom E.M. Forster wrote:

> *I believe in aristocracy, though—if that be the right word and a democrat may use it. Not an aristocracy of power, based upon rank and influence, but an aristocracy of the sensitive, the considerate and the plucky. Its members are to be found in all nations and classes, and all through the ages. . . . They represent the true human tradition, the one permanent victory of our queer race over cruelty and chaos. Thousands of them perish in obscurity, a few are great names. They are sensitive for others as well as themselves, they are considerate without being fussy, their pluck is not swankiness but the power to endure, and they can take a joke.*[1]

Like in New Guinea years ago, when they began having competitions between schools of different areas—string bands, choral groups, dance groups—and ran into trouble. When they gave prizes, the youngsters were indignant that only the winners got awards. "How can you win without losers?," they asked. "The losers deserve a prize, too; they tried." A competitive society awards only winners. A more communal culture has more sense. And so do we.

Gethsemani
February 7, 1988

20
La Vierge Enceinte
The Annunciation

I knew a man down in Maine who was for all practical purposes a Catholic, yet was not. Very well-read, exceptionally informed, he was nonetheless frustrated in his desire to be wholly
of the Church by his problem with the cult of the Virgin Mary. It
was altogether too much for him. Catholics made too much of a
good thing. Not so much doctrinally, but in style, in attitude, in
practice. With his background and tradition, Catholic emphasis
on the Virgin seemed overwrought, precious. Yet he suffered
much over this. He was troubled in spirit. In that frame of mind,
he was a tourist in Europe off-season one time and came to Mont
St. Michel off the northern coast of France.

There, wandering around by himself, he came upon a
charming little chapel, bare save for a statue in one corner, a medieval relic. He went closer and discovered it was *La Vierge Enceinte*, the Virgin with Child. Ancient piety in an ancient place.
He stood before it, reflecting, and without warning or plan, all
his difficulties vanished, fell from him like old clothes. "Of
course," he said. "Of course. How absurd I am. She carries within
her the Son of God. He will be born of her. He is the Son of God.
And she is His mother. Of course. Of course." And he went to his
knees, quite overwhelmed. Not long after, he became a Catholic.
And later, I believe, a priest.

A few years went by and he happened to be in Europe
again, and thought to himself, "Out of thanks, sheer courtesy, I
will go and pay my respects to *La Vierge Enceinte* at Mont St.
Michel and I will thank her." Which he did. He looked for the
chapel, found it again, and then discovered that the statue was
gone. He sought out a custodian and asked the old man, "Sir,
there was a statue here before and they have moved it. Do you
know where they put it?" And the old man said flatly, "There
was no statue here and so nobody moved it." "Sir, you do not
understand. A couple of years ago I was here and there was an
ancient statue of *La Vierge Enceinte* here. Now it is gone." "My
good man, I have been here all my life. I know this place like the
back of my hand. There was never a statue of *La Vierge Enceinte*

here." And with that, our friend was so overcome that he had to turn and leave. "Now I understand," he said. "Now I understand why Catholics are so devoted to this tender woman."

On this day, Mary was visited by the angel. He asked her consent and was given it. And the Holy Spirit came upon her, and she is now one who has conceived of the Holy Spirit, bears divine life within her. Such poetry!

Some years ago, my sister was here. Mrs. Gannon [the manager of the Ladies' Guest House at Gethsemani. At present, there are accommodations for women in the Abbey's Retreat House, ed.] made us our noon lunch, and my sister and I walked to the top of the knob where I had a tent then. We ate our lunch there. (Discipline was slack in those days.) And in the course of the lunch, my sister told me of her daughter, with child. "She is simply radiant. She takes on a new beauty. She glows with light and love. I never saw anything like it." I recall the women in New Guinea who, when with child, walked like queens, regal in dignity, proud of their state. Perhaps we should revive devotion to *La Vierge Enceinte.*

For will we not attend her these months to come, and with her ponder the mystery so deep, so dark, so beyond us? Today's feast calls us to that, to rediscover beauty. That it is not too much, we who know beauty. For we, too, had our Annunciation. The angel came to us. And asked our consent. And the Spirit came upon us. For surely no one of us thinks coming here to this holy house was his own idea. It was of God. Who of us, young or old, would have had mind enough to fancy such a venture? God called us. And called us also, I suppose, to be mother, to bear God, to bear fruit. Can we think of celibacy as sterile? Are we barren? Is not man also maternal? I daresay he is. For I did not come here to be fruitless. Nor did you.

I knew a priest in Australia, a Theatine, I think. I'm not sure. A priest exceptional in competence, in ability for loving service, dedication to people, all people. In association with his apostolate, he came to know a remarkable woman. They became good friends, and the friendship slowly led to love. And one day he realized that he wanted to marry. He was torn in anguish over the situation, turned to prayer, to counsel, his peace shattered. After a deal of that, in the midst of his anxiety—for he dearly loved the priesthood—he had a dream. In the dream, Christ appeared to him, warm, bright with love for him. And the Lord looked at him directly, said with telling emphasis, "I want you. And I want all of you." And with that, he took the priest in his arms, embraced him with great affection. And was gone. So the priest told the woman he loved, "I cannot. I cannot." And in his heart found enormous strength and joy.

If we rarely have visions, many of us have had significant dreams. And we have around us such great beauty to spur us on: a beauty we need attend anon. This chaste church and its liturgy, the handsome refectory and its liturgy, our noble chapter room and its liturgy, the community of love of which we are a part. Maybe we need to share them a bit more to rediscover, in the stunned response of those who experience them fresh, some renewed awareness of all we have.

As we have in the Holy Mother, the Virgin from this day bearing within her the Son of the Living God. A mystery only silent pondering can cope with. And such pondering cannot but awaken in us freshened understanding of what it is to share in the mystery of the redemption, knowing that if celibate love is sacrificial, it is, for all that, one with Jesus and Mary in magnificent fruit almost totally hidden from us.

No one said it is the only way. No one said it is something we had to do. And yet, given the Annunciation, we understand not what any other must do, but what we must do: in the darkness of faith, hidden in the womb which is the Church, until the great day when Christ is born in the everlasting fulfillment of all that is to come.

Amen.

Gethsemani
March 25, 1988

21

For Eric

Eric entered the Abbey of Gethsemani in 1975. He left the community some years later. In the course of his battle with AIDS, he visited Gethsemani and asked the Abbot if he could be buried near the entrance to the Abbey. Permission was granted. This sermon was preached at his funeral.

A well-known figure lost a young beloved son in an absurd accident: he drove off the road into a river. Perhaps a few drinks, perhaps too fast, perhaps asleep. A pious neighbor, bringing food to the wake, said to him by way of comfort, "I do not understand the will of God." At which all the suppressed anger and resentment hidden so carefully broke out, and the son's father tore into the hapless woman. "Indeed, you do not understand the will of God. You think God arranges accidents and tragedies? Absurd horrors? You think he is the agent behind so much misery?"

Is he? Easily asserted, easily denied. Most of us assume that in the end, God is in charge of this world, everything is somehow in his dominion. And since his dominion is one of love, we can assume that love is the answer, even when that answer emerges with great difficulty from the ashes of disaster.

Primitives I knew and loved were docile to the world's laws in the death of the old, the infirm. The death of the young shattered them. Since poisoning was an aspect of earlier ways of life, the answer to sudden death was always the same: poison. Someone poisoned him or her. Even when it was obvious that this was not the case, the answer remained. It was easy to live with. It was an answer, however inadequate. It worked.

Humankind is good at faith in a Savior. Someone to bear our burdens, suffer our pain, share our cross. We are always on the make for a Savior, an answer to our riddles. If you are Boston Irish, the memory of Yankee contempt in a past generation is not yet laid to rest. The Irish were scum to the Yankee. And treated as such, a generation or so ago. When I was a seminarian, no black male could get in a seminary . . . or Catholic college, for that matter. The Society of the Divine Word [the missionary congregation to which Matthew Kelty belonged before joining Gethsemani, ed.] built a seminary and trained excellent black priests: the bishops, the pastors, the people would not have them. The first of them became a monk here, perhaps with a broken heart. Years ago, Poles were so shabbily treated that a group left the Church and formed the schismatic Polish Catholic Church. The Germans, at the hands of the Irish bishops, were perilously close to the same. Would you choose on purpose and with intent to be Hispanic today, Mexican, Latin? We need someone to pick on. To crucify. We need someone to hang from a tree, as was the custom just a few years ago. The custom has an Irish name: Lynch.

Do you know what it is like to be gay? Today? Yesterday? Do you know what it is like to have the finger on you, guilty and cursed? We go on making saviors of anyone who will bear it and on those who will not. It is my generation which will live forever with the Holocaust of the Jews. Not to mention Stalin and his kind. Have you ever lived in a small town and known the vicious human tongue?

Which is what the Mass is for. Why do we go to Mass and what do we do there but put to death again the Savior God sent us. Mystically, yes, but mystically does not mean not really. Who put Jesus to death? His history is eternal, abiding, goes on.

We put him to death here and ask his forgiveness for it. And receive it. And so are wounds healed, sores closed, hurts assuaged. And more importantly, lessons learned. For it is in forgiving that we are healed. When we do not forgive, we are doomed to do again what was done to us. What was done before. What we did. That we learn at long last the lesson so hard to learn!

And in the process discover Christ. For the mystery is that when we do another to death one way or other, as we did Christ, the one we do to death becomes Christ. Christ dies in the black, the Hispanic, the poor, and the plague-ridden. This is the horror and the glory. You lay the whip on another's back and then discover whose back you whip.

We are all together in a mystery of life and death, of suffering and pain. Of glory in an eternal resurrection. That is what this Mass, every Mass, is about. This death, every death. This laying into the earth of one who will rise. Who will rise.

Every once in a while the heavens open and we see the glory to come. Usually such moments come only at the price of enormous pain and sorrow. Like now.

Amen.

Gethsemani
April 23, 1988

22
Mother's Day

This homily was given at the early Sunday morning "milkers' Mass"
at Gethsemani. As a service to the local neighbors, many of whom are
farmers, early Mass is celebrated for those who must awaken very
early to do the milking of the cows.

The deeper our response to faith, the more pure will be our love for others. That is to say, when the love of God for us and our love for him is not very well-developed by prayer and practice, we will tend as a result to expect from others the sort of love that only God can give.

Human love is a glorious beauty, a gift of God. And yet, no human is divine. And since the hunger of the human heart is infinite, it will know fulfillment only in God. We do a human wrong when we expect from him, from her, God's love. And it is just as true to say that when our love for God is real, the quality of our human love will improve for being more real, less demanding, more human.

Sometimes the love of a woman, the love of a man, the love of a mother (since this is Mother's Day) or the love of a father can be so glorified that the love becomes theatrical, that is to say, unreal, and is to that extent dishonest. Human love can be great and a marvel, but it is still human love. And there is no human love that can wholly satisfy the human heart because there is something of God in every heart.

It is a great grace to have had a good mother: it makes it easy to believe in a good God. But good, middling or indifferent, the gift of life is what matters, and that is greater than any specific person's goodness. The reason is simple enough: we are immortal. We will live forever. And that life forever cannot be without life here first. There is truly no way of grasping this mystery. It is beyond us. A matter of faith, yet written deep within our being. And it is for the gift of life that we are most grateful, for it is the greatest gift of all. No question. After which is our life in God, our life in Mother Church.

Many of you people are descendants of the early migrants from Maryland. You have been Catholic since then, and for how many centuries do you think your line has also been that? God alone knows how long the faith has been part of you. A most splendid heritage. Which makes one weep when a youngster will casually drop his faith, her faith, as if it were small matter. And so break a continuity of centuries. And without awareness of loss, no concept of how arduous is the road back to faith, how dearly purchased. Nor how sad a life without the faith which gives scope.

For we are a wounded people, a people who have been hurt. The child leaves the paradise of the womb and comes forth into a new, frightening, unknown world, and that often enough by a very painful route. Hopefully, he or she will know love on arrival. But even when he or she does, how long is it going to be before he or she knows there is good and bad, right and wrong? In other words, sin. And how big will he or she be when suffering and death are first known, or those bizarre trials and afflictions that come into every life?

How great a strength in such questions is a faith we got with our milk! For it is in the loving mercy of God that we know love and forgiveness and meaning. Here is the healing of our personal wounds, our cosmic wound, our original sin.

For who does not sometimes feel that it is because we are somehow cursed or forgotten or at least not on his list, when things go hard? And then human suffering serves to prove what I suspected all along.

Not so. That would be a denial of faith. In faith we know we are loved.

How good, then, to have a good mother and love from her from whom we received life; how good to have Holy Mother Church from whom we have faith in a God who died for us because we matter. Indeed, we do. We matter.

And *matter* is from the Latin *Mater*, mother. Which is to say: matter, material, this world, our mother is the source of all we are in God.

Amen

Gethsemani
May 8, 1988

23
The Monastery Sings a Song
Sixth Sunday of the Year
Mark 1:40-45

One of these days, maybe not this month or this year . . . maybe not next year, but somewhere down the road, a new man will be appointed to the tailor shop. And the next day he will come in, take one look and say, "Something's got to be done about this." And he will see Brother Ephrem, and the two will decide on a renovation, getting rid of rickety tables, fruit-cellar shelving, battleship-gray curtains, assorted cabinets, and much clutter from so many yard sales. A safe prediction and a likely story.

We are never done renewing, redoing, reviving, revitalizing. It is in the blood. Our very body constantly renews itself. If you cannot change, adjust, discard, adapt, then the first signs of death are at your door. We believe that and we live it.

Too much change is not good. It inhibits normal, healthy growth in children, makes them rootless and uncommitted. Too little change is stultifying and makes for intolerance, stubbornness, narrowness of mind.

Monastic life is probably as good an example as any around for the ability to maintain continuity with renovation. The proof is that it has been around so long. The Catholic Church even as institution, a body politic, is the oldest on earth and still very much alive. Recognizably Catholic in every era, boldly innovative and original for all that, in each generation.

A monastery even physically differs from other buildings or complexes in ways that manifest the character of the place. It may, as I have noted, look remarkably like a prison. It may have less resemblance to a boarding school, college, even a hospital. A ship in many ways is like a monastery, especially a freighter. Yet it is different from all these. Monks are men, celibates, for one thing. This changes everything. They live under an abbot, by a Rule. They praise God, work for a living, remain apart. And hence the place is the monk: the food they eat, the way they eat it—in silence—makes a refectory rather than a dining room or cafeteria. And the significance of the communal meal means the room must be significant. It is not just a room with tables and chairs, but suggests a church more than a restaurant. The monks are community and relate to one another, to the abbot, not only one-to-one but as community, specifically on major issues. Hence the chapter room. Not any room, anyhow, but of purpose to emphasize dialogue, face-to-face, the whole community in touch with the whole. A circle might do as well, but in the circle the abbot is lost and the sense of open-endedness also. Hence it is that through the ages, choral-mode refectory and choral-mode chapter have perdured. They may wither and languish, get overwrought or minimized, but they always come back.

The church, too. Not just any church, like a parish church, a college chapel, prayer room, mission station. The choral context is the major difference. Only monasteries of men or women put major emphasis on choir. And the church is significant because what goes on there is significant. It is not just one room in the house, a sort of multi-use area, now serving as this, now that. It involves size and scope, is not stingy, mean, impoverished, but splendid in the pure sense. Otherwise, the place belies the function.

All this is linked with a cloister and an inner garden. Cloister more than anything else has come to symbolize monastery. This is an odd development for it does not rank with chapel/chapter/refectory in importance. But it ties all three together, and round an inner center gives a role to it that is happy and deep. It says so much that needs saying when words want.

When we talk Cistercian, then all these basic forms will have a quality that reveals family wealth of tradition. Library, infirmary, kitchen, shops, gate, guesthouse—who knows what would constitute a monastic, let alone a Cistercian configuration for these? Not clear. But for the serious and basic elements, the scene is obvious: we can recognize a Cistercian cloister or chapter or refectory or church, both when they are what they should be or are not.

Put these celibates in their proper clothes and the setting is complete: let them put on cowls, chant the psalms, sing the Mass, go to chapter, eat their meal, do their work, resort to their rooms, their books.

All of which we can get on video, show on slides, record on film, publish in a book. But, like primitives who cannily sense when we are hiding something from them, one knows there is more to it than that.

There is indeed. The wall around the whole tells as much. The enclosure is not mere privacy, as people of property favor private worlds. It is not austerity, doing the difficult, making life a burden to carry. It is rather climate control. A setting and context in which virtue can grow and vice waste away. A world of peace and quiet, of nonviolence, of no aggression, self-assertion, domination, competition. A world of tolerance, compassion, forgiveness. A world in which envy and jealousy wither on the vine, manipulation and maneuver want for room. The whole life programs this, cultivates this by its nature, like some instinct. Not to make a charming people, pleasant company, but to quell the inner storms that drown God. For no one can ponder in whom passions rage, in whom strife and contention whip up a dust that hides the light. And pondering is what matters. About which no word can be spoken, for there are no words for it. Which is more real than reality, yet undetectable, undefinable. With it a monastery sings a song all can hear; without it, it becomes a quaint memoir.

When the real work of the monks flourishes, one need have no fear. They will do by instinct what should be done, and avoid by insight what is to be avoided. Without anger, without strife. A pondering people knows there is no power in a powerful ego, that allowing God, letting God is everything. Absolutely everything.

And so, by a stance we make a break with a world we knew, both the good of it and the bad of it, lest the impact of so much association rob us of vision. For just as people travel to see new sights, other ways, strange faces, and so gain a better knowledge of their own world, the monk lives in a foreign land to sharpen his vision of reality. As we know our own land best when we return to it from other shores, so we touch the Gospel most powerfully when we are free of the customary, the usual, when we live in an alien land of other ways. And to keep that freedom, we keep that distance, maintain that stance. Which does not mean that we cannot share it.

For who does not on occasion need to get out of the kitchen? Out of the house, out of town, to taste something a little different so that we may know who we are again?

It is in renewal, in the new, that we discover the old. What is private becomes public; what is secret, manifest; what is hidden, revealed.

Gethsemani
May 8, 1988

24
Sts. Peter and Paul

A few times a year, I would get on my motorcycle and drive the hundred miles to Alexishaven, headquarters of the Catholic mission in the Madang [Papua New Guinea, ed.] diocese: for teeth-trouble or supplies or renewed license or books. And while there, would always listen to some music . . . like Simon and Garfunkel's *Bridge Over Troubled Water*.

A striking figure, a Jesus figure: to lay one's life down for the cause of peace, to spend one's self to lead from here to there, over the chasm that separates, from evil to good, from Old Law to New, from time to eternity. By whom, if not by Jesus, do we cross the troubled waters? What are Peter and Paul, in God's drama on earth, but first pontifex, pontiff, bridge-builder, and first apostle to the Gentiles, breaking the barriers of tradition, of history, bringing the Gospel to far shores?

Peter as man among others is surely a #4 on the Enneagram [a personality-type indicator, ed.]: ardent, impulsive, terrified of tough women, enthusiastic, responsive, gullible and naive. It is not difficult to understand his admiration for Paul: the idealist, the Puritan prophet and preacher, staunch defender of the truth, the zealot. A real Enneagram #1. Paul: vigorous, tireless, passionate and consumed in his commitment to truth as he saw it. Worn out in the service of the Gospel, and frequently reminding us of it, fearless before Peter, righteous, forthright.

And yet, they loved one another, needed one another.

Paul had his world turned around in a moment. Peter gave his world away without 10 seconds of hesitation, the fisherman's world he knew just as quickly as the apostle's world he entered on. The same Peter who wore grooves in his cheeks in a life's tears of regret. Paul needed Peter's human warmth; Peter needed Paul's courage.

Totally different, totally Christ's in the end.

I wonder how you and I would fare in the face of his three questions: "Brother, do you love Me?" I know your answer. But if he repeats it? I mean, you know, with the way you live, the way you've acted, the way you've been—how are you going to answer him? "Do you love Me?" Someone may overhear you and snicker.

Could any of us do as Peter did, and three times answer the thrice-put query, "Do you love Me?" And risk the laughter of demons. I think long on it. Paul, too, learned. He was hard and full of assertion and sureness, but he grew warm. By Jesus. More maternal. He uses maternal words, motherly words. For we are born of mother and are bonded with her, then break the bond and sever the tie to move on.

And then are bonded to father, only to sever that bond, too, if we are to live.

And then are bonded to a male-mother. A man who will teach us manly love and male tenderness. This was Jesus for the apostles and the chosen band. He opened them to a richer life by teaching mercy and compassion, surrender, docility and nonviolence, so that, leaving him behind, they might move on to an integrated humanity in which they are wed to the inner spouse, the genuine man who is a Jesus, both a tough and a tender son of God.

We speak not of psychological development, but of holiness. There is no human love unless we are human, and we are not human if we are adult adolescents.

It is this as much as anything that Peter and Paul teach us. What good was Saul's zealous pursuit of Christians in the name of God? How much value was there to Peter's charm and warmth when he would betray his love to avoid embarrassment? What good an archbishop's piety if he cannot bring himself to listen to Peter? What good your early rising and your psalms and sweat if the abbot dare not tell you what to do? What good the rein in your hands if the horse has the bit between his teeth?

The Lord told Peter, "When you get old, another will lead you where you do not want to go." The Lord says the same to you, too. You going?

The Lord said of Paul, "I will show him how much he must suffer for my name." Has he shown you?

We had a mother we loved, and we left her. We had a father we loved, and we left him. We had a mother/father in Jesus who taught us to be men tough and tender, that we might be like Peter, like Paul, taught the bitter lessons of our own duplicity, our own arrogance. And raised by Jesus to life in the Spirit, that we might lay down our life in love for the Church, with Jesus, like him a bridge over troubled water.

We live surrounded by beauty, the beauty of God's world, the beauty of structure and of rite, the beauty of vesture and appointment, the beauty of communal love. Men beat their beautiful wives and their beautiful children for want of manly love. To live blind to beauty is a similar want. Be it forever alien to us.

Amen.

Gethsemani
June 29, 1988

25
Feeding the Multitude
Seventeenth Sunday of the Year
John 6:1-15

I have a question for you: did your prayers bring the rain? Your answer will reveal a great deal about how you respond to divine intervention in your life.

One time I was in Wewak, a small town on the northern coast of New Guinea, trying to get some help for an infected ear. I was there only a couple of days, and the last evening the priest from the old mission on the hill asked me to come up. He had a problem. On the hill was a local community of religious brothers who ran a center for delinquent boys, teaching them a trade or craft. The priest and the Divine Word Brother told me their problem: spirits.

Strange goings-on: like the sound of huge sheets of glass shattering with great noise in a field outside the church during Mass. And afterwards, no evidence whatever anywhere of glass. Sounds of huge truckloads of timber being dumped with much din—no timber. Tables and desks and chairs knocked about at night in a locked classroom, with a certainty no one had been in the room. These events had the boys on edge, and the priest feared if this continued they would all run away.

The hill in Wewak had been the scene of severe military action in the war. Many Japanese had been killed, and their bodies had never been recovered or taken home. Several times a year, Japanese tourists would come to a little Shinto shrine on the hill and burn incense sticks for their dead to do them reverence.

So I said to the priest, "Maybe the Japanese dead need help. Prayers. Intercession. Pardon. Why not offer a few Masses for them? You could do it privately. If that is not enough, then a public Mass. And more yet, then the bishop with cope and miter and staff, a procession and exorcism, prayers for the dead." Later, I heard from the priest. He did offer the Masses. Peace was restored. All was quiet.

What is one to make of that? Intrusion of spirit into matter? The beyond into the here?

Brother Lavrans told me that when he was a boy, they moved into a semi-basement apartment in Brooklyn. They were not long there when he woke them all at night from his bed in the living room with screams of terror. He had seen a dead man hanging from the chandelier in the middle of the room. Next day, his mother sought out the landlady. "Anything odd ever happen in that flat?" The woman replied, "What do you mean?" "You know what I mean! Anything odd ever happen in that flat?" After some dodging, she finally told her. "Yes, a man hung himself from the fixture in the living room." "Why didn't you tell me?" "I tell people and I'll never rent the apartment!" The Nielsens moved.

In 1972 in El Paso, Texas, a prayer group in Sacred Heart parish decided to help the poor in Juarez across the Rio Grande on Christmas Day. They took Christmas dinner to the poorest families living at the town dump. With burritos for 125, some fruit, a few tamales and a ham, they arrived, dismayed to find 350 waiting. They started feeding the group, deciding to do so as long as food lasted. There was more than enough: enough for seconds, enough to take some home, enough to feed the eight cars of people from the prayer group, enough leftovers for three orphanages.

What goes on here?

Such intrusions are disturbing to most people, an encounter which is a bit stressful.

Just as, say, Medjugorje. Some are almost embarrassed by it, or distinctly incredulous. Others are highly enthusiastic. It is hard to be matter-of-fact.

For all that, the miracles of Jesus, both in his day and in ours, disturb many. Some take the stand: give me Jesus, never mind the miracles. His life, his death, his teaching . . . yes, and his Resurrection. But leave out the wonder-working. Others find in the opening of the divine the clear intervention of greater power in the midst of our lives, our land, our time; something positive, challenging, a confirming of faith whether weak or strong.

Such contacts of one world with another, something like the lightning coming out of the cloud to enter the earth, are perhaps more common than we think. Not as rare as one imagines. The Middle Ages knew holy wells and blessed springs, sacred trees and holy hills, places visited by angels and saints. Andrew Greeley, among how many others conducting surveys, discovered that significant spiritual experiences intense enough to alter thinking, to change lifestyle, are not nearly as rare as he himself imagined. Very many people have at least one in a lifetime. What is also interesting: they never talk about it. Too personal, too sacred, too intimate to expose to possible ridicule or misunderstanding.

Despite the "ravages of atheistic communism," what are we to make of Russia celebrating the millennium of Christianity, of establishing contact with the Vatican? Mere expediency? Politics? What goes on here?

I believe meditating on such events as this miracle of feeding the multitude today ought to do something to us to bring on some reaction: resentment or embarrassment, incredulity or enthusiasm, a willingness to tolerate a divine intervention and take the consequences; some sort of matter-of-factness with human and divine. We can fancy one of the disciples saying to Jesus, after the event, "Lord, you ought to be more careful. Avoid these great wonders. They attract the wrong sort, looking for signs and free food. You do not know these people." Or someone, hearing of it all, might comment, "Go easy. These things start simple and end up momentous. Someone provides bread. Many share it. Wonder indeed. And the story grows in the telling."

Or, as a missionary put it to me, "It was a multiplication for the sharing. For Jesus took bread from those around, broke it, passed it out. And others with a loaf did the same. And because all shared, there was more than enough for all. That was the lesson." Plausible. Not factual.

Is this the faith? Miracles for the credulous? Miraculous bread? Roses in January? Voices to children? Springs in the Pyrenees that heal?

It is the faith indeed. Not all of it. But much a part of it. Dismiss this part and you end up at odds with the whole. Sometimes the human opens and the divine appears.

And the question, "Did the rain come because of our prayer?" I answer for you, "Of course it did."

Gethsemani
July 24, 1988

26
Brother Charles' Golden Jubilee

*B*rother Odilo died on the 18th. He was 66. Today Brother Charles is 50 years here. At Brother Odilo's place in the refectory is a cross that will be there for 30 days. A Gregorian series of 30 Masses will be offered for him by the priests of the monastery.

These are customs, traditions. They come, they go, but there is always some way of customarily saying something that has meaning in life, our life. A ritual, a ceremony, a function or rite. All very human.

Also very human is the contradiction that can arise between inner and outer, the words we say and what we really think, the gesture we make and the lack of sincerity in it.

The Pharisees were a pious school among the Jews of Our Lord's time: they followed certain customs and traditions. Good men (and women, presumably) who, like good people everywhere, were not lacking a certain contradictory quality. Great sticklers for the formalities, yet with no great love back of them. Sometimes.

They took it on themselves to chide Christ and his disciples because he was an affront to them in his casual attitude toward much they took very seriously. In other words, if you do not like someone, it is not hard to fault them. There are flaws of some kind in all. Or apparent flaws. The trouble is, your fault-finding reveals you, too.

We are constantly having to redo our attitudes. We build with care a relationship to God, and he shatters it. We think we have a deep understanding of someone, and discover one day that we misread them, we are wide of the mark. We think we know ourselves, and one day we say something, we do something, even dream something that shocks us dreadfully. We are filled with shame and confusion, very much upset about something only *we* know.

It is good that children learn to confess their sins early on, for children cope with evil tendencies in themselves: every good little boy and good little girl needs some way to deal with evil. Better that than acting it out.

Jesus is at pains to tell us that interior and exterior are related. Must be related. One of the pains of prayer is an awareness as we pray that we are not good, and so we are tempted to see our prayer as useless. We confront God in the Eucharist and are confronted, too, with our sinfulness. We wonder what we are doing in the presence of God.

We are sinners all, and it is for us that Christ came. The first step toward healing is to know this and to accept this. Mercy in God, then, becomes personal and it heals. There is no point in painting over old wood. Better renew the siding. No harm in staying youthful as long as you know how old you are.

The reconciling of inner and outer is a life's work. Maybe at the end we will be able to have our cup clean both outside and in, with the help of God.

Pious practices of every sort are very good, and should be part of our life. They ought never to be made gross by using them as covers for our sins. Indeed, they ought rather to lead us to greater awareness of how poor we really are, come down to it. And this leads to trust in mercy. And your trust in mercy begins to be real when you find yourself being merciful to others. And being merciful to others is a world away from a constant fault-finding, in which there is no healing.

The Pharisees talked, walked, ate with Jesus. They completely missed him, blind as bats, as ignorant of who he was as they were of who they themselves were. We can learn from them.

Gethsemani
August 28, 1988

27
The Book of Hours

A while ago, in a reply, I sent a lady that cream-and-blue folder with photos and text about the abbey, and some picture cards of the chapel. Not long after, she returned them to me with the comment, "Sad, sad, sad! It is all so plain, so barren, above all so Protestant. Like so many of the new churches today." She was, of course, quite right.

When, over 20 years ago, the two Brothers went looking for an architect/designer for our church renewal, having found one they thought most competent, they had but one question to put to him, "What do you think of the Shaker style?" When he told them that he was much taken with the Shaker style, that it was a major influence on his work, they knew they had their man. If he was in sympathy with Shaker work, with its simplicity, purity, integrity, they knew he would appreciate the Cistercian style from which descended the Shaker and so much of the Protestant approach. The old Congregational churches of New England have a Cistercian directness which is more than just their being white.

The first Cistercians were innovative in art and otherwise. We tend perhaps to think of them in conservative terms, see them as anxious to return to early observance, the pure Rule, and miss the innovation that was so much theirs. They did return to earlier ways, but they approached the Rule with freedom to interpret it afresh. Thus, the mode of governing the Order was a new departure which, if they did not invent, made good use of the assembled abbots as the supreme governing body of the Order. Like the architectural style they developed, this too had a profound impact on consequent history in religion and religious orders.

Most innovative of all was their acceptance of lay people into the Order. This, too, was in the air at the time and not their idea. But they adopted it with such vigor and success that it was a major aspect of their phenomenal growth. Into a monastic life, then priestly and reserved for the most part to the educated (that is to say, literate nobility and upper wealthy class), they admitted lay associates. These were from the lower classes. With their own quarters in the monastery and a simple prayer form instead of the Latin Office, they would, through dedicated, competent labor, share and actually make possible the monastery's life. It was a move that caught on very soon, had enormous influence not only on the Cistercians but on monastic life, religious life ever since. Slowly, over the centuries, the lay men became Brothers, more and more integrated into the life of the monastery, right down to our own time. Choir is no longer clerical. The lay and the cleric are one in being all of a kind, monks, with a variety of service according to one's vocation. The integration is complete.

What now? Perhaps a new era is at hand when once again we will open the door to the laity. Once more we would be well within the tradition by being innovative.

The piety of our time changes. For one thing, far more emphasis is on the Eucharist, with a great deal of participation, a great deal of variety. For another, far less emphasis is on the paraliturgical. So much has gone, and little has replaced it. We had devotions: Sacred Heart devotions, May devotions. We had novenas, triduums, Holy Hours, First Fridays, Stations, Benediction, much else. Though I cannot assess contemporary parish practice, I do think patterns have changed.

I hazard the hunch that the next trend will be at once traditional and innovative: a return to the Hours. The Hours as public practice and as private devotion: Lauds and Vespers in the parish church, not only in the cathedral—for Sundays, for feasts, maybe daily. And in the privacy of the home, the Hours of prayer. A return to the psalms, to Scripture, to prayer linked to the Church Year from Advent through Christ the King, tied to the saints along the way. Rich, deep, abiding, rewarding.

This renewal was called for by Vatican II:

> *Pastors of souls should see to it that the chief hours, especially Vespers, are celebrated in common in church on Sundays and the more solemn feasts. And the laity, too, are encouraged to recite the divine Office, either with the priests, or among themselves, or even individually.*[2]

Who can better guide this, inspire this, encourage this than monks whose lives revolve around the Hours? Not to make nuns and monks of everyone, but to let everyone share the privilege we know in the prayer of the Church.

In what way? I do not know. I cannot guess. That is not my point nor the issue. Nor is that a problem. When it comes to food and hungry people, ways to serve them are not long coming. I am more interested in the Gospel and how we live it. For the Gospel is a call to the innovative. Your ideas, your notions, your views, even your convictions are always subject to divine veto. To Providence. To history. The great tragedy of Jesus was that he did not fulfill the people's expectations. We, too, have our expectations of what life should deliver. What this life should be. Yet we cannot, like James and John, turn the Kingdom to our own advantage.

Ask the woman, the man on their Golden Wedding Day, even on their Silver Wedding Day, "Was it like you thought it would be?" Ask the jubilarian priest, the elderly monk, "Had you any idea what you were in for?" It is not just sickness and suffering, poverty, worry, disaster; none of these are conspicuously absent from most lives. It is the deeper things, the landscapes of the soul that shake us so profoundly. So radically opposed to my plans, my ideas, my notions. Who counts on the life of faith being darkness? Why is God so elusive? How can I help agreeing with the mother who tells me, "Life is not fair"?

In other words, being innovative is interior. It is a disposition of the soul, a spiritual quality one learns from sailing a small boat in a large sea with an unreliable wind. If you dare, you can cope. If you do not cling, you can be free. Change as such is not the issue. The depth of our love for God is.

I entered my first novitiate in 1939 [the Society of the Divine Word, ed.], and my second in 1960 [Gethsemani, ed.]. My experience in an active order and in a quiet one has much encouraged me. The one and the other were both highly innovative. The Cistercians have no corner on this market, even if they have been around in the business 900 years, and perhaps for that very reason. The service of God is a great school of youth for it keeps you young, and only the young survive. Who would follow Jesus must have a young heart, wide open to love, willing to dare, able to accept, eager to endure. It has nothing to do with strong stands and self-assertion and absolute demands. They are for the old who live by willpower.

The Church is a youthful Church. And those who are loyal to her keep youth. The Christ is a young man, and those who would love him must love as the young do. Fresh, joyous, lovely as those Books of Hours that have come down to us from the piety of past ages. We can do as well.

Amen.

Gethsemani
October 16, 1988

28
The Great Day
1st Mass of David De Vore
Feast of Christ the King

Some years ago, 1951 actually, the year I was called back to this country after a few years in New Guinea, I first went up to the Highlands to visit a priest friend, to see some of that wild country. We came back from a neighbor missionary one day by horseback, along difficult mountain trails, and got caught for the last three hours in heavy, cold rain that made us miserable and travel dangerous. As we came into sight of his little house, he saw someone on the front porch waiting out the rain. "It's the Seventh Day Adventist pastor," said Al, for Europeans were then few and he knew them all. "And I don't care if he doesn't like it, we're going to have a glass of rum after all this." Which we did. We changed, sat down, sipped, said hello. And we had scarcely exchanged a pleasantry or two when the pastor said, apropos of nothing, "Well, it's gonna be a great day!" "Sir?," I said. He repeated, "It's gonna be a great day!" "What do you mean?" "You know: Armageddon, the great battle in the Valley of Jehoshaphat." I was so surprised that I laughed. And he was startled at this reaction from a Catholic priest. I thought afterwards, "That good man had the Last Judgement, the Final Coming, the end of all right up here in the foreground, center stage front. He lives with it."

Yet we believe in the Last Great Day, too. It is elemental in the faith, part of our creed. And we celebrate it today in the person of Christ the King. Scriptures are at a loss trying to cope with this mystery: some of the scariest writing in the Bible is on the end of time. Blood on the moon, the stars falling from the skies, the end of all things, the great judgement, doomsday.

In the words of the Second Vatican Council:

We know neither the moment of the consummation of the earth and of humanity, nor the way the universe will be transformed. The form of this world, distorted by sin, is passing away and we are taught that God is preparing a new dwelling and a new earth in which righteousness dwells, whose happiness will fill and surpass all the desires of peace arising in human hearts. Then with death conquered, the people of God will be raised in Christ and what was sown in weakness and corruption will put on the imperishable: love and its work will remain and all of creation, which God made for us, will be free of its bondage to decay.[3]

In other words, we are at a loss for words, for images to describe something beyond description, at once an overwhelming change which is so radical that it amounts to destruction: a coming of peace so splendid that it is beyond conceiving.

The Word of God, through whom all things were made, was made flesh so that as perfect man He could save all and sum up all in Himself. The Lord is the goal of human history, the focal point of the desires of history and civilization, the center of humankind, the joy of all hearts and the fulfillment of all aspirations. It is He whom the Father raised from the dead, exalted and placed at His right hand, constituting Him judge of the living and the dead. Animated and drawn together in His spirit, we press onwards on our journey towards the consummation of history which fully corresponds to the plan of His love: "to unite all things in Him, things in heaven and things on earth."[4]

The Seventh Day Adventist pastor was quite right: it *is* going to be a Great Day!

A day in which we have a place. As that day is described, positively and negatively, so our share. All we do in building a world in terms of family, of service, of creation, all that is good and noble for love and dedication and sacrifice has meaning not only in the immediate now, but also for its abiding in the world's ultimate development. So, too, all that is borne in suffering, trial and trouble, sickness and death, the more so was lacking in obvious meaning. Because it is related to Christ by his life and death and rising, it becomes one with him, with his life for us and for the Father.

A priest not only takes part in this mystery of the Incarnation by his priestly service at the altar, his ministry of word and sacrament, his care of the people, but also, and perhaps no less significantly, by his life. Who can fathom the mystery of a human life when we reckon on human life as eternal? Who knows what life means in God? So, too, a priest by his suffering and death enters into Christ and in Christ with all humankind.

For the call to be a Christian is to make articulate what is deepest in human destiny, just as a priest makes articulate for the people the passion and death and rising that is Christ's and every human's.

One time, when David De Vore was in the midst of personal trial, seeking God's will, searching for the next step he was to make, I went with him to visit some monasteries, to make inquiries, to have a look. We pulled into the parking lot at Mt. Saviour's, near Elmira [New York, ed.]. I got out and, while waiting for him to get his bag, noted that the car next to us had the sticker of an Episcopal parish. I told David, "Someone here is an Episcopal priest." And seeing another decal, I said, "And he went to Nashota. Isn't that the seminary you went to?" He made a grim face. "Yes. Man, I hope I don't know him." He was in no shape for socializing, clerical or otherwise. Too burdened in mind and heart. It turned out that the priest was a very good friend of his. And since God is often tender in dark hours, it also turned out that the good friend was in the midst of becoming a Catholic priest. The visit turned out to be great comfort in a difficult time.

This, too, is a great day. The culmination of a long search. Beginning a new life in the Church of God. Of great personal meaning. Of what significance for how many others? This is comfort for us all in responding to grace given. Salvation is singular but is never solitary. For each it is, "What would You have me do?" and the doing of it is for all. We venture each day to build a world that will surely end, and will surely be recreated in Christ, the King. It is to know that suffering is the lot of us all, in whatever form. And in no sense meaningless, but deep in the mystery of God and his world. David takes paten in hand, he takes his own life and yours, and mine, and the life of all the world, and "Christs" it. It is no small thing to be a priest. It is no small grace to love one. And it is great joy. That is why this is a Mass of Thanksgiving.

Amen.

Gethsemani
November 20, 1988

29
Thanksgiving Day
This homily was given following a reception
for benefactors at Gethsemani.

*A*fter that lovely expression of hospitality and intercession for gracious friends of the Abbey, I got to thinking about it and wondered if I would have done it the same. I let my imagination play and considered that perhaps I would have come up with something maybe not better, maybe not even as good, but in a somewhat different style . . . which I venture to share, not in any sense in a critical mode, but because it led me to considerations which moved me.

Perhaps I would have favored Vespers in choir so as to give the guests a taste of choir worship in the manner of monks. And then I think I would have served dinner in silence with reading, to offer a sense of participation in the monastic liturgy of the refectory. That done, we would have all gone to the chapter room, the guests on the upper tier and we, at least some, on the lower, the abbot then introducing the guests to the monks:

> *Mr. and Mrs. Sloan Ketterell: Mr. Ketterell is an engineer, went to Ohio State, is a great supporter of the Louisville Symphony. His wife is also musical, a graduate of Wellesley, and plays in a string quartet in Louisville. Mrs. Louise Humphrey is a widow, a graduate of an art school, a friend of our late benefactor by reason of common interests . . .*

And so on. And then he would introduce the monks to the guests, down the row:

> *Brother Egilhard came to us from Nebraska in 1959 from a Catholic farm area, came early, has worked mostly on the farm, is an excellent cook, served as chef for the monastery in Rome for several years. Father Jonas is from Cincinnati, son of a doctor, studied at St. Meinrad's and with the Jesuits in St. Louis, has been our infirmarian, archivist, teacher . . .*

And so on.

I went through the community—you might try it sometime—and tried to sum up each in a sentence or two, discovering what a fascinating group of men we are. From all over, of a great variety of backgrounds. Some came early, some late; some after a career in the world, some fresh and youthful; some with educational accomplishment, some with wide travel. Some with neither.

What moved them to come here? What graces touch a man to inspire him, maybe slowly, maybe suddenly, to leave all he knows and enter this monastery? What chance circumstances, what inner conviction, what suffering? To come here for why? What is this all about? Where are we headed? What journey do we make together?

Like the first ships to Australia, as we read in *The Fatal Shore*,[5] we are off on a journey we know so little about, to places we know nothing of, for reasons we grasp only in the light of faith.

Years ago, when this church was much wooden—floor and stalls and sanctuary—and a great old steeple tottering overhead, a monk would come through here on fire watch in the middle of the night and hear ominous creaking and groaning of wood on wood, ever so much like an old ship sailing silently through a dark night on a rolling sea en route to far-off places.

I was reminded of that just last week when a blustery wind was whipping those huge sheets of plastic that sheathe the side of the retreat house against rain, sounding for all the world like sails snapping loose and wild as we change course.

We are much a ship. And we are on it together. We certainly could not trip alone. I know. I tried it. And we need everyone on board. Who could we spare? Name him. We need all, can spare none. Every single one. If he is not here, it is not Gethsemani. If you are not here, it is some other place, some other time. The infinitely complex web of divine genius that led us all here is only the beginning of a mysterious love that keeps us here, treasures us, loves us, delights in us.

For we are so few. The ship so small. The sea so huge. What are 12 monasteries but one small fragment of Catholic America, not to say whole America? And even worldwide in the Church, we are a modest Order. In the world at large, so trifling. Procter and Gamble soap is a bigger enterprise.

Like butterflies. Why does God bother? So delicate. So fragile, so beautiful. Yet God watches over them in his delight in them. How else could they find their way south, and back? They of no use.

So on this Thanksgiving Day we might join hearts in thanks for grace, for gift, for privilege underserved, unmerited, to play some role in the mysterious drama of God in the world. Something so deep, so intense in meaning, that no song can say it, no poetry.

I stood there watching them raise the cock to the steeple, and Mr. Clark asked me, "Why a cock?" "Why, Mr. Clark, to announce the end of night, the banishment of evil spirits, the coming of dawn, of the new day, the rising of the sun who is our glorious Lord, victor over darkness, death and the powers of evil. The cock is like a watch at the top of the mast, Vigilant for his coming, first to gild in the glory of the rising sun."

And we below take delight in the joy of this endeavor, enthralled with not being able to grasp it. This fascinating group on this fascinating journey. No. Be it said, "You can never introduce them. Better not." How could you put in two sentences the meaning of such a person? Like assuming you know the mystery of a butterfly because you know its Latin name. Better simply thank God that we are here, beg God bless our voyage, make it significant for the world to come.

Significant it is. For who knows how? For who knows whom? So many sinners convicted by grace to a journey of atonement for us, for all. Little knowing—not knowing at all—what is to come of it. Like pilgrims on the edge of a continent thanking God they are there, that they live, got through a year, unable to imagine what is to come. We join them in *Deo Gratias*, thanks be to God.

Amen.

Gethsemani
November 24, 1988

30
Immaculate Conception

$\mathcal{M}$any times, when people write in to have Masses offered for their intentions, they give dates, usually marking an anniversary of death or a birthday, a wedding and so on. This generally annoys me for it means fuss for me and others, and I am tempted to write back, "Why not now? Why wait? After all, there is no time with God, and certainly those gone into eternity do not experience time as we do." In the end, though, I acquiesce. For it is true: the marking of times does mean a lot to us.

In the cemetery out front is a large slab of black granite with the names of 106 persons who lie there and who do not have a stone, or whose stone or cross has long since disappeared. A long list. Is there any meaning to this? Why is this tradition so deeply engraved in us? Is a name chiseled into rock enough to halt time, keep a person alive? Does a Mass offered for you a year from your dying day have special point?

One Veterans' Day, the former Armistice Day, November 11th, a monument to Vietnam veterans was dedicated in Frankfort, a work sponsored by the efforts of Ron Ray, friend of the Abbey. It is a large sundial on the Capitol grounds, with the names of 1046 war dead inscribed in rows on stone slabs in such a way that the sun's shadow from the gnomon point of the dial crosses the name of each on the day he died. So young Kentucky fallen are remembered.

What does it mean? A shadow crossing a name, shadow from a sun 93 million miles away, its light eight minutes in reaching us. Are these notings of name and time real? Once we are gone, our dust too disintegrated, what does it mean to be remembered in human years or incised in stone, recalled at the altar?

It does not mean much of anything unless time be something nearly a delusion, a construct we use to deal with life as we know it, not unlike marking distance by inches and feet and yards, rods and miles, changing space not a whit, yet somehow necessary for us.

We celebrate the conception of the Virgin Mary, the Mother of God. This is a yearly commemoration of an event we know in our faith to have taken place. Our faith is nothing if not historical, and this feast is to attest it. It is our memorial Mass, an anniversary, our inscription in stone, a shadow from light passing over a person. Theologians of an earlier time were much puzzled for explaining how what happened did happen. For they figured time linearly in a rather narrow sense, and so were at a loss to know how the Redemption could take effect before it happened. Later theologians said it was "anticipated," and that proved satisfactory. Today, we might not be so skittish, for our views of time change and we are not so sure anymore that time is always before and after. For God surely, for us also. Conception is not temporal, but is an entry into eternity. Time is but an Advent before birth.

What we can do, then, is to relish the joy of the eternally present, to know in faith. That is to say, in reality Christ lives and dies, rises in glory, reigns among us. Now. That the woman who was his mother is no mere memory but, in a way we have no way of understanding, is present to us, present as the one who was conceived as humankind was first meant to be conceived. Here for the first time in history, human love was what human love was meant to be. And in Christ can come to be once more. Just as her Assumption is what human death was meant to be.

To believe in the conception of Mary as one without involvement with the sin of our first parents is to believe in the full glory of human nature redeemed. Just as to believe in her Assumption is to state with finality the ultimate glory of our kind in the grace of God.

And these mysteries are present to us now, even if we have to time them in order to cope with them. The Redemption is going on, the mystery of our conception, birth, death and rising is present in Mary. And is at work in us.

It is worthwhile to remember, to mark days and anniversaries. It does matter to carve names in stone, it does make sense to note the passage of sun, solstice and equinox, the succession of day and night, the year. For we live in eternity already.

A great conception takes place, the union in love of God and humankind, soon to be revealed. This feast is to assert that it is so, that we know it, believe it, and love it.

Gethsemani
December 8, 1988

31
Dreaming

The other day I was going out the door with a bag of trash to burn when a monk from behind called, "Have you got a minute?"

"Yes, I've got a minute."

"I had a dream."

"So, you had a dream!"

"Well, not a dream really, but a scene. A couple of scenes."

"Well?"

"I am in this room and all there is in it is a bird cage with a very colorful bird inside. And my brother is standing by it. And I said, 'She wants attention. Put your fingers together and she will peck them.' And he did. That's all. And then a second scene. Another room. And in this rather large room, a big glass box, like a plastic cube, big enough to hold a person. And it had a very pretty woman inside, obviously distressed. And I went over and put my hand to the glass. And she did the same inside, palm to palm with my hand. And then she wilted and fainted. That's all."

"Well," I said, "it looks as if your anima needs a little love, a little attention. I would guess the bird in the cage is your anima, and the woman in a cube. I wonder how you relate to your other side. That seems the obvious message, wouldn't you say?"

He replied, "Could be I'm not exactly in love with my feminine aspect. I do not relate well to it. Which reminds me—there was a third scene. I am in a waste country, a big desert, only rocks, a wilderness. I am alone. And there is this large prehistoric monster, like a dinosaur with an enormous tail. And oddly, I am not afraid of him. In fact, I feel my power over him and sense that he fears me even though he is huge and I am so small by comparison. Let's talk about it. Let's talk about it." He said I could.

Relating to our other side. Coming to terms with the other pole of our bipolarity. In a man, this is often pictured as a feminine spirit. And the opposite in a woman. If women find their integration easier than men, it may be because our culture is so male-oriented. No one will question a male emphasis. But if a man tries to emphasize the feminine, he may run into trouble. I mean an opposition from the man himself, an opposition that is typical of our kind of world. But it is no mere matter of a man being a little feminine now and then, allowing something soft and tender to emerge, some show of tolerance and patience: qualities we think women favor. Or for a woman to be tough once in a while, as men are supposed to be tough.

This is superficial, a veneer. Christianity is not a charm school or a course in personality development. Christianity is to follow Christ, to be Christ-like. And this is the business we are about.

We deal with healing and wholeness. It is beyond us. It is the work of the Spirit of Christ. Only God can lead us in the sunshine of another kind of love.

No one can set about to be like Jesus on their own power. They may do well enough, but this well-doing will be restricted and narrow, end up a caricature of Christ, not a resemblance.

In any case, our resemblance to Christ is not an imitation but an interpretation, which is to say we do truly be ourselves, the self that God planted in us, our Christian image, the person we would be for love of him.

So we learn surrender to the Spirit and descend in him to where we really are, and so begin to be, to discover what Christ meant when he said, "My yoke is easy and my burden light." True indeed. Nothing is easier than being yourself, your true self.

But you may be a while getting there, given the warped, one-sided, unbalanced sort of world we live in. For we live in a man's world, my brothers, a man's world. I hope you have that clear. For if you have that clear, then you realize that woman is no great part of it. Not really. Even our prayer at the altar, even at the Eucharist, the love feast, we make it clear by the way we speak that it is a man's world. Which, of course, is not the world of Jesus or of the Church. It is an aberration born of a breed of vultures who fed on decadence.

So if you would be Christian, you cannot go along with things as they are. You are going to have to face the fact that if you are going to be a real Christian, then you are going to be odd, something curious. It can be risky.

Archbishop Hunthausen tried it. He did not set out to be anything other than a Christian. Merciful, compassionate, tolerant, fearless. He helped those who most needed help. They who are so little loved in our day: the divorced, poignant victims of failed love, the gay, lovers of another kind and therefore contemptible. And he confronted the military, caught up in a nuclear madness conceived in the depths of hell.

The bishop did not know what he was taking on. And in short order, pious Catholics were writing to Rome in growing numbers and in loud words that this man was breaking the rules. And so Rome humbled him. But such an uproar followed that Rome relented and reinstated the humiliated bishop.

Quite by accident I came upon an editorial in the *Boston Sunday Globe*. The astute editorial writer made this point:

> *The federal government of USA has been served notice in the reinstatement of Archbishop Hunthausen that the bishops of this country who oppose the nuclear madness of our military have more support than was realized.*

It is people like the Archbishop who are truly Christian, truly integrated. And such people have enormous power because of Christ in them. They are people in whom the Spirit is present in power. The Spirit can work only in the person who is free, has moved beyond one-sided reflections of the worldly pattern, who are in touch with their own wholeness.

To resist the pattern of the competitive, aggressive, assertive, violent world we are part of is to take on a formidable task. So it appears to be. As if we cope with some great dinosaur. But once you enter into the world of grace and of prayer, you learn that the dinosaur is timid and afraid, much show and much bluster.

Living in accord with the world's pattern is very hard because it is so unnatural, so inhuman. It is not possible to be a Christian and live so, not without inner contradictions that will tear you apart.

To walk in Christ's way, to become a whole person, to be complete in him is song. Is joy. And our hopes continue to grow in a way of joy and of peace. And will make us fearless even against the mighty.

And I will end with a little dream I had: someone gave Brother Simeon a box of 24 ice cream bars, chocolate-covered. And so he put them out for pickup supper one night. The monks came and went. But the box of 24 bars was still intact. No monk would take one, but left them for the others. Is such tenderness unreal? I do not know, except that I am not capable of it. Not yet. I am still trying. For surely Maximillian Kolbe, who gave his food to others in concentration camps, did not start being unselfish at that stage of his life. He had years of practice. So I, too, will look to my anima and feed my bird and set free my lady that I may yet become a Christian.

Gethsemani
Circa 1989

32
Bad Press, Good News
Ash Wednesday
2 Corinthians 5:20

So, we are ambassadors for Christ; it is as though God were appeal-ing through us; and the appeal that we make in Christ's name is: be reconciled to God.

Judging by what small amount I see, I gather that in both secular and Catholic press the Church, the Pope, the bishops and priests come in for a share of criticism, complaint, biased report-age. This is nothing new, and God knows other times have known far worse conditions. That does not make me reluctant to say that reading about Christ's Church in the press, especially some of the Catholic press, can sometimes be disheartening. One does get weary of fault-finding, nagging criticism for news. It does not wear well. Having had a mother who was prone to nag-ging, I am sensitive to this and find it counterproductive. And when things go wrong, as they sometimes do, I am not likely to praise champions of liberty and honesty who think everything must be told, that detraction is not a vice, that good is served by spreading evil to no point. So one feels for a priest in these Inqui-sition days.

Which feeling I do not have for monks. In times past, monks have had their share of false report, prejudice, contempt, even ha-tred. In our own times, this is still true of some lands. In our situ-ation, we are in that sunny land of a general good feeling toward us. The comments in our guest book are almost without exception positive, even flattering. We are not above mentioning that our cake or cheese have been served in the White House. Catholics and those who are not, even those of no faith at all, in general think well of us. Even a rather messy involvement with Texas money was handled at length in *The Wall Street Journal*, yet fairly enough, it would seem. Or at least it tried to be objective. Our books are known worldwide. A voice heard in this secluded clois-ter 25 years ago now is heard in Hong Kong and Chevy Chase and a thousand other places, while listeners trod a treadmill or drive to work, in some cases. So we have good press. We fare better than pope or bishop or priest. It is not only His word:

"Alas for you when the world speaks well of you. This was the way your ancestors treated the false prophets . . ." that makes me chary. Public taste as exemplified in the press can be very fickle. Monks can go out of fashion very quickly. And vocations, for all that, are few. Read history: we are a superb target for abuse and ridicule. And given the consistent thread of anti-Catholicism that runs through our nation's story, we must admit that as monks we are fortunate. Even nuns are more abused than we are.

Yet we do share some of the cultural values of our land. I do not think I reveal secrets or betray any when I say there is a certain amount of anticlericalism in the house. Just as there is in our society at large, in the Church. Not as bad as in some countries, especially so-called Catholic ones. But there.

A recent reflection on the morale of priests in our country, coming from the National Conference of Catholic Bishops, describes in competent terms the overall picture today. We who live in community, know and benefit by a support group, have tremendous resources to fall back on. We ought to have some grasp of our favored position, some sense of compassion for those whose service of God and his Church is in many ways more heroic and more generous. And I think we might express that compassion better than we do.

I single out but one aspect of priestly life that was mentioned in the study of the bishops, if not at length. There is the opposition and criticism of self-righteous faithful who are proud of what they construe as orthodoxy, who insist on an understanding of the faith as they see it. This carping can be very destructive in parish life, as in any community. But worse, no doubt, is the unspoken resentment, the inner rebuttal, that comes from a nonacceptance of Church teaching in some area. In good conscience, one can disagree and act on that, as we know, but we know also how hazardous a route this is. It is, for example, hard to live under an abbot when you disagree seriously with an aspect of his teaching, his authority, or even something no more momentous than his style. Much more so in the parish. An unconscious attitude of hostility can easily become powerful and effective in coloring one's whole attitude in some subtle, secret way. The disagreement may be with the Church, but the brunt of it is borne not by pope or bishop, but by the local pastor. This, in my mind, is a major element in vocational decline. Though a word against Church and priest may never be spoken in a family, the unconscious message is clearly read by the young: the priesthood is not an ideal to pursue. For things do have a way of working through in time: you do not listen to your priest, and it will not be all that long before there are no priests to listen to.

When I told Father Louis (Thomas Merton) that the fruit of a year of novitiate was a sense of having lost the faith, he told me that was typical. Any desert experience exposes the poverty, the shallowness of our faith, and challenges us to deepen it. The desert of cultural shift and breakdown, a breakthrough to new modes and manners, will lay bare weak faith. And since the service of God in religious, priestly life is first of all a life of faith, no one can be too surprised at the revealed inadequacy of Catholic faith, nor the call to depth in faith. Pope and bishop and priest, monastery, convent, parish, family piety, personal holiness are meaningless without faith. And so priests leave, monks quit, nuns depart, families break, the practice of faith abandoned in a bleak desert of emptiness. What I know and what you know is that precisely in that desert we find God again, anew. And so come to renewed faith that brings back to life what had died. So we stand beside the priest, back of him, with him, in response to faith.

And that brings it home. What we monks can do for priests in some practical way may be problematic. But in the essential there is no question: we must pray for them and pray deeply. Lent is as good a time as any to thank God for Christ and for the Church, to pray daily for it, to commit ourselves wholly to it, to fulfill our role in it as best we know how, since we relate in Church to Jesus Christ, Son of God.

Amen.

Gethsemani
February 8, 1989

33
Everything I Have Is Yours
Fourth Sunday of Lent
Luke 15:1-3, 11-32

A week or two ago, I received a letter from Pat Barder, a priest friend. We were in the seminary together. I have not heard from him in years. He wanted to tell me that he had been to Snowmass Monastery in Colorado for a retreat. He signed his letter "Cassius." Cassius was the role he played in a showing of

Shakespeare's *Julius Caesar* we put on in the seminary. In picking leads for amateurs, it is a help to find players who in some way resemble the character. And he resembled Cassius. Shakespeare, like any good literature, is deep, and no rehearsal went by without some new insight emerging, making the production a very rich experience. No surprise he recalls it 45 years later.

Scripture is like that, even more so. The stories are deep, very deep, and keep offering new insights when we enter into them, see ourselves playing in them. And among stories, this is a classic of a father and his two sons. Think of the two sons as failing in love for their father, each taking his own course in not truly believing in the Father's love. The elder, in the way of many elder sons, took the route of duty and steadfast service, hoping thereby to prove his love, to win paternal approval, be accepted. The younger son, as is also the case frequently enough, took a completely different approach. His style was lighthearted, carefree and indulgent. He put the father's love to the test quite dramatically in asking for his inheritance when he was of age. The father perhaps surprised him by granting his wish. The young man was then off, and ran through it in no time at all, unconsciously, no doubt, bringing about what was in the back of his mind all along. When he was in desperate straits and not able to cope, he returned to his father with a well-rehearsed story. He was testing again a love he doubted. And again was surprised.

In that crisis, both sons were exposed: the elder making evident that his service was a calculated one, the younger revealing his foolish behavior and utter want of love. The only hero is the father who loved the elder, service or no service, and loved the younger, foolish or not. We are sometimes the elder in winning God's favor by genuine service, and as often as not the younger by a foolish testing of God because we assume we mean little or nothing to him. We talk much of love for God, but the good in us and the evil may reveal a doubting heart. The father was munificent to younger son and elder. We call the parable The Prodigal Son because we favor the elder: he appeals to us. Yet his love was as shallow as the prodigal's.

In either case, it is clear where we go when events in our lives reveal the quality of the love we are so assured of. We go home to the Father who loves, loved us before, loves us now, loves us after, irrespective of our posturing.

I was reminded of the same profound truth by something told me last week by Paul Mareschal, who was a monk for a while 10 or 12 years ago. A good friend told him that once when she was big with life within her, for no special reason, from some sort of whim, she laid her hand over the child within her and spoke, "Listen, love. I want to tell you something and don't you ever forget it. If you are ever in trouble and do not know what to do, turn right onto Underwood Row." Then she smiled a bit at her notions and went about what she was doing. The child was 4 or 5 and in the kitchen with her one day when, out of the blue, he asked her, "Mommy, what is Underwood Row?" It took her breath away, but she was able to tell him, "That's where we used to live. We had to move when you were not born yet because your Daddy's work changed." The boy was onto something else. A year or two later, when the older sister was upset about something and carrying on in distraught fashion, the little boy went up to her, put his arm around her and said seriously, "Don't worry. Just turn right onto Underwood Row." The girl looked at her mother. "What's he talking about?" She told them how it all began. And the meaning of it: "Home is where you go when you are in trouble. When you run out of love. For home is where there is always someone who loves you."

True enough. If we have ever left home and foolishly squandered our love, if we have been faithful to God and yet know how thin is our love, we turn right to him to be assured anew of an undying love. Then we enter more deeply into our drama, this brief interval we have on stage, where the curtain rises for us in promise and will one day come down in climax. And the name of the play?

"Everything I have is yours."

Amen.

Gethsemani
March 4, 1989

34
For Charlie+
Jeremiah 20

A curse on the day when I was born,
No blessing on the day my mother bore me!
A curse on the man who brought my father the news,
"A son has been born to you!"
Making him overjoyed.

May this man be like the towns
That Yahweh overthrew without mercy:
May he hear alarms in the morning,
The war cry in broad daylight,
Since he did not kill me in the womb
While her womb was swollen with me.
Why ever did I come out of the womb
To live in toil and sorrow
And to end my days in shame?

This passage from Jeremiah the prophet was read the other night at Vigils. It is one of the most daring in Scripture. Only the cry of Christ on the Cross as one abandoned by the Father can compare with it in intensity.

I do not suppose one would normally or even comfortably apply it to St. Joseph. Yet it may be only long familiarity with the events that causes us not to reckon what an extremely taut demand was made upon Joseph when he learned his bride-to-be was with child; when he learned by a dream of God in the night the even more amazing revelation that the life within her was divine. Think on it sometimes and fancy, if you can, how straitened he must have been. Just as impressive for us is his prompt response to God's action in his life. A man of profound faith, enormous courage.

Do you not suppose in the days that followed, the years, that in dark moments he must have been assailed with trials of doubt, with puzzled wonder why he was called to such a destiny? As a pious Jew he would have known well enough of the promised Messiah. Yet what Jew, however pious, would have easily embraced an acceptance of his coming that would mean a baffling mode of that coming, mysterious and unique? Joseph's own virginal call was as unusual as anything could be in a people so enamored of family and children, seeing in a lack of progeny some sort of divine displeasure. I do not find it beyond conjecture that dark shadows would at times drift over the soul of that wonderful man, and the words of Jeremiah come to mind. What, after all, did he know of what was to come? Or what could he have had in mind at the episode in the Temple when the Child spoke so sagely of himself? A holy tradition has it that Joseph died while Jesus was still on earth, becoming thereby patron of a holy death in the arms of Jesus and Mary. So or not, he is a superb advocate of our life and death in Jesus, a great deal more than Joseph the Worker.

Do you suppose others echo the brazen words of Jeremiah, others who find in the challenges that God's Providence thrusts upon them a plea that borders on despair, the familiar refrain, "Why me?" You have only to look around you. One does not need to live very long before coming upon events that try one's faith to a dangerous point.

Death, if not always like that, often is. The absurd is not always remote in our days on earth. Who we are? Why we are? Where we are? When we are? Each a mystery.

What do you suppose it is like for a young man to realize of a sudden what he knew all along and now no longer can deny - that he is gay? What it is like to be dying of cancer? To be ill-favored when it comes to intelligence, to beauty, to place in life? And yet we need not go so far. Into everyone's life God sometimes steps with an unfathomable touch of darkness.

We know in the end that for Jesus, for Joseph, for Jeremiah, for us all, love is the key. Love is the meaning. Love is the reason. We better believe it, for it is the essence of our faith in a Christ who himself sustained a destiny that we relive this week.

We meet to remember Charlie, to pray for him, to commend him anew to God. More than that, to say again our love for him. That is so good for us to do. So sound. So worthy. Death is not a morbid necessity, but an interval on our route to eternal life that is most wholesome to ponder for all that it can reveal to us.

If we are tempted to doubt God's love because of the darkness that sometimes overwhelms us, as it did Jeremiah, Joseph and Jesus, we are also called to reaffirm it time and time again. This is the beauty of death. It reveals love.

We are here a community of men. We love God and we love one another. Yet that love can be clouded by what God does and by what our brother does. If life can sometimes be absurd, so can my brother. The absurdities can loom large. This brother I love: why is he so slow, so stupid, so fussy, so noisy, so moody?

And my brother dies, as they all must soon or late. And in his death my love for him comes home clear and bright. I see him now in focus. I no longer cope with his frailty. I love him whole as I never knew I loved him. Has this not happened to you? Death reveals love.

And that is the lesson we learn. That to keep the whole in mind, it is good to keep the end in mind, for then the love I have for you can be larger, wider, deeper, more whole. I still see you exactly as you are, but I see you in focus.

Charlie, help us to love on earth as they do in heaven. Taking ourselves as we are, making the best of what we have, taking life as it comes and refusing to be overcome by it. Being rich or poor, bright or dull, handsome or homely, gifted or garden variety. And others the same. And if at times I wonder aloud why God is as he is, I am as I am, and you as you are, I can rise to the call of my faith and assert with a divine defiance that love is the meaning of it all. He died for it. And so will we. To rise to glory. Amen.

Gethsemani
March 18, 1989

35

Grace
Fifth Sunday of Easter
John 13:31-33a, 34-35

*I*n a recent issue of the *New York Review of Books,* one Conor Cruise O'Brien writes of nationalism supplanting religion as the major ethos, and notes that, far from emerging a benign development of recent centuries, it has instead just as much arrogance, intolerance and oppression as he feels the Church once had. He then notes that a document Pius XI prepared against Hitler and his treatment of the Jews, which his death forestalled issuing, was never taken up by Pius XII. In the author's view, it might possibly have averted the Holocaust. God alone knows the answer to that. No human does. But what I do see as having having relation is a hostility to the Church and a supposed inability of the Church to act vigorously in a crisis. There is no graceful action without grace.

Another story will illustrate this. One time, years ago, the Superior General of an Order I know was in the States at a meeting of the several provincials. The issue at hand was the choice of a novice master for a common novitiate. The provincials maintained that they had decided what sort of man they wanted, and found that a careful scrutiny of a long list of possibles turned up no one suitable. They therefore asked the Superior General to supply one from another country. He refused to do so and said they should make the best of what they had. Then, in a gesture of dismissal, he said, "That's what I do." With a sweep of the hand across the several priests before him, he said, "I take what I get and make do with them. Have you never heard of the grace of God?"

Making do with what you have is as much a matter of grace as of nature. In the great struggle between the forces of evil and of good, we deal not only with human capacity but also with the capacity of God. The grace of God is always at hand, gratuitous and potent, yet in some sure way is also related to human response to God. There is a price on everything in this world. You can have what you want if you are willing to pay for it.

It seems gross on the one hand to denigrate the Church, and therefore a world of grace, and on the other to expect the Church to act effectively in enormous questions of good and evil. Even the Pope has to deal with what he has in grace and nature. He is no *deus ex machina*, a divine Mr. Fix-it, even for those who revere him. In other words, the world of grace has definite relation to the human scene. God's intervention in the world is related to the human response to God. People are involved in human redemption. At all times, the nations stand under the judgement of God, may be found wanting in the weighing, be abandoned to consequence.

This is both profound truth and profound mystery. Nothing is as significant in the world as response to grace. The whole of our faith is rooted in this truth. And it is obvious that our life here is barren of meaning apart from it.

One of my two visitors at my vows in 1962 (before the restoration of the church at Gethsemani) was a provincial, a close friend. Afterward, he reminded me of something I had told him. "Charlie," he said, "remember how you told me you were not upset that the monastery was not an architectural beauty, for it made necessary a very pure motive? Beauty of place was not the reason you wanted to enter. Charlie," he said, "what you said is true. It's not much to look at."

Years ago, we had a most splendid farm operation. Really very impressive. Visitors would be mightily taken. Farmers and non-farmers alike would rub their hands together enthusiastically: "Man, these people really know how to farm." Well, today we have a beautiful monastery and I dare say a better place than we had 20 or 25 years ago. I do not think beauty has everything to do with it. And our farm now does not amount to much. And that we have a better place does not make that especially relevant.

We deal rather with the world of grace, the interior life, the acceptance of all that it is to be human, wedded to the magnificence of God's love. It is testimony of enormous consequence for the Church and the world. Almost wholly hidden. And a matter of making do with what we have and making the best of it.

And this labor is far more arduous than building a handsome monastery, running an effective farm, or whatever else. And it is the basic work of God; in the message of Christ, *the* work of God.

There is no dearth of vocations, but calls will never take root, sprout, blossom where there is no real love for Church, for priest, for religious. Even choice seed needs sun and rain. There is a climate that stifles vocations, even when no word is spoken. It is deeper than that. Some folks in a small country parish were giving their pastor a hard time. They did not like his ways. "Be comforted," I said. "It is a problem your children will not have. They will have no priest. And maybe no faith either."

There is a frightening word in this morning's Gospel. Christ, on the day before his death, says, "Now is the Son of Man glorified." This is astounding. It reveals to us that suffering and death are as much glory in the Christian mystery as Resurrection and Pentecost. This makes human history baffling, makes clear that only the grace of God, the life of God, in the midst of the human scene is what matters. The Christian lives in the world of grace. Redeeming grace. Salvific grace. For us. For all. This is the only way to make the best of what we are. To make do with what we have. The only way. So we walk in light, shed light, are a city on a mountain in a world of the blind. What is true of every human we shout from the housetop in the deaf darkness of night.

Conor Cruise O'Brien could come and spend some days with us and go home and write about it for the *New York Review of Books*. If he did not write in faith, he would write the place off in total truth as folly in the Knobs, however handsome. And wonder why his world is dark, his Pope inept.

Gethsemani
April 23, 1989

36
Abundant Mercy
Eleventh Sunday of the Year
Luke 7:36-8:3

*J*ust preceding the selection from II Samuel (12:7) is this touching parable Nathan the prophet told David to bring him to his senses:

> *Judge this case for me: in the same town were two men, one rich, the other poor. The rich man had flocks and herds in great abundance, the poor man had nothing but a ewe lamb, only a single little one he had bought. He fostered it and it grew up with him and his children, eating his bread, drinking from his cup, sleeping in his arms; it was like a daughter to him. When a traveler came, the rich man did not take anything from his own flock or herd to provide for the wayfarer who had come to him. Instead, he stole the poor man's lamb and prepared that for his guest . . . and David flew into a great rage with the man.*
> (II Samuel 12:1-7)

David, as we learned, was the man for making off with another man's wife by way of murder. And Nathan predicted death for the coming child, not to say further misfortunes. David, for all the favors God had lavished upon him, would yet have what he would have because he could have it. And at any cost. The man had no sense of proportion and no sense of restraint. Which amounts to saying that he so far knew very little about love.

The relation of Nathan and David to what we heard in the Gospel is perhaps not at once obvious, and yet a second look reveals that in the Pharisee who entertained Christ at table we have another David. He was another David, our Simon, for his enormous self-assurance and ego. In asking Christ to dine with him, he thought of himself as a host of admirable generosity, if not piety, in having this homeless wandering preacher, of whom there was so much talk, into his own home, together with his rag-tag band. So impressed was he with his own munificence that he thought it perfectly acceptable form to omit the usual courtesies in welcoming a guest, and so spared Jesus what Simon was sure he was neither used to nor expected. He was as blind as David to his own arrogance.

If that were not enough, the woman of the street who attended Jesus with kisses and perfume, far from moving Simon, served only to convince him that Jesus was not really a genuine prophet, so confirming a first suspicion. If he were, he would never let this dirty woman touch him. Jesus must know *that* much of the Law. On guard, wary, when taken up by Jesus with a story and a question, Simon parried carefully, "The one who was forgiven more, I suppose." "I suppose," he says.

Jesus surely smiled as he looked at this impresario and pointed out gently the kindness of the woman in offering to wash his feet, kiss them, anoint them. "Something you did not do, Simon."

Nor is Jesus done yet. Now his face grows serious, his eyes penetrating, in a carefully firm voice, "I tell you, her sins, many as they are, have been forgiven her because she has showed such great love. Who is forgiven little, loves little." And then to the woman, "Your sins are forgiven." Now hear these merciless men, "Who is this that even forgives sin?" Jesus ignores them for the woman, "Your faith has saved you. Go in peace." This cannot be fiction. No one of the evangelists could write such fiction.

There is nothing in the words of Jesus that worries me more than his harsh words to the religious people of his time, his place. The hazard of being professionally religious, I take it, is a serious hazard, given the attitude of Jesus.

Reasonably good men, assuredly, Simon and his friends, as the word goes. A bit taken with themselves, perhaps: impressive and anxious to impress, aware of prestige and reputation, public repute and professional stature. Yes, and blind.

Blind most of all to mercy. Mercy for themselves, of course, was not called for: they kept the Law. Yet if mercy has not been received, it cannot be given. They were blind to mercy at work in Jesus and in this woman who was a sinner in the city. They could not see what was in front of them, as blind as David to his own arrogance and pretension. He saw a pretty woman and he wanted her and so he got her. As was his way and wont. What has mercy to do with any of that?

We are no Davids—even if we would be—and we are no Simons, though we may have a bit in common with him. But as professional followers of the homeless Christ who wandered the land with his own, it is good to return every day, every night, if not even every hour of day and night, to mercy. For God's mercy on us sinners. And then, like the woman pouring out her love on Jesus, pouring out mercy on others for the great love we have in him.

Take it as a bad omen, my brothers, my sisters, when you find yourself muttering in your beard or behind your hand, about the doings of others. For you reveal in your act a heart barren of mercy. And if that be so, you know nothing about Jesus. It scarcely calls for heroic virtue to love the likes of us who are but middling sinners at whom Heaven's butler will snicker. But if not us, what if you cope with real evil? For mercy is not blind. A man who beats his wife is evil. It is mercy to be his Nathan and confront him. Mercy does not condone, it forgives. There is a difference. And even so, the mercy will be long coming if we have not long since known it in the heart, in the face of personal and cosmic evil, met in secret, in silence, in watching and waiting, in prayer.

If we are open to reality in the power of the Spirit, we will be able to cope with impoverished humanity and redeem all with Christ. And that redemption begins here within, and thence spreads.

David learned his lesson from the Bathsheba he got so deviously. One hopes Simon learned and shed his pompous ways. And one can almost be sure that the woman who was a sinner followed the Christ who loved her, up and down the land to the end.

A forgiven sinner is a lot better off than the proud, pious person who needs no mercy, for the forgiven sinner knows what love is.

Gethsemani
June 18, 1989

37
Evil's Return
Seventeenth Sunday of the Year
Luke 11:1-13

*A*rchbishop Arkfeld, coastal bishop in Wewak, New Guinea, had a nephew who was a priest missionary in the Highlands. Among other work, the nephew ran a youth center where he had games, dances, roller skating and such. One night at a dance, two young drunks turned up late, hoping to raise some mischief. He would not let them in. As you'd expect, the two brothers were angry and began a scene. In the end, they beat the priest mercilessly, breaking his jaw in the process. In a later court case, the two got off rather lightly. The whole affair did not go down well at all among the people. Priest-bashing did not appeal to them. It happened a year later, almost to the day, that the father of the two had been drinking with them and, by way of showing off, began to play with his rifle, aimed it at the elder and more brash of the two, and pulled the trigger. Since empty guns are always loaded, he ended up killing his own son. This spread like a grass fire all through the Highlands and had enormous impact. In everyone's eyes, without exception, it was God's reprisal for what the youth had done to the priest. From then on, the family had no name.

If this is not primitive thinking, it is close to it. We, too, sometimes read into events some divine interference. We find a certain satisfaction in that, like the words of Longfellow, "The mills of God grind slowly, yet they grind exceeding small."

It is, for all that, a dangerous business, and one should be very wary. In this world, there is much injustice and to all appearances neither God nor humans do much about it. Not to say that perfectly innocent people are as often as not victims of insufferable evil and our faith much tested in the knowing it.

It is very necessary, when reading or hearing the Old Testament stories, to keep in mind that it is the Old Testament. And the Old Testament has been completed and fulfilled, if not corrected, in the New. The Old must always be read in terms of the New. The psalms the monks love so must always go hand-in-hand with the Gospels; otherwise their often violent and vivid language may lead us to omit parts and will be misleading.

There are two points in Abraham's encounter in the Sodom story that are very pertinent to us. The one is that God hears prayer. Abraham's argument is that for the sake of the good, however few, God should not punish all. Though God listened, apparently, in view of the story, even a few good could not be found. The other point is that suffering of any kind is related to sin. This is a universal law: it applies to all and it is always at work. How it works is what we do not know and never will know in this life: that is, the relation between personal sin and personal suffering. We suffer because we are human and, as humans, we are sinners. We all die. We all have some share in common misery: some more, some less. There is absolutely no definable tie-in between how much we suffer and how much we sin. Only God knows that.

And what we do know in Jesus Christ, living in New Testament times, is that all suffering and death is redemptive in him, beginning with death and everything this side of death. It is God's grace in us that keeps us from the primitive notion that we deserve the suffering that comes our way because we are sinners, because God is displeased with us, condemns us. The matter has already been taken care of: Christ's suffering and death have ended forever whatever we had coming. The indictment, the verdict, the sentence have been nailed to the Cross, and so voided.

One is amazed at times to learn of how some small injury was inflicted on us when we were young: not by vicious people but by simple, ordinary people who slip, who fail, who are not perfect, who sometimes do wrong. Why can such a relatively minor hurt—for if sometimes the hurts are major, they are often minor—why can it have so devastating an effect on a person, live with him for years, affect her behavior, attitudes?

Why? Because that small event gets linked to the deep primordial event: original sin. We are born bruised, wounded, blameworthy and guilty. Any hurt, small or great, can by chance only serve to confirm that, confirm the cosmic, genetic, universal in us. Only the love of God can heal such. And does heal. When that original wound is healed, the healing of life's later wounds can be much more hopefully expected.

Therefore, we need to be fearful of any love for suffering and misery, any desire to be further hurt and wounded, because we are no good or deserve no better. This is to reject Jesus and the New Testament. We are sinners and we are loved. Life being what it is, we can expect a certain amount of suffering, and we all die in the end. But by Jesus, we need not love any of it. We bear it for love because that is what Jesus did. But we are not in love with it.

The primitives thought God punished the boy by having his drunken father accidentally shoot him. God didn't. The primitives thought God punished Sodom for gross violation of hospitality. But no. If there were no righteous in Sodom, the same is true anywhere. No one is righteous before God.

We do not live in the Old Testament, but in the New. When we call, he hears. When we knock, he answers. Because he loves us. If the likes of us will lend three loaves, be decent enough to give a child what is asked, how God-insulting to think he will not do as much. God loves us. What happens to us in this life can never undo that, unmake that, unravel that. His blood on us proves it.

There is thus no sweeter solace for the soul than prayer. And God hears all prayer. And all prayer is answered. Somehow. Some way. It is prayer that keeps us from the precipice of despair, from the dark satanic mills of hatred for self and others. You can do a child no greater service than to teach the child to pray. You can do your own heart no greater good on earth than to pray. You can do your love no greater good than to pray for him, for her. The best revenge on any enemy is prayer. Only prayer can keep us from indulging in that lethal notion that, in the end, God will get us. As he got Sodom.

No, he won't, for we have a righteous One among us. His name is Jesus.

Amen.

Gethsemani
July 30, 1989

38
Gratefulness
Twenty-eighth Sunday of the Year
Luke 17:11-19

*W*hen Naaman the Syrian leper, at the suggestion of a pious Hebrew girl in captivity at his court, journeyed to the Holy Land and the holy man, the prophet Elisha, he went with some hope and some misgiving. The hope was manifest in his making the journey; his misgiving in balking at the ritual expression the prophet asked of him. He overcame his misgiving, strengthened his hope, and he was cured. That he was a man of good will became clear in his profound gratitude and in his determination to worship the true God of Israel in his own land.

If the world is God's and the glory thereof, it is also true that there are both persons and places, items and actions, that are marked with a special presence of the divine. Thus Naaman asked leave to take what two mules could carry of the earth of this holy place to his own land that he might erect an altar over it and thus worship: the earth our mother, God our father, heaven and earth united in prayer, the feminine and the masculine one. Naaman was made whole, soul and body.

We have our holy places and holy things in the seven sacraments that unite us to divine life, to Christ's redemptive work, making us whole in every area, through life and death, in love and service. We are not foreigners, but citizens of the Kingdom. Yet Naaman was a foreigner, and the only leper to thank Jesus the same. Of the 10 lepers healed because they asked to be healed, only one returned to thank him who healed. Jesus made clear his disappointment.

What of the nine? Who knows? Presumably they had faith, for healing is of faith, even if wholeness be not, fulfillment not. What do you suppose was at bottom in their lack of gratitude? No one knows, but it is not unlikely that they saw no need of thanks.

Anger may rise when someone is afflicted with some great misfortune, and certainly leprosy is that, and was that for centuries, even into our own time. Lepers were isolated, segregated, shunned, barred from society. The Church provided a ritual for their banishment and, up until recent years, there was in our land a colony for them in the South. So tragic a fate may very well have aroused in our 10 people a resentment, an anger, a fury at a God who would do, would permit so gross an evil. This reaction is scarcely unpredictable, the more so in the pious, the good, the religious. People who feel they do right by God are hurt when God's response seems uncalled for, unmerited, as it were, and certainly not asked for. That being so, the removal of an affliction would not necessarily call for thanks. No one thanks an intruder for leaving their home. Is that the way the nine felt? Could be. And they were all Israelites, people of God.

Jesus expected better of them, for there is no necessary connection between what happens to us and what we deserve. In olden times, as in present, good and evil come upon good and bad alike. We are all sinners, and the fruit of sin scatters itself at random over us all.

The coming of Jesus is to make that clear. Children of darkness that we are, victims of our own misdeeds, communal and personal, we suffer the blows of what the world calls fate and we call Providence. By faith, we enter into a new level of relation to God in which we are rooted in his love for us. That he loves us does not suggest that our belief in the fact guarantees a life without woe.

A lady wrote to me that she thought God was good to her and so steered Hurricane Hugo further down the coast. Is one to gather that God is angry with Charleston, displeased with the monks who saw their lovely old oaks stripped to hulks? What sort of thinking is that? I will tell you what kind of thinking it is: it is very human thinking.

Yet we must be more than human for our being children of God. We avoid what misery we can avoid, and we accept what cannot be avoided. And thank God for all. Not that we are all that grateful. Who of us think to thank God that dedicated research found a way to cope with leprosy, Hansen's disease? How enormous the good we enjoy and take for granted. I boasted years ago to a primitive about the sewing machine he had never seen. "Make us one," he said. Absurd boasting. Absurd request. I can make neither needle nor thread, let alone machine. Nor can you. Surely one of the graces of an age of communication, whose like has never been known, is that we come to realize how graced we are and how widespread is wretchedness. How few we are who know the good life. We dare not suggest we merit it. Nor can we be so gross as to think the rest of the world deserves its lot.

So, like lepers healed by the sweet ministry of Jesus and the holy Virgin, we must at least do this much: thank God for all we have, a long litany. And not only ask that those benefits be spread, but do what we can to spread them.

Even in the matter of earning our living. Capitalism without love becomes monstrous, a world of greed and envy, cutthroat enterprise, ugly accumulation of power through wealth, while people haunt the streets, children are homeless, education is failing, advertising inane. Some try to Christianize capitalism, share our material and spiritual wealth, and avoid as some diabolic interference any assumption that what suffering we know entitles us to anger, vexation with God. Or, not bold enough for that, with his Church.

Indeed, let truth be told, most of the human suffering we know is of our own making, could be avoided, is not necessary. In this situation making so evident the powers of darkness at work in humankind, how serious our need to ask God to heal us lepers. "Jesus, Master! Take pity on us!" And he said, "Go! Show yourselves to the priests."

Gethsemani
October 15, 1989

39
Immaculate Conception B.V.M.

A week or two ago, a lady sent the Mass Office $1,000.00. She asked that a Mass be offered once a month, beginning January 1990, until the offering runs out. That means that for 16 years and 8 months a monthly Mass for her departed parents. Until August 2007. What is one to make of that? I asked the abbot and he said, "If that is what she really wants, we can accept it." I do not plan on being around that long, and surely many of you will be with me in a better country by then.

Fashions in piety vary. The abbey has one obligation taken on in earlier days for two Masses every November for the Miles' dead, as long as time lasts, or at least Gethsemani. Whichever. People make much of dates, birthdays, anniversaries, of time. Pearl Harbor, for example. I tend to favor God's time, an eternal now. Then we offer Mass as we can, as time goes by. But people cling to their notions and find a reality in dates.

We enter into the mystery of time with this beautiful feast today, recalling the conceiving of Mary in the loving union of Joachim and Anne, and aspects of it that came to be realized only long after. The most beautiful union of man and woman in love that history has known, for once in the original scenario of Paradise. Unique in history. A haunting loveliness that the Church has always loved. And when theologians took to delving into the mystery, they were long at a loss how to explain the effects of the atoning death of Christ predating the event. Entering into God's time, they finally declared that what he did for us was anticipated in his Holy Mother. Alone of us all, she was without the results of the first and worst human sin, preparing her for her dramatic part in the salvation drama.

What is puzzling is why many Christian bodies who are strong in the faith are reluctant to credit this marvelous Providence of God. Puzzling because, after all, what was done in her will be done in us all in measure. We will not enter heaven save without sin and the effects of sin. If we were not conceived immaculately, we will be born immaculate into the Kingdom by the grace of God in Christ. What was done from the first for her will be done for us all at the last, please God. Our pondering this feast, then, is a pondering on our salvation, our life in preparation for it, our share in the salvific work of Christ in his Church. The glory of the Virgin does indeed far surpass any glory we will know, for the reason that personal sin never defiled her, not to say original sin. And her being the Mother of God exalts her to heights in human destiny, the glory of all, queen of a redeemed people.

As her beginning was unique in human history, so, too, her end. She anticipated once again the resurrection of all the redeemed in Christ by her Assumption into heaven when her earthly life was done. If this mystery, too, seems too much for many Christians, then how can the resurrection of all at the end not be? Here, too, Mary is our symbol of hope, for as she was welcomed to the realms of glory, full and perfect human, so too is our frail hope that we may also know human completion and wholeness before God and with him and all his saints. Her glorious Assumption, like her glorious conception, far exceeds our own, and yet our own will be, for all that, a marvel of God's surpassing love.

If, then, as sinners we know the darkness of evil and the torment of guilt, we know also the light of grace and the power of mercy. Living in that context of mercy for ourselves and for all in the redeeming Christ, we can live in joy for all our poverty and weakness.

In faith we enter into God's time, and we are now and forever one with Christ, his holy Mother and all his saints. It may take earthly years yet before this is all accomplished, but the years will surely end, and what has been promised will be delivered. If that be not reason enough for joy, then there is none. Be that joy yours and mine, now and forever.

Gethsemani
December 8, 1989

40
Elitist Entitlement
Fifth Sunday of the Year
Matthew 5:13-16

When, years ago in Chicago, whites began suburban flight and abandoned their neighborhoods with fine homes, churches, schools, convents, rectories, because they could not abide blacks living among them, the devastated parishes were not abandoned. When the Catholic community was no longer large enough to support the parish enterprise, Cardinal Mundelein would ask a religious order to take over. Their answer was simple and direct: convert the newcomers and so build a new community.

In times of cultural breakdown, disintegration, massive shifts and the ensuing chaos, the tendency to exclusiveness is intense: the desire to build a safe haven against barbarian forces. We witness it today.

A bestseller of a year or so ago was built around a series of simple teachings one presumably learned in kindergarten. You have, no doubt, heard them:

Share everything.
Play fair.
Don't hit people.
Put things back where you found them.
Clean up your own mess.
Don't take things that aren't yours.
Say you're sorry when you hurt somebody.
Live a balanced life: learn some and think some and draw some and paint and sing and dance and play and work every day some.
Take a nap every afternoon.
When you go out into the world, watch out for traffic, hold hands, and stick together.
Be aware of wonder.[6]

They seem original and fresh, now heard, yet they are almost obvious. What you would tell any child. But in a time of upheaval almost a revelation.

Why a bestseller? Because people recognize in the text something they believe in and want others to believe in. A good code.

I need not point out a sad lack in the list: "Pray some every day." A child needs God. Not to teach a child to pray is really a form of child neglect. Awareness of wonder is a start. But wonder is a reaction. Prayer is a response. God wants response.

People have memories. They remember when you never had to lock your house when you left it, when you could walk the streets alone at night, when churches were always open, when you could take a subway without fear, use a park without being mugged. These memories bring home to us a hard truth: nothing works without God—life or love or family or marriage or children or society. We are barbarians again in many ways.

That being so, we can do what the Wasp Ascendancy did and build ourselves a fair haven within the mass, a club of our own kind. I have been reading another text, not a bestseller, about the exclusive preparatory schools that prepare the young elite for prestigious colleges, build close bonds of good connections early on, and determine that wealth and name and power will be ensured, nourished, passed on by those endowed with it and thus entitled to it.

These cultured, refined, elegant people are at the top or near it. President Bush comes from the same town I do, only I went to public schools and he did not. He lived in the same town but in another world than I knew.

Is that what we are here in the monastery? A private place? A hidden life? An entitled enclave walled up against barbarians? The poor, the ignorant, the trash? Should our chief endeavor be to keep the wall high, the gate locked, the phone unanswered? Did we leave a world whose kindergarten did not come true, where people did not share, did not play fair, where people are violent, steal, hurt, and never say "I'm sorry"?

Call it so if you will. We do have a vast estate. We do have good facilities, if not academy quality. We do enjoy privacy, peace, the woods and fields and hills, a community of gentle men. We know leisure. Add the grace of a life rooted in God, the service of God. Nor is it hectic, driven, mad. Yet in no way would anyone here think it all something he is entitled to. Nine centuries of tradition make us what we are, what we have. And the will of God has us here. Nothing else and no one else.

This endowment constantly challenges us to response for the sake of the Kingdom: interiorly in grace and through the entrance into the mysteries of Christ as deeply as we can go in God. And exteriorly, by permitting others to do what we do, do it with us, so far as can be. This twofold life makes the monastery a most splendid gift to a time, a country, the Church and the world. And to be called to be part of it is superb grace. Grace far surpassing endowment with superior intelligence, distinguished family, great wealth. If gifts of that kind are good, and they are, and are a call to service which is answer to entitlement, which they are, our call, too, is the continued call to love.

The small handful who attend prestigious schools are urged, indeed insistently taught, that they must by entitlement contribute to the common good with prestigious response. And they do.

If they mostly end up heads of corporations, they also serve as trustees and board members for libraries, museums, operas, symphonies, hospitals, art centers, galleries, parks and gardens, and numberless endowed enterprises. We need not point out the gross lapses, vulgar display and greed that make the papers. Rather, we acknowledge that privilege is so often distinguished for noble service.

We can be inspired by that to do what we are called to do with ever-deepening love. If we are aware of failings—even of little things we should have learned in kindergarten—we are aware, too, of heroism, the heroic love of so many who have lived and loved here the last 150 years.

Our response is not withdrawal, but engagement. The barbarians devastated the monasteries of northern Europe for centuries, but in the end the monks won out. They converted them. The Norse became Normans. We do not condemn modern barbarians—we convert them. By salt. By light. As vessels of grace, even if clay. And constantly test the validity of what we do by trifles that manifest a loving heart or a hateful one. The heroic is usually a matter of such trifles, for so we reveal the essential. Genius is in trifles. So is love. Just a little salt is quite enough. One small candle dispels the dark.

Amen.

Gethsemani
February 4, 1990

41
Being in Relation
This talk was given to the University of Notre Dame
Folk Choir while they were visiting Gethsemani.

Two-handed cups from the pottery shop in the refectory suggest something. It is supposed to be that way. Our context for living tells us who we are and reflectively makes us what we are. There is unending dialogue going on among very many parties.

This is so true that if monks make monasteries in a certain way, it is because they are monks, or better, want to become monks. And because dialogue is perhaps central in a monk's life, dialogue becomes a theme of his monastery, the place where he lives or works or prays or spends his time.

The abbey church is a double or triple row of choir stalls facing one another. The heart of the monk's prayer is the Psalter, a book of poetry which lends itself beautifully to antiphonal chant or recitation, verse by verse, back and forth across the chasm. The dialogue between us and you, you and us. We face one another, see you as you are, receive your seeing, chant back to you in an exchange that is stylized, ritualized, to lend it credibility, beauty, elan. And God is on each side and in between.

The scene around the altar is something else. Here centrality is expressed in a gathering around the altar, the force that pulls the monks together, identifying the One around whom the whole life finds focus. God is the point. Here is Calvary, Upper Room, priest, victim, bread and wine, body and blood, the universe. Here time dissolves and we enter into another kind of time in which yesterday and today and tomorrow are one. And day by day, in small portions fit for us, we ponder through the year the mysteries of Christ's life, relive them, enter into them, each an allotted span: some 10 times, some 20, some even 50 times, before the curtain parts and reality becomes real.

But the chapter room repeats the original theme: two facing rows before the abbot. The principle once again clearly stated: the monks dialogue. The abbot listens, adds a word, directs a trend, but does not dominate. The dialogue done, and sometimes long in getting done, he sums it up, expresses the consensus, and replies to it. Better than democracy for it is not majority rule; better than autocracy, for all have a voice. It is rather the fruit of genuine exchange done in purity, poverty, simplicity. Chaste love makes chaste dialogue possible. The Spirit then can emerge.

In the refectory we sit in choir form in long rows facing each other, seated at one side of the table only, not that such sitting was never intended for conversation, not that this makes serving easier, but that the notion of dialogue is essential. I live in touch with reality. And reality is my brother across from me. And me across from him. I accept him as I know him, truly, and he me. Because God is in us. Otherwise, the Incarnation does not matter.

These three: church, chapter, refectory, are the basic places of a monastery, the regular places, as they are called, and their form is not accidental. It is deliberate. They tell us who we are, who we should be.

And, of course, this is but an echo of God's world, full of contrast, full of dialogue: day and night, summer and winter, darkness and light, here and there, time and eternity, life and death, male and female. It never is and never can be one or the other; it must be both somehow. Lacking that desire to use both hands and take both aspects makes a deprived life, an impoverished life.

So a monastery is an endeavor in reality. It is called—this place, this life—a contemplative monastery, a contemplative life. But that is only because of the darkness of our times. The one-sidedness of our disastrous culture would make us one-sided, and so we are weird because we are balanced. In other words, we build a life of dialogue in which eternity matters as well as time, death as well as life, God as well as humankind, woman as well as man, prayer as well as action. It is a balance we seek to achieve, a neat response to the other side.

For example, who better than the celibate expresses the duality of the human person—the union of male and female aspects that is so deep, so rich, so fruitful? And what better proof of the sickness of our times than the endeavor to force one-sidedness of the human? And what more cheering than the return to acknowledgement that we are, all of us, dialogical? We are two. And we two must relate.

And so we talk to one another, we pray to one another, we eat facing each other, we argue, we discuss, we discern the Spirit in communion. And we all of us gather around one Lord, one faith, one cross, planted in the midst of our ground, one world.

So take this home with you. The solitude of the human is a duality. We are never, can never be alone. That is why monks love solitude. It proves that what we've been saying all along is true: there's always two. There's always the other.

About the cups. Actually, we never knew why they traditionally had two handles. For how many centuries. Until concelebration of the Eucharist came back. At first, we used a large number of chalices for the Precious Blood for the monks' Communion. But this was clutter. So one of the monks made a very large cup of hammered silver. A beauty, but it was awkward to handle. He made a second huge cup and put two handles on it. It was simple to use and safe. And then we knew why we had two handles on our refectory cups: to link table and altar, human drink and divine. So you see what I mean. We use two hands.

Amen.

Gethsemani
Winter 1990

42
Mockery
First Sunday of Lent
Matthew 4:1-11

Some months ago, an unfortunate Kentucky man named Mahoney drove down a throughway on the wrong side—being drunk—and ran head-on into a busload of young people. A terrible tragedy. Later, at the time of his trial, I asked one or the other of the monks, of people I ran into, what they would recommend if they were on the jury. The answers were a mix: one suggested the death penalty, another—and he a long-time prison chaplain—that the man be given a life sentence, another three years in prison and lifelong abstinence from alcohol, another that what he eventually got (an extensive prison sentence) was about the best you could do. I myself thought that a fitting sentence would be his visiting every high school in Kentucky and talking to the students about drunk driving. That would be of some use to him and to others. Even if the state paid him, it would be cheaper and more effective as therapy and penance than prison would be.

As a country, we are busy again building new facilities, as they are called. An American idea, I am told—the penitentiary—and we have more of them than any nation of our kind. And one gathers that prison is not very effective as a deterrent, for we rank very high in crime.

What disturbs me is the likelihood that monasteries were the inspiration for penitentiaries. The monks' way not so long ago laid heavy stress on their life as penitential. What better penance for those who offend than to live like monks? Surely you have seen such a place. They have a wall, as we have, if higher and better maintained, and a gate no winter wind will blow open. There is enclosure, then, and stability. Life in common. Each has a cell. At least until overcrowding. There is a common table. They usually eat in silence. There is work. No doubt a library. There is enforced celibacy, an amazing demand. And even optional solitude. So the similarities are many. Yet the comparison is gross, obscene. Where is love? Where is God? Where is anything of what gives a monastery heart? It mocks the monastery. With noise, among other things.

Satan mocked Christ at the end of his fast. If you have fasted on water for a long time, you know it is no great feat. The stomach folds in sleep, and hunger disappears after a few days. The mind is exceptionally clear, and the exercise therapeutic in the widest sense. But after 30 or 40 days, depending on your condition, the body has used up its available resources and needs input, the stomach awakens, and clamorous hunger ensues. At that moment, Satan approached Christ. His tactic was mockery:

"You are a great wonder-worker? Very well. Make bread of these stones."

"You are the favored one of the Father whom angels guard? Throw yourself from this parapet."

"You are the King to come and Lord of the Universe? Take it. I give it to you. Just bend the knee." He mocked Jesus.

Mockery is a great weapon. There are about two-and-a-half million weddings a year in our land. *Bride's Magazine* says their readers spend about $13,000 on a wedding. 190 guests is the average number. Yet half these weddings will end in divorce. No wonder some young people do not bother with a wedding.

And since most married people use birth control, mockery is made of love: there are flowers but no fruit. And since control is such a hoax, 50% of the million-and-a-half abortions in a year stem from contraceptive failure. So one mockery leads to another. It is called Planned Parenthood.

There are 57 million dogs in our country, in 31 million households: a $7-billion-dollar business. Hallmark Cards keeps an eye on trends and says there are more households with pets than with children. So they introduce a sympathy card to send when someone's pet dies. Touching. Last week, a family showed up at the abbey. Mother and father and two children. Homeless. They said they were living in their car. They looked it. Just some of our homeless. A sort of mockery in the face of the good life that even most dogs live.

Public schools are reputed to be a mess. Maybe it's because religion is missing. Education without religion is mock education. Yet public funds cannot be used for public religious schools. Because of the Constitution. More mockery. The Constitution says nothing of the sort. 2,000 Catholic schools have closed since Vatican II. The people cannot support a double burden, financing two systems. The more so with lay staff. A great loss for the nation. Based on mockery.

To bring the matter closer to home: priests consecrate themselves to God, to Church, to God's people. And change their minds. And so do religious and monks and nuns. Careful selection, careful training notwithstanding. A mockery, sort of.

Robert Bly conducts workshops for men. He sees the male as an endangered species. A beleaguered lot. Grievously troubled. One of the more serious troubles, he teaches, is that men do not know how to mourn. How to grieve. Men are not supposed to cry. And this cripples them. For they, too, suffer this human condition we are in. Caught up in mockery.

Lent is time for mourning. Weeping time. A time for remorse and repentance. Monks call it compunction. It is the sequel to looking into one's heart, so guilty of mockery. These people I have spoken of, from Mahoney on down, are not wicked people. They are unfortunate. Poor. Weak. And confused. Misled. Quite unknowingly.

You know. I know. Does not every homilist preach to himself, to herself? Do you, as I, feel shame when you hear the Rule for monks read each day at dinner? Feel the mockery that is your life, this awareness of our situation, this sense of being a mindless Mahoney driving east into western traffic, all unaware? So we turn to compunction of heart lest we run into tragedy over the hill. Lent is time for tears over the human condition. Yours. Mine. Everyone's.

So we turn to Jesus, you and I. His first work in the program of salvation was to reject mockery. And its source. That's what we do in Lent. For ourselves. For all. And so heal and are healed. Amen.

Gethsemani
March 4, 1990

43
Ascension Thursday

Only one of the Gospels—St. Luke's—specifically tells of the Ascension. The selection from St. Matthew assumes it. St. Mark speaks of it in his last verses. Only Luke has details. And they are somewhat puzzling: "They went back to Jerusalem full of joy, and they were continually in the Temple praising God." Puzzling because a "return to Jerusalem full of joy" seems rather an assessment made later, a looking back on the event. For there must have been some sadness in the farewell. But it is Luke in the Acts of the Apostles who is most enlightening. "After Jesus was taken up into Heaven, the Apostles went back to Jerusalem from the Mount of Olives...and when they reached the city, they went to the Upper Room where they were staying." Then Luke lists the group, including Mary, the mother of Jesus, and several other women, ". . . all joined in continuous prayer."

Can we suppose the "Upper Room where they were stay-ing" was the same Upper Room of the Last Supper? Luke uses the same word. That proves nothing, but would not that room, so full of warm memory, appeal? Their last meal together . . . and engaged in prayer, going to the Temple services. And what else? We know what else: talking about Jesus and their years together with him. Here the first Gospel accounts are beginning to take shape. Each calls on memory, revives a scene and what he said and what he did. And that leads to another. It is not hard to see them at it those days before Pentecost. And that in the very room where they spent their last evening together with him.

The Upper Room "furnished," as Jesus said, for dining. The room with the table of the Lord. Where the first Eucharist ever was offered. So the question comes: Do you suppose they had the Eucharist during this time? We do not know. Nothing is said. It would perhaps be too much. The impact of the whole story, their life with him, his passion, death and rising, his appearing to them, and now his departure, would have been a great deal to absorb, even to begin to understand. Slowly. Slowly. And with the coming of the Spirit would come light and power and insight. Even so, they are in the first church, and where the Church took form. And every church since has been built around an altar ta-ble: not the cross, not the book, not the pulpit, but the table of the Lord. It is where the disciples naturally went when the story was over, when the story was about to begin.

Monks keep alive the close union of three factors: taking bread together, the presence of God, and the expression of love. The most important rooms in the monastery are three, and they are all significant, rooms of meaning. And they look it. The church, the refectory, the chapter: the church where we gather round the table of the Lord, the refectory where we break bread together in love, the chapter where we hear the word of God ex-pounded, where we break the bread of exchange, dialogue and colloquy. What the disciples did in one room we do in three, but they did three things: they broke bread together, they shared the

Lord's Supper, they exchanged their views and memories and dreams in love for one another.

If we dignify the simple rite of the Eucharist with all that art and grace can devise, it is only right. From the beginning, monks have loved liturgy, a fitting church, glorious praise in song and dance of some kind. From the beginning, monks have seen taking food together more than a function, but as social, religious, sacramental love. For how many centuries monks have met in chapter, heard, expounded, expressed, voted. Many parliaments sit in chapter as monks do, even derive from it.

Who is Jesus? What he said . . . what he did . . . what he means. This is the point of Christianity, of monastery, of Gethsemani, of church, refectory, chapter. All three are of a piece, all three have much in common, all three deal with love.

There are still families who gather round the dining room table to hear the word of God, who break bread together in a family meal, who talk things over and talk things out around that table. That family prayer, family meal, family fellowship weakens, disappears, is sadness beyond telling. It can bode little good.

We are called to gather in this Upper Room, this Cenacle, as it came to be called in later times, and do as the disciples did. We remember the Lord Jesus and his death and rising, his sending of the Spirit, and we eat the bread of life, drink the cup of salvation every day. For ourselves, for all. We take bread together in dignity and peace, in quiet and in love, anticipating the day when we will do it together in the Kingdom. We gather in chapter to share in dialogue what God has told us, to listen to our father in Christ, to rise to spread the Good News by being good news worth spreading.

We do not stand as those of Galilee, looking up to heaven, chided by some angel. No, we are very much on earth, building the city of God among his people, preparing an Eternal City that will surely be rooted in this one as much as ours is in that one.

Amen.

Gethsemani
May 24, 1990

44
About Half My Life
Feast of St. Benedict

*A*bout half my life has been with an active community, the second half with a contemplative, monastic one. This past week, I visited a community that successfully combines both: St. John's [Collegeville, ed.], deep in the woods and lakes of Minnesota, is the world's largest Benedictine community. It manages a thriving monastic life, together with a university, major seminary, boarding/day school, and a large number of parishes and houses, at home and abroad.

What struck me was how architecture and forms of prayer express orientation. In the active apostolate I was familiar with, places of worship were in the usual parish form we are accustomed to. The community gathers in prayer before the altar, as a body. Here in our monastery, we have choir, with monks facing monks in the praise of God. Though at the end of the Office we turn to the altar, as to Christ. The usual understanding is that we pray to God present in the community, the Christ found where there are two or three gathered in his name.

For the Eucharist, we move forward in the church to the Mass area and gather around priest and table, a distinction I remember was made by Father Louis (Thomas Merton). He made the point in the very first meeting of what was to become a long series of building committee meetings: one area for the choir, one for the Eucharist.

The orientation in Collegeville is different. The choir gathers around the altar in a large, modified semi-circle: the Office is there and the celebration of the Eucharist. The open arms of the assembled group not only embraces a large number of worshippers, but enfolds as well the whole church, actually or symbolically. It is a neat expression of the combination of the monastic life and the apostolic life, and is very impressive.

The particular forms that have been used down the centuries in monastic prayer are varied, many of them lost in history. Common was to stand facing East; just as common the use of solo recitation of the psalms to the praying monks, sometimes in a circle, a group or in rows. By the time of the Middle Ages, the style that we know, choir facing choir, had become traditional.

All prayer is, of course, apostolic in virtue of the Mystical Body of Christ. The form we know makes clear our call to be not only a praying community but also a Christian community of love that embraces ourselves and each other in the love of Christ. This is constant challenge and constant joy. We do not become in the act some sort of house of prayer—which we nonetheless do - but rather seek to enter deeply into the mystery of Christ's redemptive act in *this* place, with *these* people, in *this* time.

It is not the only way, not necessarily the best way, but it is the way God called us to. This is our share, our role, our participation in the Great Work. No one is exclusively active, no one exclusively contemplative. It is all of a piece. Externally, modes/expressions differ. We need only look at a place to know it is a church, a monastery, a contemplative house. If our way of life has its difficulties, so do other forms, and life itself. The point is: how well do we do what we are called to do? And let it be said that a daily standing in choir before your brother across the aisle is a kind of action some find impossible, most find difficult, all find demanding. In the end, whatever can be said of contemplation, it is not necessarily easier than action.

This feast of St. Benedict is a renewed call to joy in God's favor to us, the response that joy makes, the determination that we shall continue our song and dance to the end, one with so many other servants of God all over the world. All Christians are a privileged people, elected for the good of all. We no less. We pray that God will continue to bless our land, our world, and maintain and increase the gift of houses of men and women who make God the heart of life for the good of all.

Amen.

Gethsemani
July 11, 1990

45
Of Angels and Bears
Twenty-second Sunday of the Year
Matthew 16:21-27

I have been reading a book about angels by Sophy Burnham.[7]
About angels in the strict sense, their engagement with us,
and about angels in a wider sense, the odd combination of circumstance, the coincidence that seems so inspired as to bear the
mark of transcendence. Surely something like that has happened
to you? A seemingly accidental cluster of incidents that you are
sure was born of grace, of God?

The author is gifted. So was her mother. But her mother was
as difficult as she was accomplished. She was a put-down artist,
and she practiced her art on her favored daughter. When poor
health and approaching death finally came, the situation got
worse for the mother's vexation at being sick for the first time in
her life. The daughter dearly loved her and hoped to God that
she might at last get close enough to exchange some worthy
words of heart before the end. Instead, she sat slumped and dis-
heartened in a chair by the hospital bed and listened to her
mother carry on about this and that. Then the cleaning woman
came in, a black woman from Jamaica with a marvelous smile.
She mopped the floor, the heedless mother carrying on with her
harangue. It took but a few minutes to swish the mop around the
small room, but before she left, the charwoman looked at the two
and said, "I grudge you the mother-talk." Mother and daughter
looked up, startled. "What was that?" "I begrudge you the
mother-talk. I lost my mother when I was 12, and this is the first
mother-talk I've heard since then." She smiled a smile full of gold
and left.

Mother and daughter were stunned a minute. Yet the word
of the black woman broke the spell. Here was this mother cuffing
her cub when the cub was long since grown. For the first time,
mother and daughter talked together. And a week later the one
was dead and the other forever indebted to a black angel she
never saw again.

A bear will cuff a cub to teach it manners. To curb its assertion. To teach it to live with others and save strength. A good

mother will cuff a daughter, a father a son, to teach breeding. Not violence: that is savage. But love, by teaching the necessity of restraint. To heed others. To live in communion. The more so with the gifted whom all admire and none admonish. Otherwise the child becomes an adult who must always have its way. Cannot dialogue. Cannot abide criticism. Pouts and is full of self-pity when crossed. A terrible handicap. The mother in the story had never been cuffed as a cub, and became impossible by making a life work of what she had been deprived of as a child.

Peter was such. Gifted. Given to impulse. Generous. Assertive. And with no sense. Jesus knew his man, though, knew he was a prince. But too full of ego, too impetuous, too sure. See Peter on the mount with James and John when Jesus was transfigured. Right away he takes over: "We'll build three huts here. And stay here." An absurd idea: live in glory on a hilltop with the Messiah. Jesus is exasperated, leads them down the mountain, warns them, "Say nothing of this until I am gone." Peter, on the stormy sea, sees Jesus come walking on the waves. "Lord, bid me come to You." Foolhardy man. "Come, if you will." And he cuffs the sinking Peter, "Where is your faith?" Peter at the Last Supper: "I will never betray You. I will die for You." Every crowing cock since reminds of fickle heart and boasting words. So in today's Gospel. Only last week we heard his glorious confession in Capernaum, writ large in Rome for all to read, that Jesus is no Elijah or one of the prophets, but truly Messiah, Son of God. Jesus commends him and reminds him of the source of that light, this grace from the Father. And today Peter is his old self. When Jesus speaks of blood and tears, his shameful death at the hands of foreigners, Peter is aghast. "Never, Lord. Never. No way." Jesus stops in his tracks, with anger to the man: "Get behind me, Satan. This is man-talk, not God-talk." Strong language. How long since any of you called anyone a child of Satan?

So Peter learned, if late. Jesus was no put-down artist, but Peter was the uncuffed cub, full of self and self-assertion, ready to wilt at someone critical.

Angels come to us sometimes. Sometimes in a startling way. Sometimes as black angels because we fancy them always golden. That is to say, sometimes in very ordinary events, in very ordinary people. To give us what we need, to free us from our addictions, to throw light on what we have so artfully hidden. When once in a while we catch ourselves putting others down, read what is written. Who has never been cuffed make the best cuffers. They're professional because they were so deprived.

We were talking at the last Council [the abbot's board of elected and appointed advisers, ed.] about Alcoholics Anonymous, and all agreed that the movement was one of the most significant spiritual developments of our time. An American gift to the life of the spirit. All agreed that thousands have achieved sobriety, freedom from addiction through AA. All agreed, too, that progress within the movement could vary: that some would go on to real holiness in a life totally committed to God. Totally. Fulfillment. Ego gone, laid tragically low. Now, free of addiction, totally dependent on God.

I asked the abbot afterwards, "I suppose monks, too, in their program reach degrees of fulfillment. Thus, when a question rises, a project comes up, you would ask each, as in the Rule, what he thinks on it; and all being asked and heard in turn, you could think it over and do as you saw best. That being so, all being enlightened, being an abbot must be a picnic. Is it?" "Not quite," he said. "Not quite."

But we can learn. We can grow. If as cubs we were not cuffed, the cuffing comes later if we accept it. Peter did. And died Rock of the Church. Martyred for Christ. This is the month of the angels. They'll be around.

Gethsemani
September 2, 1990

46
A Monk's View of Asceticism
A conference originally given during
a retreat for missionaries serving in New Guinea

We may divide asceticism into several categories and thereby understand the scope and significance of the art. Asceticism can be SOCIAL, CHRISTIAN, MONASTIC, GENETIC and COSMIC.

We may gather under the term *SOCIAL ASCETICISM* all that enormous set of practices that we begin to learn early on as characteristic of anyone who would be thought well-bred, civilized, of good manners, to some degree at least refined and cultured. It is enough to mention some: being pleasant, being polite, answering letters, returning calls, paying bills, being honest, minding one's own business, being neat and clean in one's person and with one's belongings, modulating the voice to the occasion, lending when one can do so, returning what one borrows, and so on. The list is as long as it is variable. People who are religious and people who see themselves in no way religious can be accomplished ascetics in view of the way they live. Both would see this as an important part of being human. A Christian would try to motivate the whole by love for God and for neighbor, aware that the cultivated life can be noble in its inspiration, and also ignoble.

As a monk, I find it appropriate to recognize the high level of asceticism that many people achieve. The dedication of artists, craftspeople, scholars, scientists, public servants, is often heroic and a great deal more than good manners. One need only think of a good family. All this can be an inspiration and example for those who may think of their cause as perhaps more noble, even if their level of commitment to it often be less.

CHRISTIAN ASCETICISM is our dedication to virtue, and is neatly summed up by noting our goals:

the theological virtues of faith, hope and charity;
the cardinal virtues of prudence, justice, fortitude and temperance;
the gifts of the Holy Spirit: wisdom, understanding, counsel, fortitude, knowledge, piety, fear of the Lord;
the fruits of the Holy Spirit: charity, joy, peace, patience, benignity, goodness, longanimity, mildness, faith, modesty, continence, chastity;
the beatitudes: poverty of spirit, mourning, meekness, hunger/thirst for justice, merciful, single-hearted, peaceful;
the works of mercy:
corporal: feed the hungry, give drink to the thirsty, clothe the naked, visit the imprisoned, shelter the homeless, visit the sick, bury the dead;
spiritual: counsel the doubting, instruct the ignorant, admonish the sinner, comfort the afflicted, forgive offenses, bear wrongs patiently, pray for the living and the dead.

And likewise, from the opposite point of view, we avoid the capital sins: pride, covetousness, lust, anger, gluttony, envy and sloth. As Christians we are dedicated to this asceticism and practice it to the extent that we are graced and able.

MONASTIC ASCETICISM involves us with all those practices that are specific to the monk's life, are noted in the Rule and customs of the monastery. It suffices to mention a few of the more significant:

> love for the abbot, the brothers;
> love for the Divine Office;
> love for manual labor;
> love for silence and solitude;
> love of the cloister, for the habit;
> love for poverty, simplicity, the poor;
> love for reading, for Scripture.

These and others characterize our life as monks and are cultivated by the community as an embodiment of the monastic life.

GENETIC ASCETICISM is the result of self-knowledge, the subsequent acceptance of all that we are. This asceticism is the fruit of coping with our own history, acknowledging and accepting it, immersing it in the mercy of God continually, rending him thanks. It is further an awareness of trends and qualities that are part of our nature, sometimes acted on, often not, but nonetheless present. These, too, must be presented to God in thanks for all good, in atonement for all evil, actual or potential. Such asceticism goes further than our own person, but extends itself into our family, availing ourselves of a knowledge as complete as we can make it, of family history. This is more than curiosity or a cult of genealogy, but rather a spiritual ascesis in which we accept good and evil in our familial history, expressing gratitude for the one, atonement for the other. Called by God to be monks, it is our function and duty to accept this obligation as much as we are able, thus presenting to God not only ourselves, but our larger selves and all that the term means. We make all that has been evident in our family, as far as we know it, the subject of our lives before God: murder, incest, abuse, addiction, violence, birth control, divorce, abortion, infidelity, loss or abandonment of the faith, fraud, injustice, greed—all is placed before the mercy of God. Just as seriously ought we express gratitude for blessings lavished on us, the more so when the blessings are taken for granted. This is an asceticism of high order and of great significance. It makes our prayer life, our worship, our work fraught with meaning. If as celibates we do not pass on our genetic pool to progeny, by spiritual ascesis we do what in effect is more significant: we purify the inheritance, cleanse it in Christ, make it wholesome and holy. So are generations freed of the tyranny of sin. So is a holy people built up through generations.

We may call COSMIC ASCETICISM entering into our world in Jesus, identifying with it, responding to it before the Father. We are identified with this generation far more than with any other. If it be true—and it is—that our roots are ancient and that our history goes into a past too remote for us to comprehend, and yet present within us, it is also true that our union with those who live on the earth at the same time as ourselves is very close. Their good in some sense is ours. Their evil, also. We are not alone. Neither are they. Our relation to one another, our dependence, is much known. Yet what is beyond our knowing is far more vast and complex. The simplest things we do involve others. And even if we dismiss this as poetic, we are yet united in time. Does it mean anything at all that we are here, all of us, at the same time? A monk would suspect that it rather does. And therefore that we are accountable in some way. We thank God. In the first place, in the name of all, for all. We ask forgiveness of God, in the name of all, for all. The good and evil of even one calendar day on earth is beyond human measure. What then of a lifetime, of many millions of lifetimes? We reach into the infinite. And yet in Christ must do so, can do so. This magnificent world must glorify God in explicit praise, thanks, atonement. Such a cosmic ascesis extends our hearts, expands our faith, diminishes us while adding to our stature. And who else, if not a monk, is called to this? No doubt many others, very many, enter deep into the life of the world and, in prayer and suffering, thank and atone in Christ. Or God, as they know him. And we join them, now and for eternity.

Gethsemani
October, 1990

47
All Hallows

I wonder if there be any feast in the year of the Church that is so splendid an expression of faith as the feast of All Saints and its sequel, All Souls.

Faith in Our Lord, Jesus Christ, our greatest gift after life, is a relatively easy response because we posit our belief in a person who was conceived, born, lived, died. We know him. And before his death he gave a body of teaching, backed by signs of his source, then departed with a promise to send the Holy Spirit. That he did. The Spirit was to found his Church, his continued presence on earth. Which happened. And into that body of faith we have entered: in it we live and hope.

And now? The saints? We do not know who they are. At the utmost—and who presumes the utmost?—we know only a handful. How many are they? God alone knows. Uncounted legions, one assumes. Where are they? We do not know. They are in heaven for certain, a heaven that is both state and place, we agree, yet where it is and what it is, we do not know. What we do know for certain is that there are Saints, capitalized, and they are in heaven. And this on the testimony of the Church. But beyond this very limited number, we know none. We believe, nonetheless, that the saints in heaven are an uncounted, uncountable number. And this belief is countered by this qualification: that uncounted legions, we assume, atone in a state of penitence for past sins in view of their entering into the ultimate joy of God.

These mysteries are a delight for their splendor, their extravagance, their calling us to reaches we dare not dream of. It is a refreshment to the soul so unduly confined to this small world we live in: the people I know, the places I know, the time I know. Now we are called on to open our eyes, to listen, to answer to realities truly beyond our consummate imagining. To be as little as we are, to be as great is, at the end of the Church year, in the culmination of all, to rise to the unthinkable, unknowable, pure land of faith. The mysteries of our Christian faith reach their ultimate.

The asceticism we practice as decent human beings, as serious Christians, as monks given to this particular and ancient form of Christian service, or to some other pattern of life, is to enter into the depths of this truth by vivid, living participation. For we are called to move up and out of a mere personal commitment to Christ to such a personal commitment as engages us also in the whole of Christ's body, an engagement written into the original endeavor. We are not Christian alone.

Thus, an ascetic life involves us with our own response to grace, an acceptance of it in wider terms so that we express it by a love that is, we may say, genetic. By that love we encounter our whole family and its history, that complex of inherited good and evil that makes us a person. Who but God knows the ancient roots we have, the past history we have inherited and is somehow present in us? What sins in our line there undoubtedly are? Sins that left wounds passed on to us. This vast inheritance that constitutes me. A present, living person must be redeemed, sanctified in Christ. Thanks must be given for all good, atonement for all evil. I recall the woman who sent in a Mass offering some years ago, for some unknown murder in the family history, she wrote. One gathers that she was haunted in dreams by a past evil in her tree. And wisely set out to atone. This genetic asceticism involves us with our history and makes piety of wide scope.

The feasts of All Saints and All Souls bring us face-to-face with greater, more amazing truth: that our kinship in Christ extends to all humanity, certainly all now with us on earth, surely with those gone ahead of us. But like us, still en route to eternal life.

So personal history becomes cosmic. We enter into the world scene in Christ, and thank, atone, petition, adore God for all, in all, with all. Our union with others in Christ is like our union with our forebears. There is no way you can separate yourself from all who proceeded you. They are in you, part of you. That celibates do not pass on this inheritance is not at issue. In any case, redeeming the genetic pool is as significant as passing it on as best one can. What *is* at issue is that the whole must be purified, healed, redeemed in Christ. That is for each to do so that humankind can be healed. And on the wider scale, we engage with all living on earth now, our contemporaries now and for all eternity. We embrace all in Christ, thank, atone, speak in their name, as we hope they do for us.

So is that final Communion of Saints prepared for by this magnificent drama here on earth. This short hour or two on the stage of life, this play so fascinating to watch, to be in, with Christ our Lord.

Amen.

Gethsemani
November 1, 1990

48
Times
Second Sunday of Advent
Matthew 3:1-12

December 9, 1990. In the year of the Church, it is the Second Sunday of Advent. The difference between these two identifications of this day is profound. On the one hand, we have secular time and on the other, religious. And yet we speak of the same day.

Yet the difference is even more disturbing. Secular time comes in several packages, the most obvious being linear time and circular time. Days go by one after another: the sun rises, reaches noon, sets, and night follows. One day after another, month by month, year by year. All the same. Except that cyclic time makes each day different, unique in the great circle of the day, each truly so not only in time but also in place. And if that cycle does not suffice, the whole universe may be cyclic.

Most days celebrated in the calendar are linear feasts: New Year's Day, Memorial Day, July Fourth, Labor Day, Washington's birthday, Lincoln's birthday, Martin Luther King's birthday. As we move along the line of the year, their days come up. And we note them. "He died 102 years ago." "This is the 215th anniversary of the signing of the Declaration of Independence." "The Armistice after World War I was signed this day 72 years ago." Even the saints are linear: each in turn, those commemorated by a memorial, as most are not. "He/she entered heaven this day 120 years ago . . . 400 years ago."

There is linear time. There is cyclic time. And there are other times as well. But what concerns us today is God's time. Perhaps we could call it liturgical time, dream time, festal time. For when we celebrate Christmas, we do more than remember the day when Christ was born 1990 years ago, more or less. We do that indeed, for the birth of Jesus is a historical event that is remembered. But when we celebrate the feast of Christ's Nativity, we do so also mystically. That is to say, time as we know it is left behind, and we are into God's time, timelessness, the eternal now which we are at a loss to understand. We do not need to understand it, explain it. How many things there are, even in the natural order, which we truly do not understand but gladly make good use of.

Liturgical celebration is a matter of reliving in grace the original event. In God's time what is temporal becomes perennial, timeless, removed from the limits of time. We are at Bethlehem, we hear the angels, see the shepherds, we are at the crib with the Wise Men. The original witnesses are no better off. Our response is on a par with theirs. So is our participation. The way we react to Christmas now is the way we would have reacted then, since it is the same event and we are the same person here or there, now or then.

And we share with the original participants the grace of returning each year to meditate on, ponder on what cannot possibly be absorbed in one exposure. We need to return over and over to the first scene, in reading, in pondering, in prayer, in participation, as we will do 15 days from now.

Mystical time, grace time, liturgical time means that in the cycle of the year of the Church, we pass through the major mysteries of Christ's life by actual participation in grace. We respond to the event. We are graced by it. We become part of it and it of us.

There is no other human activity that is similar. In remembering past events by holidays, we do not in any way assume that we are doing over, reliving, witnessing anew what once took place. It is all over and done with. We merely remember it. The saints' days, too. We are not with Francis Xavier or again with Vincent Ferrer. We rather recall their lives, their witness, their day. And recognizing them, we live in the Kingdom and ask their prayer. Unlike national birthdays, we recall not the dead but the living, and commune with them.

But when we celebrate Christ, we do so in a quite different way. We enter into a kind of dream time, our first modest taste of eternity, in which history disappears and what was past becomes present, remote becomes here. For we deal with realities so deep, so profound that one encounter would scarcely do. We need to return again and again if we are to enter into them. Hence, from the beginning, the Church has done again in mystical mode the events done before.

The first lesson we learn in so doing is how genuine the narrative of the first event really is, the narrations we find in the Gospels. For we see what a variety of responses there was to what took place: enthusiastic acceptance (relatively rare), indifference (the most common), and rejection (the most effective). We like to think how noble would have been our response had we witnessed the passion, the death, the rising. Yet we have only to look at our response this day, this season, this year, to confirm the truth that our response then would have been the same as now.

How graced we are in being able, year after year, to relive the life of Christ each year given us, and hopefully increasing in us a deeper sense of what takes place, what it all means, seeking in prayer to enter into it deeply, share it, live it.

In New Guinea, they were wont to mark the year by Christmas. And so, in asking someone, "How old are you?," we would ask, "How many Christmases have you?" I do not necessarily inquire your age, but I do ask how many Christmases have you had. How many more can you count on? And how deeply have you entered into this profound mystery?

So now, yet once more, we are invited to leave time and enter God's eternal now and gather at the crib of the Child born of woman and born of God.

Amen.

Gethsemani
December 9, 1990

49
Premonition
Fifth Sunday of Lent
John 12:20-33

*J*ohn Guise was a New Guinean who emerged as a leader around and after the time his country became independent in the Commonwealth of Nations, 1975. A man of integrity, quality, competence. He was the first governor general of his country, a prestigious office of consequence in the political order. He served his country well. For all his status, he remained a man of his people, deep in a culture many thousands of years old. Thus, when a memorial betel nut tree died that he had planted in a ceremonial row of many such outside the Government House, he and all knew what it meant. Only a week before he died, he made out his will. And shortly before, he had asked on his knees a blessing of his Anglican bishop, something he had never done before. And at lunch on his last day he had rice and tinned fish, a common meal of the poor and a favorite of his. He turned at the end of the meal to his son and said quietly, "I'll be going now," and then died in the arms of his wife.

Premonitions of such a sort are not at all rare among people not far removed from a primitive, ancient culture. I am not sure they are unknown among us. What makes us different is that we pay them no heed, if indeed we notice them at all. And even if we did notice them, we would have no skill at interpreting them since we never heed them.

It is not difficult to see premonition written in many events of the last days of Jesus. In the Gospel, we have Greeks seeking him out. He who was Jew among Jews, come for Israel, hints at a wide world, the whole of time. And gives to them basic lessons on the role of death, so vital a part of every Christian life.

We can complete a picture of the scene from what details are given. A spring storm has brought in sudden heavy, dark clouds...ominous. Jesus talks of losing one's life to find it, of dying in order to live . . . against a background of thunder and lightning. Further, he speaks of tragedy to come in terms of glory. He who has just entered the Holy City in triumph: "All the world goes after Him," his enemies angrily remark. So there is conflict and victory, there is talk of glory in the midst of a threatening storm. Thus, when a heavenly voice attests to his glory, some hear it, some think it thunder, all are disturbed. Christ assures all that the testimony is to their good, not his. They need it, not he. So his young life now moves more speedily into its final stages and he knows how shattered his followers will be. How frightened and disillusioned.

Do you have premonitions? About death? About anything at all? Do you think it matters whether you do or not?

One might ask how you read the covenant written in our hearts if you do not listen to your heart. It is well to search the Scriptures, but we know, too, that there is another book that needs careful reading . . . a reading done by listening.

If there was drama in the life of Jesus, there is drama in ours, too, by reason of our being high-born, our high living and our ultimate high dying, since we are Christian, immortal. Our life is open-ended. Which is to say, ending in God. Does it seem all that unlikely that we who are temporarily in time should have no intimation of eternity? One feels that in the life of Jesus. He was hard-pressed to contain the divine lest the divine usurp his life among us. Now as the end nears, he appears unable to hide the God he is. The voice of God seems void and thunderous, threatening and terrifying. We need his assurance that it is to our good.

It seems wise to be chary of all that dims intimation of God: assertion and anger, contention, vindictiveness, the stubborn, scheming heart—these darken the day. Rather say with Edna St. Vincent Millay, "God, I can push the grass apart and lay my fingers on Thy heart!"

In those last days before the end, then, we sense a foreboding, a worry over dark skies and rolling thunder, of the hate of hell let loose, set to destroy love. Would there be anyone who does not sense some vague dread at divinity about to die, catch in the wind some sense of disaster near? Unfortunately, we know well enough that your intimations are well-founded. The worst is about to happen. And so we are involved. And the worst in the end will turn out best.

> *The soul can split the sky in two,*
> *And let the face of God shine through.*
>
> —Edna St. Vincent Millay

Gethsemani
March 17, 1991

50
The Pansy Sermon
Fifth Sunday of Easter
1 John 3:18-24

W *hen Saul had come to Jerusalem, he attempted to join the disciples. And they did not believe he was a disciple.* (Acts 9:26)

This is a scenario we are familiar with. We are disciples of Jesus, no doubt, but we are still afraid. It is hard to believe. This may be the climate we live in, the sort of country we come from. Anyhow, who knows his own history, who has any awareness of where she is at, will have some difficulty accepting the full impact of the basic truth of our faith: that humankind is loved by God. *Genetic* sin and personal sin, like massive mountains about us, hide the sun early and late. Only for a brief time do we perhaps live in the light of love, and soon enough move into shadows.

The thought is repeated by John:

> *Let us not love in word and speech, but in deed and in truth.*
> *By this we shall know that we are of the truth, and reassure our*
> *hearts before Him whenever our hearts condemn us, for God is*
> *greater than our hearts.*

Who does not know the condemning heart? Who is not betimes saddled with guilt, carrying a heavy rider on our back?

Let me my own heart more have pity on. (Gerard Manley Hopkins)

Who does not know the put-down artist that is much a character part in our self? And the giveaway is, of course, the neighbor, for we invariably, inevitably treat him, treat her, as we do ourselves. We are of a piece and we do be ourselves despite ourselves, and stand revealed in word and deed. Small point in acting love for others when you do not love yourself. It is, in fact, an unattainable goal. Spare yourself.

Begin at home, where charity begins, before you go abroad. Not that it is a matter of doing. More a matter of concession to reality, believing in the name of Jesus. If you have not such love, you need not say so, for you have already said it when you do not love me. You love me as you love yourself, and neither is possible in depth save in that grace which made us all lovable.

"Abide in me and I in you." It is strangely put. "Abide in me" is a command, a call, an invitation. "And I in you" is not. It is a statement of fact. We cannot abide in him unless he abides in us. And that he does in his love. Through our faith we abide in him. That so, it necessarily follows we have love for ourselves in him and love for all because he abides in all, actually, potentially.

Which brings me to the purple pansy with gold trim I picked in the courtyard under the oak. Where is the pansyhood that made this lovely thing? Whence the color, the pattern of petal, the velvet sheen? From the pansyness planted in this spoonful of earth from which it drew loveliness, loveliness no one on earth can fashion. One asks, "Where is what makes it what it is?" It is, they say, in all the cells of the whole plant, the program thus printed out in detail, followed perfectly. The program is not part of the plant. It *is* the plant.

So with the superior grapevine, so complex, intricate, extended. What genius fashioned it? Surely not human! And where is what makes it what it is? It isn't anywhere in the vine, we know. It *is* the vine. It produces sturdy stock, disease-resistant grapes that ripen slowly in the heat, in clusters that are large, with this special aroma when crushed, fermented. And where is all this? It is everywhere in the plant, in every cell. It was in that first small sprig from which it all grew. Who could believe it? Who could do it? We cannot make the simplest living thing, let alone something as magnificent as a pansy or prodigious as a grapevine.

He says he is a vine, Jesus. What does He mean save that as extended as the shoots and branches of the vine be, they come from one stem: the same life flows in all. If we cannot explain what that life is, and how it is in each part, so too we are at a loss to tell how Jesus is in each and all, and each and all in him. It does not strike me hard that if earthly life surpasses our grasp, that heavenly life should do the same.

So, too, Christ's love for you, for me, is nothing we can fathom. This is a truth we are all afraid of. It is hard to believe I am a disciple, which in turn makes our belief all the more glorious. No one believes the obvious. No one is challenged by what is clear. So pick a pansy and explain to me how it comes to be. I gather that the presence of Jesus in you would be easier to handle. Easier, say, than your soul, so much you, in every part of you. And yet no part. All of you and yet more than that. Separate, but still you. In that soul, that body, lives Christ. Christ abides. That it is hard to believe does not mean it is not true. It is both one and the other. Like the pansy, impossible and sure. Like Saul, the suspect disciple . . . soon Paul.

Amen.

Gethsemani
May 5, 1991

51
In Heaven, All Will Be Catholic
Eleventh Sunday of the Year
Luke 7:36 – 8:3

I would assume there is a sense in which it can be said that in heaven all will be Catholic. This is scarcely an appropriate approach in a day that makes much of geniality in religion and little or nothing of what is called triumphalism, that is, the glory of the Church contemporary and ultimate. Even so, Jesus is the Son of God and there seems no likelihood of there being another. Further, he is second person of the Holy Trinity, who sent the Holy Spirit on the community he formed when he came to earth, establishing a Church that would embody his teaching, continue his life, work and death on earth, and in that Spirit return to him in glory at the end. Meanwhile, he united himself to the human family in a very special way. He is present in our person, our lives and our history in ways largely hidden to us, for all the clarity of his teaching on the matter. "What you do to the least, you do to Me."

It would follow, would it not, that if his presence in his Church in the Spirit is a very special and preeminent one, he is present also in all humankind, not least in religious leaders of all kinds who have sincerely sought God and the good and the Kingdom? He is in all truth, absent from all not true. But the search for God, which is so much a part of human history, surely receives response from a sought God. "He enlightens everyone who comes into the world."

His particular family unites with him in very profound ways, remains a very special presence of the divine. This perdures despite the tumultuous history of the Church, heavy with human frailty and failure, propensity to schism and error, to quarrel and disobedience. If Christianity is a congeries, it is witness thereby not only to the glory of God but also to human weakness and depravity.

The teaching is clear: He is among us. He is in human history, in humanity. He may be hidden, but he is here. He is present in every search for him and reveals himself in how many ways. If then the Church be specific and one, and it is, if all of humankind be one, and it is, the bringing of the two together continues to be the splendid dream of Christ, a dream that will come true in the end of time, when the Christ will be revealed in his redeemed world.

Meanwhile we who have a very particular call to him and his Church know nothing of triumph. We know only tragedy—a Church here so long and still so small, a mere segment of the human race. We know it torn by strife and contention, dismembered by disagreement. We are sad for it with a sad Christ. Yet we are of faith and know that the Church is his, that it lives, that as remnant in the world it is a yeast that ferments the whole, a light that penetrates the darkness, a salt that saves and savors the whole. This is both glory and disgrace. Glory for the truth of it, disgrace for the shame that we have done so poorly.

For all that, we look to the future with joyous confidence. The Great Day will dawn. We will one day be one in him, suffered, died and risen with him to a glory we cannot conceive. And it will be all of us, not some, each a work by God's grace and humankind fully realized. In times that are as dark as ours in human poverty, it is good to reckon our union with Christ as a great calling, a great challenge, an enormous responsibility, and joy unending—given us for the sake of all. In this great drama, who can think any part small, oneself a mere extra? The mustard seed is smallest of all, yet see what it becomes?

> *A sower throws seed on the ground—night and day, while he sleeps. When he is awake, the seed is sprouting and growing, he does not know how. And when the crop is ready, he loses no time; he starts to reap because the harvest has come.* (Mark 4:26-29)

Nothing is trivial in the Kingdom of God. And how touching that twice every day, in specific form, we commend all the world to the love and protection of the Holy Mother of God, she, Mother of the now Church, Mother of the Church to come.

Amen.

Gethsemani
June 16, 1991

52
The Sacred Brought to Speech
Eighteenth Sunday of the Year
John 6:24-35

*I*t is well-enough known that those born deaf need the earliest possible development of a mode of communication, often enough by way of signs with other deaf people. One of the more amazing endowments of human nature is the inbuilt ability to use sign and symbol as the way to communicate with another. To all appearances, we talk naturally and naturally create language. And talk, of course, is the use of symbol. A French priest of the last century is credited with first taking seriously the ability of the deaf to construct a language by sign. He codified it, tried to generalize it, and ended up founding schools to teach it and to prepare teachers for the same purpose. Sign language became general and very effective, continuing until some decades ago when an attempt to replace it in favor of speech took over. There is now a return to sign, and a lot of interest in it. The source of major interest is that sign is a language, a mode of communication through shapes and movements of the hands. It is not English or any language translated into hand action, as our Trappist sign language tended to be. It is language every bit as much as speech is language. And it is founded on the human situation: that as body and soul we communicate not directly, but through sign and symbol. Angels do not need signs. We do.

When deaf people do not learn early a language—a mode of communication—they do not develop mentally, but remain, as it were, retarded. Perhaps this is the origin of our relating mute to stupid.

I do not think it too brave a step to say that no human develops fully or normally who does not see symbol as an inbuilt dynamic of life. It is not that we communicate only through speech, the most obvious sign or symbol, and its companion, the written sign of word. It is that the whole world is sign and symbol. It is in some way God communicating with us. We need to know that sign language, too.

We usually reserve to poets the cultivation of such ability, but since poetry appeals to all, it seems clear that interpreting the signs ought to be a common right and privilege.

There is no way to understand Jesus without an ability to see the meaning of parable and simile: His use of symbolic action. The Church continues enamored of symbolic communication. When we are not developed in this capacity, religion becomes cerebral, all in the head: creed and code and cult neatly drawn up and preached and practiced. It will not wear. It will fade out in a generation.

One of the ailments of our times may be a weakening of a capacity for symbol, the more so in religion. This is a consequence of the cult of noise and distraction, unending input, the flight from silence, the fear of quiet. For it is in quiet and peace that the double nature of reality comes home to us. In psychological terms, we perish without relation to the unconscious. In poetic terms, we wither with no reference to the heart. In religious terms, the world is filled with the glory of God.

Edna St. Vincent Millay is right:

God, I can push the grass apart
and lay my finger on Thy heart! . . .

The soul can split the sky in two,
and let the face of God shine through.

To live bereft of insight into the hidden reality of all that exists is to be mute willfully. For it is a capacity we all have, since we are made for such a dialogue, so function, so operate. It is not alien to us, it is proper to us. Body and soul constitute the human and the human relates as body and soul.

Jesus dealing with bread today is a simple example. He plays on the many meanings of bread, daily bread as sustenance for mortal life and for immortality. In doing so, Christ was not being strange. He was being perfectly human. We do not speak any other language than sign language, for language is sign, and everything created speaks. We are not mute, but return in kind and so take part in the dialogue between God and us. It would seem to me that the monk, by vocation, is a specialist in this area. As the world needs poets, priests, dancers, dreamers, artists, singers, prophets—all of them devotees of sign and symbol—so, too, monks who live in touch with reality. This in turn becomes both model and inspiration for all caught in the materiality of the material, out of touch with the hidden glory that is all around us.

Gethsemani
August 4, 1991

53
Priests and People
Twenty-fifth Sunday of the Year
Mark 9:30-37

You, however, are a chosen race, a royal priesthood, a holy nation, a people He claims for His own, to proclaim the glorious works of the one who called you from darkness into His marvelous light. Once you were no people, but now you are God's people; once there was no mercy for you, but now you have found mercy. (1 Peter 2:9)

"What were you discussing on the way home?" At this they fell silent, for they had been arguing about who was most important. (Mark 9:33)

*A*s any teacher or preacher might do, Jesus asked his disciples what they were talking about after he had instructed them. Perhaps he overheard them, perhaps humanly speaking he was curious. More likely, he knew well enough that they had poorly understood his words. And as any teacher, he would be disappointed that they did not grasp what he had said.

In a day when interest in the order of priesthood seems not great, when numbers entering it are modest, when needs are really serious, it is worth asking ourselves what is thought of the character given the people of God as a "chosen race, a royal priesthood, a holy nation." It would seem that a developed awareness of such priesthood would be reflected in a high regard for those who are specifically ordained. If there be an undeveloped grasp of this, would it be any surprise if it were evident? And it is evident. We know, for example, that there has been a great falling off in attendance at Sunday Mass . . . in the whole sacramental life, for that matter. For if priests' roles pertain to "worship" and "teaching" and "leading" by the very term "priest," public prayer is a priority. So a certain coolness in participating in worship reflects a lessening of regard for the priest.

On the other hand . . . such marvelous developments are at work that any conclusion is hesitant. The enormous interest in the spiritual life, an involvement with ministries of all sorts, the engagement with serious social issues, is so intense that one cannot be other than grateful to God and profoundly impressed.

Yet the truth remains: lay priesthood is not merely secular but also sacred. Ordained priesthood is not only sacred but oriented toward the secular. The prime stance must look beyond its locus. Lay priesthood totally secular is barren. Ordained priesthood articulates the sacred in the secular.

It follows that a contribution we could make to the common good is to rediscover and reshape the entire notion of priest, asserting in our lives an emphasis on worship as prime. Nothing whatever is preferred to the work of God: a keen appreciation of the role of evangelizing by our love for the Gospel and by living it, a sharing in pastoral building of the community, rather than any passive indifference that leaves it to others.

Our position is superb. We are both cleric and lay, we are "priests and people," in one sense of the terms, and "all priests" in another. The dynamics are stimulating. It is perhaps a rather important function for us to contribute to a more healthy love for priesthood in all senses and counteract a certain disenchantment born of the exigencies of our faith.

For let it be said, Christianity is not easy. And when we find this so, it is no small matter to stay on course. Disenchantment is as common as rain and not nearly so fruitful. A coolness to any priesthood is self-defeating for we are *all* a royal priesthood with Christ. Any coolness is thus demeaning.

A climate of positive love will make prosper the works of the future. No one knows the shape of things to come, what forms priest and people will assume, how worship and teaching and ruling will take place. It is clear that we come to the end of an era in many ways. The new is not yet evident. We are in a period of flux. If this be stressful, it is also necessary as part of growth. How serious the need, then, to love and love dearly, not forms and modes and manners, but the inner reality. There are ordained priests and there are people, and this is of divine origin. And the people of God are themselves a royal priesthood, a chosen race, a holy nation, a people he claims as his own. This, too, is divine in origin.

So, what were you discussing among yourselves out of earshot of Jesus and the abbot? For there is your thinking revealed, your attitudes manifest. And it is good at times to call our thinking and our attitudes into question. So Jesus. He would root our significance in our priesthood with him, our engagement in full measure with the drama of salvation. He would never demean. Nor rate our importance on anything less.

Amen.

Gethsemani
September 22, 1991

54

Veterans Day

"In Flanders Field"

In Flanders Fields the poppies blow
Between the crosses, row on row,
 That mark our place; and in the sky
 The larks, still bravely singing, fly
Scarce heard amid the guns below.

We are the Dead. Short days ago
We lived, felt dawn, saw sunset glow,
  Loved and were loved, and now we lie
    In Flanders fields.

Take up our quarrel with the foe:
To you from failing hands we throw
  The torch; be yours to hold it high.
    If ye break faith with us who die
We shall not sleep, though poppies grow
    In Flanders fields.

—John McCrae

There is a hill of stones in County Meath in Ireland, called Newgrange, which dates to 3,000 years before Christ. In the middle of this mound of brook pebbles, perhaps the size of St. Joseph's hill [on the grounds of Gethsemani, ed.], is a vaulted burial chamber. And leading to it there is a long corridor from outside, a corridor lined and roofed with massive stone slabs, the entrance, too, blocked by one. But above the doorway a narrow slot remained open, and only in 1963 was its purpose discovered. Once in the course of the year, at the winter solstice, the morning sun passes through the slot and sends rays down the narrow passage to flood the inner chamber with a few moments of brilliant light. And is gone. What deep people, how observant, those early Irish.

Not much different from ourselves. In Frankfort, the names of Kentucky's Vietnam War dead are inscribed on marble slabs laid flat on a plaza overlooking the state capitol. The names are by month and day of each soldier's death. And in the midst, a large aluminum sundial. All of this so set, with the help of the U.S. Naval Observatory, that the sun moving east to west across the sky each day, and north and south from solstice to equinox each year sends the finger point of the sun's shadow across your name on the day you died. Very moving.

The passage of time is so profound a mystery. We are at a loss to plumb it, use sign and symbol to convey in some way a word we cannot speak.

You need only grow older to know for certain that time is a very fluid construct. A day to a child and a day to an old woman cannot compare. A long night of pain is not the night of sound, healthy sleep, an evening of pleasure. Nor is a day of exhilarating enterprise one with a day of wait in a terminal.

The cycle of the Church Year is so great an introduction into eternity. The round of the daily Office, continuing through centuries from ancient times, links time to eternity inseparable, qualifies time as almost fancy and fiction, an artificial interval before we enter the real.

This is obvious most of all in the Eucharist: no repetition of a past event, but a continuing of a single event through what we call time. It is just as true in our celebration of the mysteries of Christ's life and death. We do not repeat or merely recall his birth, his death, his rising. We are present at the original event. Time is lost in an eternal now.

The flooding of a secret burial chamber with light each winter solstice for thousands of years in an effort to express eternity in time, this renewal of light each year a witness to the dawn of eternal light. The shadow of the sun passing across your name on the calendar day you were born to life years ago is testimony to life's meaning, death's significance. Not for nothing do we put our names on the cross beneath which we rest. We are somebody and we live. And that life is eternal. Temporal death is temporary. Life is not. The sun rises each day and each year because light is eternal, not darkness.

In this very church, Vigils and Lauds and Vespers, Terce, Sext, None and Compline have been chanted thousands and thousands of times. And even those 50,000 days and nights is a modest number compared, say, to some ancient Cistercian abbey in Spain. In terms of time, it is all meaningless for not even an echo remains. In terms of eternity, it is an undying song, a praise that goes on forever.

We are surrounded by eternity. It is just over the ridge, just beneath my mind, within earshot. We live in it as surely, more surely than we live in time. We are eternal, time is not.

To you from failing hands we throw the torch. Be yours to hold it high. What could the torch be but commitment to life, death unto eternity? We do not break faith with those who die. We keep the faith and die with them now and forever.

Amen.

November 10, 1991

55
Christmas Eve

*L*isten again to the solemn tones of the Latin creed come down to us through the centuries, words worn silk-smooth on stone:

> Credo in unum Deum,
> Patrem omnipotentem,
> Factorem coeli et terrae,
> Visibilium et invisibilium.
> Et in unum Dominum Jesus Christum,
> Filium Dei unigenitum,
> Et ex Patre Natum,
> Ante omnia saecula,
> Deum de Deo,
> Lumen de Lumine,
> Deum verum de Deo vero.

And still magnificent in our own tongue:

> And I believe in one Lord, Jesus Christ,
> The only Son of God.
> God from God.
> Light from Light.
> True God from True God.
> By the power of the Holy Spirit He was born
> of the Virgin Mary and became man.

There is no drama in all the world, in all time, more profound, more living, more real, than the drama enacted here at this altar. There is nothing on earth that can come even remotely near it. This sanctuary is the stage, the roles are assigned. The celebrant dons a vestment, a costume. He enacts a rite. He personifies Christ, speaks his lines, his words. And pretends that Christ does again what he did before. Only this drama is not just pretending. It does what it acts. For as there is stage time that transcends time, so there is a God time: Spirit time, grace time, eternal time. And we enter it.

Good drama is first of all good performance. Good drama is also participation. If the audience is not involved, there is no drama. Good drama is life made articulate, human experience witnessed, my humanity revealed. The better the drama, the better my entrance into it.

Good liturgy is first of all quality performance. But far more than good performance, it must also be quality participation. Here history is not reenacted, it is accomplished. History is made. In the one action, Christ and all his mysteries. How? With us!

So we are there. If good drama be quality performance and quality participation, we are shepherds, we are wise men, innkeeper and Bethlehemite. We hear the angels, follow the shepherds, see the star, feel the warmth of the cattle. Not in imagination. Really. For I am involved in this drama. He came for me. He came for you. There is no one he did not come for.

This is not a play you just come and watch. You cannot just come and watch. Even your watching is your languid response, your way of being involved. You are a witness, after all. You were there. You can be summoned as a witness.

So we look at this child. This lovely child. And the mother, so young, so pretty. And Joseph, so serious, so absorbed. And the words ring in your ear:

Deum de Deo, Lumen de Lumine.
God from God, Light from Light.
True God from True God.
Come down from Heaven.

What is one to make of it? And if it be true, it is too good to be true. And yet it is true. And still too good. So we come to sense that what affects us most is most difficult to express. The words are clear: *Deum de Deo. God from God. Light from Light.* But it takes more than words. The head is not enough. The heart must be involved. As we say, "The heart must act." I act it out. I pretend it. And the acting, the pretending, the staging begin so and move so soon on to another level. My acting becomes participation. My pretending becomes real. We are children again. We pretend. And the world of make-believe becomes the world of faith. For only the Christian takes the play seriously. Knows good theater, understands liturgy, recognizes quality. Moves drama into the eternal. In time, touches the timeless. Tonight. Here.

This Christmas is one more allotted you, allotted me in the Providence of God. How many so far? How many more to come? Each a re-entrance onto the eternal stage on which is played the eternal drama of humankind's redemption. Day by day. Year by year.

For in our union with Christ in grace, our human reality enters divine reality and, one with Christ, transfigures everything. Without him, life is a play without meaning, significance. The drama is then lost to us, becomes mere history. But our life with Him becomes reality with his reality, at once historical and mythical. Drama which is history. A story which is ours. Forever. There is every reason, then, to say as I say to you now, "Merry Christmas."

Gethsemani
December 24, 1991

56
Be Not Ashamed
Fifth Sunday of the Year
Matthew 5:13-16

*B*e not ashamed.
These are the words of a Kentucky poet [Wendell Berry, ed.] and express a human response to exposure to light, to revelation, suggesting that far better than shame is a rejection of it, a belief, rather, in goodness.

The Scriptures speak of the same situation. Isaiah's first response to a vision of divine glory is:

Woe is me. I am doomed. For I am a man of unclean lips; yet
my eyes have seen the King, the Lord of Hosts.

His eyes saw, his ears heard, but he speaks of unclean lips. We reveal ourselves in our speech, perhaps that is the reason. St. Paul sums up the teaching he received, but cannot help recalling his unworthiness; he says he is the least of the apostles. None of them persecuted Christ's followers as he had done. He says he does not deserve the name, gives all credit to grace, notes how hard he works for the cause to support his claim to be heard nonetheless.

In the Gospel, in the face of an obvious wonder that a fisherman would recognize as a real marvel, Peter is filled with shame. He and his partners worked all night, caught nothing. No need to tell him he might move past the shoal into deeper water, as if they had not long since done so, and more than once. But out of courtesy and respect for Christ, who was, after all, no fisherman and not expected to know much about it, he did as was suggested. He got more than he counted on, a great deal more.

And the first reaction, you note, is not thanks for the wonder, marvel at this demonstration, but self-awareness. Like being suddenly in the presence of beauty and realizing you are not much. Like singing a song and thinking you did pretty well, and then someone rises and sings like nothing you ever heard. In the presence of the good, we sense our lack of it. *Depart from me, Lord. I am a sinful man.*

Peter was impulsive, volatile, hearty. His reaction is immediate, his answer swift: *You have no business dealing with people like me. You picked the wrong man. Depart. Surely you can do better.*

A sense of human need can come on suddenly, a light in a dark room. It can come on slowly, a gradual awareness that grows clearer. Sometimes it is an abiding sense of guilt that seems permanent, present both when we do pretty well just as much as when not so well. More often, it is an occasional and usually sudden grasp of what we really amount to. And we are relieved when it passes, when we can get rid of the sensation.

All of which is a basic human experience. We are born in original sin and we never quite succeed in forgetting it. Later lapses into sin, early and late, only confirm our memories. And sometimes the way we are treated by others, also early and late, will substantiate first impressions and leave us guilt-ridden and unworthy. Sorrow over sin is healthy. Believing in God's merciful, forgiving love is even more so. All the tactics and techniques of therapy, psychiatry, psychology, so highly developed in our times, are all very helpful. But the ultimate healing is spiritual. We are a deep people. We are, after all, immortal. Thus in our faith in God, in Christ's redeeming love is our healing sunshine. A mystery often to be returned to, pondered on, mused over. Mere knowledge is not much help. It needs to be experienced. And experience for the soul means reflecting on the mystery of love.

The angel touched the lips of the prophet with live coal. This symbolizes healing, purifying. Through the symbol of speech, we reveal ourselves, the lips are touched with divine fire that we may be made whole and good.

St. Paul never forgot where he came from, but he also never forgot about what God had done for him.

Christ did not answer Peter's request, though Peter answered his. He did not depart, for he knew that would do no more than leave Peter to his situation. He rather drew Peter

closer. In the end, after a tumultuous relationship, Peter made it
to happiness and joy in God.

We can do much. Christ does not depart from us. Never. Let
us not depart from him, recognizing who and what we are, but
never submitting to shame. Rather, admit we are sinners who are
dearly loved. And loved by Jesus Christ, Son of the Almighty
Lord. We must hold our ground and fearlessly maintain it. It is
our salvation and our glory. *Do not be ashamed.*

Gethsemani
February 9, 1992

57

Beatitude
Sixth Sunday of the Year
Luke 6:17, 20-26

*A*s you may be aware, winners in the Winter Olympics
from Russia do not have a national flag flown in their
honor—part of the award rite—nor their anthem played. They are
in the unusual situation of having no country, no flag. That is, no
officially-established structure of government. That is what a flag
represents primarily, an anthem.

In some such sense the Beatitudes of Jesus can stand as a
sign of our faith. They do not constitute it, but express it. We believe in a person, not in a statement. Even so, the Sermon on the
Mount is a dramatic symbol of Christ and what he represents.

The approach that Christ takes to reality is not the usual
one. He does not, in the face of poverty, first of all set out a program. Rather, he calls the state a blessed one. We know why: poverty is never a choice, always a misfortune against which one is
usually helpless. The millions of poor in our land and all over
this world are poor because, for the moment at least, and for
longer than that usually, they are in a helpless situation. Christ
makes clear that this situation will be otherwise in his Kingdom.

No one chooses hunger. Yet many are hungry, and most of
them can do little or nothing about it. Christ does not set up a
relief program. He rather promises a better day. Mourning over
tragedy and disaster is never a choice. It is a response to a situ-

ation over which we have no control. Christ again avoids temporal solutions, and promises ultimate joy.

So all the "Blesseds" are compensation for what cannot be helped. What is never mentioned is puzzling. Who or what is at fault in all this? And what is the role they play in the final solution?

And we are led to think of that by the woes of the Lord: "Woe to you," a series. Here it is quite different. Here is choice.

Woe to you rich. No one has to be rich. It is a choice. Christ says it is a regrettable choice, and one that bodes no good.

Woe to you who are full. No one has to be full, satisfied. It is a choice. It follows on having plenty and enjoying it. Christ speaks ill of it.

Woe to you who laugh now. Laughter is a choice. It is a response to what we find pleasing, fit, joyous. And Christ finds it suspect. He does not praise the choice.

Woe to you when all speak well of you. Being well-spoken of is something most people assume to be a worthy good. As choice, we see it a consequence of a way of living that deserves good report. Christ takes not only a dim view of it, he claims it is untrustworthy.

If all this—these Blesseds and these Woes—is the flag we fly over us, the most gentle comment could only be that it is a strange banner, much at odds with the usual view!

It is good, however, to note where we come from. We speak from a privileged position. It is not that God begrudges us goods, or a full table, or the joy of laughter. The world is full of his own joy, his plenty: hear the birds, see daffodils once again emerge. Nor is he pleased at poverty, sorrow, want.

It is rather that there are more important things. And if we took the important things more seriously, other things would fall into line. There is no need of poverty, of want. And if there need be sorrow over sickness and death, there is a Christian grace that endows them with dignity, even beauty.

Christ has here no program for human living. That follows later, and is for us to develop. Such doing follows being. We are called, then, to be sons and daughters of God, destined all to the Kingdom. In that Kingdom, the nonsense of this world will be revealed, the ugly fruit of human evil brought to task. We need not wait for that: we need only look around. And choose to live as Christians among God's people, en route to God revealed there because we saw him hidden here. And so made the proper choices.

Gethsemani
February 16, 1992

58
Remembering the Monk Lavrans
This was written as an Introduction to
The Sacred Art of Lavrans Nielsen
(Kansas City: Sheed & Ward, 1992)

*L*avrans Nielsen, born in Brooklyn, baptized Donald Anthony, took after his Norwegian father and was much a
Scandinavian type: tall, fair, blue-eyed, large-boned but spare, big
hands. He was exceptional for grace of movement, though perhaps too slow to be athletic. I have a specific memory of him that
remains vivid. One night after supper, when I went to his studio
to view some new work, he offered to fry me an omelet on the
little hot plate he had. I never saw anyone crack open eggs, drop
them in a pan, stir them and serve with such beauty of movement. It struck me forcibly and made a deep impression that remains. He was usually soft-spoken, but could become quite vocif-
erous on occasion, laugh uproariously, eyes sparkling. An engaging person, interested, responsive.

He was 20 when he entered the monastery and 40 when he
left (1957-1976), and it is, of course, Lavrans as a monk that I remember him. His gifts became apparent early. I believe his first
assignment, or one of the early ones, was the wardrobe or tailor
shop. In those days, there was a large staff, since there were perhaps 150 monks or more, and most of their clothing was home-
made. Only overalls or work pants and denim jackets were not.
Socks in the medieval manner (cloth boots for the feet, plus leg-
ging underwear, shirts, as well as the monastic robe, scapular,
cloak or cowl)—one set for winter with a change (the monastery
then had little heat) and one set for summer. Making up and
keeping all this in repair was a lot of work. An early project of
his was the redesign of the monks' robe, still the pattern, and a
new form of the cowl. He also designed and made a number of
handsome vestments.

He was meanwhile using what free time he had for oil
painting, and soon moved also into woodcuts or linoleum block
prints. In the latter he became a tradition. And the community
Christmas cards, and Easter cards, all of them of beauty, not to

say many holy cards, were part of our life. Meanwhile, he also moved into icons, in the Russian or Greek style, and came to excel in this area. All this work expressed deep spirituality and a relationship to the monastic life, and even the abbey itself, by way of monks and specific abbey features: Our Lady seated in the abbot's seat, for example.

It is to be noted that he had no education in art, was self-taught. He studied artists and their work, of course, but developed on his own, moving steadily in the quality of his work. And after he left Gethsemani, he continued to grow. A later interest was large, abstract paintings in light colors, often multi-layered and three-dimensional. They remain very impressive and were featured in several exhibits he staged.

When the renewed abbey church was complete, he did a number of long banners that hung from the ceiling behind the high altar, ones in felt mostly. We still use them for feasts. In them he shows a mastery of color and of the ability to reckon with distance, for these banners close up are quite different from the way they look from deep in the nave.

When we moved into an English liturgy, he hand-lettered a number of texts for Holy Week functions: the sung Passion of Christ done in impressive calligraphy, or musical notations, handsomely bound; they remain a treasure for us.

That the abbeys have a number of monks with some artistic ability has always been more or less taken for granted. But in his time no provisions were made for them to express themselves, except in what free time they could find. We were then vigorously developing several means of livelihood, and all available monks were made use of. That came first. With Lavrans, it was different. It began in a rather droll way.

His assignment one season was to operate the vacuum machine that drew the air from plastic sacks of quartered cheese rounds and sealed them. It was, of course, a monotonous routine that would drive a man like Lavrans into a state of high exasperation. This went on, for the work had to be done, until he began to break out in large, ugly boils. So a halt was called, and the Brother in charge made a bold move and offered a deal to Lavrans. If he would milk cows each morning—no favorite among mostly city monks—and do the chores that went with it, he could have the afternoon for his art. Lavrans seized the opportunity. This was the first time any monk had been given official worktime for something like art. As it turned out, he was the right choice. We had a fine herd of purebred Holstein-Friesians, cows of distinction with a certain awareness of their class: moody, sensitive, touchy. Lavrans developed an amazing affinity for them, got to know them almost on a personal basis. His gift for animals was unusual. And the open afternoons left him free to do a great deal of wonderful work. The arrangement worked perfectly, and Lavrans was always grateful to the Brother in charge. And the monks credited the same Brother for recognizing a true artist when he saw one.

Characteristic of Lavrans was his free spirit, his sense of independence. He did not function as a group person. Though he loved the monks and the life, he had a certain inability to enter into the communal. When he entered the abbey, there were the two divisions: choir monks and lay brothers, now largely melded. It is not enough to say that lay brothers did not know Latin and hence did not go to choir, the Conventual Mass. There was more to it than that. Most of the lay brothers did not relate that easily to liturgical function, made rather their work their liturgy, perhaps finding formal worship a bit contrived. And this was more a matter of temperament and disposition than of theology. Years before the English liturgy arrived, people with some awareness (like Dom James Fox, then the Abbot) realized it was bound to come. Thus the lay brothers were introduced to an English choral office in a lovely chapel of their own, complete with choir stalls and the needed texts. All Brothers were encouraged to take part and so do in English what the choir monks did in Latin. It was hoped, I suppose, that most of them would simply move over to the abbey choir when the English liturgy arrived. It did arrive, and many did join, but some returned to the old *Pater* and *Ave* office of the lay Brothers, not comfortable with anything more. And Lavrans was one of them. For he was, in any case, something of a loner. He began to spend all his free time in his studio, first in the old grist mill within the cloister, later in another in red brick built for him by one of the Brothers just outside the cloister, where visitors could view his work. Without indulging in superstition, it was perhaps an omen that the Brother-builder fell from the roof and was killed in the course of the project. Lavrans took this very hard, for the Brother was a friend—and Lavrans had many among the monks—and used to express at times a wonder how long he would last, whether he would end his life in the abbey. The remarks upset me.

There is small point in analyzing after the event, but the opinion may be ventured that perhaps he tended more and more to isolate himself from the community—or at least had a spirit of isolation, for he took part in all that was required - so that a time came when severance from the community did not seem all that wild an idea. Who knows?

For all that he loved the monks and he loved the abbey, though, he really was not able wholly to lose himself in the group. He had an independence that tripped him in the larger enterprise.

Having him with us 20 years was a grace for us and the world. His work continues to inspire us and how many others who have come to know and love his work, recognize his genius. May he live forever in God and not forget us who love him.

Gethsemani
Spring, 1992

59
Just One Thing After Another
Second Sunday of Easter
John 20:19-31

*I*t's just one thing after another!" Had it ever occurred to you that the first disciples of Jesus the Lord probably said this or thought this or something similar in the course of their two years, maybe three, with the Lord?

We, who at this safe distance know the full story, cannot really know what it must have been like. First of all, to come into contact with the man, to be called by him, to be enthralled with him as a person. Then struck by his teaching—new and dramatic and with power. And how could they have coped with his miracles? Not one, but many, perhaps many more than the many we know of. And in some ways, miracles growing even more astounding, like the raising of Lazarus from the dead toward the end. Then there was, for three of them at least, the Transfiguration—his moment of glory on the mount that so overwhelmed the three that they lost consciousness. Who can imagine how the disciples first sensed trouble, suspected all was not well, heard his ominous words about the coming death? They could not have believed what they heard. And subsequent actions reveal that one betrayed him, the rest retreated into sleep, all eventually fled, save John.

The ghastly death on the Cross ruined all, ended all. If it was "one thing after another," that was the limit. He had led them forward in bold steps into ever-new country, challenging them to move on, move forward, press on into the new and unknown.

To cap all this with the Resurrection is to expect a great deal. Judas did not get that far, but collapsed under the overwhelming experience of this man of God. It is no wonder the disciples did not believe. It would be a natural, human response to what they simply could not deal with.

His leave-taking and the sending of the Holy Spirit was the climax, even that extraordinary event, one that forever changed life on earth. All this within two, possibly three years makes it easy to believe that the disciples might well have said, "It's just one thing after another."

Is it that way with you? And if it is, what is the relationship which you have with Christ and the work he came to do? Such concerns may very well raise more problems than we can manage, but will at least direct attention to what may be central to our lives.

We are called to life, death, resurrection in the most real way. And in union with Christ. And we deal in a most genuine way with the redemptive work of Christ, the salvation of the world. Our share in all of that drama, whatever we may assess it, is in Christ's eyes most significant. We are deeply involved in the world's redemption. Like the disciples, we may be tempted not to see, not to hear, not to believe. We may sleep in an unconsciousness that never lets on any awareness of what we are dealing with.

Told that the world's salvation, sanctification, may depend on us may seem a bit much. One should not presume. If life is one thing after another, it is no great comfort to know that it is all part of a program, a scenario we did not design in a drama we were not aware of being cast for. We may be more like the disciples than we reckon. May I suggest it would be no surprise if we were?

Even so, it might do us well to consider the matter: how real is this notion of our Christian significance in the world of things and persons? The mystical aura that pervades all reality is no mere icing, a prettiness added: it is rather the reality hidden in the appearance. And we tend to make much of appearance.

Gil Gross told Sophy Burnham this story in an interview on *WOR* New York radio. A young couple had one little girl and a new baby boy. The little girl wanted to be left alone with the baby, but the parents were afraid. They had heard of jealous children hitting new siblings, and they didn't want the baby hurt. "No, no," they said, "not yet. Why do you want to be with him? What are you going to do?" "I just want to be alone with him." She begged for days. The parents finally agreed. There was an intercom in the baby's room. They decided they could listen, and if the baby cried, if the little girl hit the baby, they could rush in. So the little girl went in and approached the crib. Alone, she came to the newborn boy, and over the intercom they heard her whisper, "Tell me about God. I'm forgetting."[8]

It would seem it is so for us all, from the first days. We are forgetting God in a land of forgetfulness.

If one thing after another in life with Christ was for the first disciples an ultimately enormous challenge to their spirit as a call to faith in a context of demand, ours is no less. Forgetting God in our context is as easy for us as it was for the disciples and just as likely. It is easy to forget. Easier to forget God than to remember him, easy to sleep. The more so when it is one thing after another. But we are called to wake.

Gethsemani
April 14, 1992

60
John the Baptist
John 1:57-66

We cannot but be distressed at the large role violence plays in the Christian drama, and that from the beginning. Today we celebrate the Birth of John the Baptist, a joyous event. Great things are to come through this man. Great things are said of him. And will be said. Yet we who read history know that this happy birth will come to a violent end: decapitated in prison, and served to a vengeful woman. And even the Lord Jesus was hardly here when he was driven from his own land, a number of children killed in a desperate hope that he would be among them. We know Christ came to a violent end. And all who were closely associated with him. This is startling, baffling. And true.

When Christ came upon the human scene, he came upon a violent one. We do things violently. It is the way we make emphatic statements. Still do.

Yet Christ is nonviolent. The scene when he took cords in hand and drove the cattle from the temple precincts is as close as he came to violence. And one is not violent in driving cattle. It is not necessary. And he never laid a whip on anyone's body.

The particular fascination that many find in gay men is that they are consistently gentle and nonviolent. Not always, indeed, but usually noncompetitive. It is one reason they are loved, and is also a reason they are scorned. To be nonviolent is to be unmanly in our competitive world.

As monks and followers of Jesus, we are surely called to nonviolence in thought, word, deed. Nor do we act in such a way as to provoke violence. For it is possible to get what you deserve. The Church has been the object of violent reaction all through history. Often out of hatred. But sometimes because she was not true to her calling. That happens, too. You can indeed deserve what you get. It is good to be aware of this. We all know, too, people who are skilled at making martyrs of themselves. Jesus has no part of this.

Nor is he impressed, one gathers, with prudence and tact carried too far. By some people's terms, he himself lacked good judgement in these qualities. And John the Baptist even more so. Their style is thought crude, primitive. Easily said.

For all that, we are not wanting for men and women in our day whom Jesus and John would praise for standing for truth and justice to death. We are not short of men and women of caliber. Quality.

And we need them to inspire us, stimulate us. Think what you will, the Church is a bold Church and a lonely one who will stand proud and maintain in the teeth of persistent disagreement that birth control does not wear, that abortion is evil, and so is divorce. And mercy-killing. And greed is ugly, as is exploitation of land and sea and air and peoples. So, too, mockery, ridicule, gossip, slander, hatred of God, his Church, his servants and friends. If you wonder then why so few priests emerge from a people who do not agree with what they hear, your wonder is odd. We have here another form of violence.

In the cloister garden and in realms of peace and quiet, one can read the soul. It is possible in grace to unravel the complex doings of the human mind and heart. For our endowment has been contaminated. The capital sins may be trimmed on the surface, but the root system is intact. Monks can be violent—in gentle ways, of course. We can get even, assert ourselves, be dominant, teach a lesson, give tit for tat, practice jungle warfare in the Garden of Eden. Yet the grace of God and vocation will enable us to see all that, acknowledge, repent and renew. That is what the vow is about: conversion of manner. It is a life work. And a life of hard labor.

The birth of John can give us much to think on. I have known many who died in the service of God, some of them violently. I have known some who suffered much for their faith in the service of truth and justice. I do not think I have known anyone who literally was put to death for the faith. But that is only circumstance. I could easily have been a witness to such suffering and death, given our times.

Do you suppose any of us will end with a violent death like Jesus and John? Witnesses to God's justice? Who knows? We leave that to God's Providence. Meanwhile, we can practice nonviolence. Practice makes perfect. It can be taken for granted that any who died so learned the art over years of love. We can do that, too, and so help tame by grace the widespread violence of our day.

Amen.

Gethsemani
June 24, 1992

61
Chasms
Twenty-sixth Sunday of the Year
Luke 16:19-31

Of great interest to us is the chasm that separates Abraham and the rich man, "so that those who might wish to cross from here to you cannot do so, nor can anyone cross from your side to us." Do we have here a first suggestion of what we call purgatory, a place of atonement and reparation? For the rich man cannot be in hell, even if we deal only with a story, for those in hell do not practice virtue. This man speaks with compassion on behalf of his five brothers.

The first reading from Amos [Amos 6:1, ed.] speaks eloquently of the idle rich who spend their time and their money on themselves. They are marked for a dim future. Such people are not lacking in our day, in fact they grow more numerous. And more gross each passing year.

It is St. Paul, in the second reading [1 Timothy 6:11, ed.], who suggests we seek "integrity, piety, faith, love, steadfastness and a gentle spirit." Noble goals in an age of disillusionment.

We have just participated, as you are aware, in a three-year, multimillion-dollar study funded by the Lilly Foundation, made at their suggestion by reason of their awareness of the significance of the religious life in the spiritual life of the whole nation.[9] You have seen the findings? They are of interest, involve some 10,000 persons in religion, and reflect the opinion of the whole religious life in our land. What the project deals with is the future: how is the religious life going to fare? There are many areas of concern. I pick up only on three.

1) *The future lies in the ability to decide between the high cost of Gospel living in a religious community and exclusively privatized understanding of vocation to religious life.*

We deal here with a *chasm*: what the demands of the life are and what my demands are.

2) *Several factors inhibit the exercise of effective leadership in religious orders. The nature of authority is widely contested, consensual decision-making processes have little form, membership is generally unwilling to relinquish authority to those given responsibility, and the concept of personal "call" often eclipses any willingness to work on behalf of the congregational ends.*

In other words, where there is a *chasm* between leadership and those who follow, we have a sterile situation: the rich man powerless and Abraham unable to do anything for him.

3) *Authority in religious life, as in the Church itself, is perhaps that most pressing question for religious to resolve. Variable understandings of consensus, subsidiarity, discernment and leadership have diffused understandings of authority. This, coupled with dynamics of individualism, limited understanding of obedience, and the separation of one's spiritual life from the life of the Christian community, has made the exercise of authority extremely difficult.*

Chasm indeed.

And the conclusion:

Without significant change, religious life in the U.S. will continue to decline.

This informed assessment—it is lengthy and deep—has a particular pertinence to us, and that for a simple reason. There is today a real groundswell of serious interest in prayer, in mysticism, in the contemplative life. This is no mere trend or passing fad, but a true shift of focus, of fundamental position. Only this week, Fr. David Tracy, theologian from the University of Chicago, spoke on it in a seminar he gave at Lexington Theological Seminary. Society moves into an era in which prophecy and mysticism have priority. It is not absurd to say that the contemplative life is to be the major emphasis of the future. We as monks had nothing to do with this. It is the work of the Holy Spirit in the human heart. It means that we are called to be what we are called to be, and in such a way that it is evident.

Gethsemani
September 27, 1992

62
Interdependence
Second Sunday of the Year
John 1:29-34

A recent article about Tintern Abbey told of the tour guide's tales of earlier times, one of them of the punishment the abbot meted out to a monk who had an affair with a local woman. He was buried up to his neck in a tidal flat and left for the rising Wye to drown. Another monk was hung in the orchard—so the story—for stealing apples. These legends sounding, as you may agree, somewhat farfetched, I asked a knowledgeable confrere if there could be anything to them. He admitted they could be historical in basis, for he had read in old chronicles that the general chapter of abbots, centuries ago, severely reprimanded English abbots for their cruel punishment of infractions. So, it may be.

The point is that the Cistercian Abbey is not autonomous, but subject to the chapter of abbots, subject also to the founding house. Both advances were made by the Cistercian founders to unify the New Order and to provide outside assistance to the monastic life in an individual abbey. St. Stephen was English and possibly Norman, and endowed with the organizational ability of these people. In any case, the founding fathers were good organizers and developed the Rule dramatically and to great advantage.

Our ways must seem somewhat decadent compared to the styles of our English forebears, excess notwithstanding. But the same dynamics are at work. Outside input is still part of our way of life. A visiting monk has suggested that our telephone facilities are rather outmoded and could definitely be improved, brought up-to-date without difficulty, making our phone service one of quality. Though it is a far cry between monks drowned and hung for delinquency and updating telephone service, the principle involved in curbing the one and improving the other—the benefit of another view—is what is to be noted.

A community just as much as an individual can unwittingly assume that the way they see things is the only way, or worse, even the best way. If everyone hears their own drum, there is no point in noting the beat of other drums and how the beat is responded to.

The principle becomes especially important in the spiritual life, both of community and of the individual. There is an ever-present need to be open. Preconceived notions and frozen customary ways can be a great detriment.

Christ himself was rejected because he did not conform to established notions of the Messiah. Compared to what they expected, what he turned out to be did not meet what they wanted. We can be so enamored of our views that we are blind to any other view. John the Baptist would seem to have had some problems with Christ, but we know that in the end he accepted what God designed.

Our own life and the life of the community is never static, but a constantly-changing reality. When our own views, when a community's harden in established positions, a dangerous situation arises.

Dialogue is built into our life, neatly expressed, as I have often remarked, in the very architecture of a monastery, the dialogical setting of choir and chapter and refectory. Dialogue is an inbuilt dynamic. We dialogue with one another, with God, as monks, as house, as Order, under the Gospel and the Rule, in the light of the Spirit.

The basic virtue is docility, an openness to inspiration, guidance, direction. If we lack that docility, we easily go astray. Who does not know the tendency to resist change, to ward off new ideas, to settle for entrenched views? This docility is put to a great test in our time, because it is a time of flux and change. This can frighten and so tighten us in our opinions.

We can see this at work in our own response to the Spirit. We are aware of the great need for community, for example. Rather than following a common trend among religions to become more and more dispersed in the world around them, losing their identity, following their own call, monks tend to go in the opposite direction and resist a trend they do not see as healthy.

So we try more and more to open our houses and share our life with those who seek community, seek prayer, seek the love of God and neighbor. We invite others to share what we have, stay with us, pray with us, dine with us, the while keeping the integrity of the way we live, that their coming not be in vain. This is a beautiful response to grace, and it is possible because we are not only a community but a community of communities, guided and directed in our interdependence on one another. We are not on our own, not autonomous as individual or as community. This is no mere check on what we do, how we behave, but a far deeper concern with the Spirit of God so active in the Church and our strange times. Here is great strength, great comfort. All ought be grateful and endeavor seriously to be at the call of God and follow where he leads.

In so doing, we are a help to all. For any life is often confusing, distressing, difficult. To have a confirmed ability to be responsive to God in everything is a real help. And when we share what we have, we inspire in a most heartening way. So we avoid wild excesses that history tells us of, moving ever forward in building the Kingdom. Even so minor a matter as telephone service improves the process. Your own service of God stands only to improve through willingness to learn, an attitude for listening, rooted in community.

All of which is a superb mode of the Church, a closely-knit community molded into one by the mothering Spirit, as Father Bede [a monk of Gethsemani, ed.] mentioned yesterday. Parish, diocese, region, and all the world is one in faith, in love. The hostility, stupidity, ignorance of this world would shatter this marvel, but to no avail. The Church is ever and always one. We are not. Thus we pray, now especially in this time of prayer for the Church of Christ and all peoples. Only the mothering Spirit can bring to full beauty the great Mother Church on earth, that glory on which and in which our Cistercian mother depends and develops.

Gethsemani
January 17, 1993

63
Back in the Saddle
Chapter Talk

Benedicite! ["Bless the Lord!" This is a common greeting in a monastery, ed.]

It has been a mere 20 years since I last spoke to this community. Since some of you have *never* spoken to the community and the same may *never* do so, the matter is scarcely worthy of note. But as a bit of nostalgia, it bears mention. Some memories are at hand.

We used to have chapter every morning for the choir monks, and on Sundays and feasts for all. The Brothers had chapter three times a week and on Sunday. And for all, there was chapter every evening. None of this optional, I may add. It adds up to 14 sessions for the choir, 12 for the Brothers. We have one [on Sunday morning after Lauds, ed.].

The morning choir chapters were usually Dom James. On feasts, one of the priests would preach, for all in church was sung. What was spoken was spoken here. The Brothers heard doctrine, Scripture talk, spirituality in the Order. These sessions for some quaint reason were called "Repetitions." Maybe it is better not to inquire into this. Brother Anthony is the first in line of a generation who never knew chapter. And all since him [he came in 1968, ed.].

But after you've been around a while, you become aware that wheels turn. Things have a way of coming around again. Tiffany glass and mission-style furniture come to mind. A recent survey of seminary teachers in the U.S. and Canada about today's seminarians reveals that they have many positive qualities, but they are a different breed. Mixed in ages and background—something thought healthy—their knowledge and experience of the faith is thin; they come not from typically traditional Catholic families; and oddly, not only are they conservative but rather anti-intellectual and much more socially-oriented. It does not seem wholly absurd, then, to fancy a return to necessarily more frequent chapters to foster depth in community. I would not wait up for this. But things do change, you know.

Just a generation ago the Army, the Services, were of no interest to men or women. The post-Vietnam scene left the military low in esteem, saw the end of conscription. Certainly gays, of all people, were the last clamoring for military service. Today, things have come around. And the military is not much taken with developments. Like when President Truman integrated blacks. A typical response from a Marine commander was, "Contrary to popular myth, men do not fight for God and country. They fight for one another, a shared sense of values, and for respect." The commander concludes that gays are unacceptable for being different.

I do not think the man has it quite right—I mean not about gays but about bonding. Close fellowship derives not from similarity of persons but from similarity of pursuits. It is facing death together that knits soldiers. Common goals make for bonding. And there are not many bonding forces as powerful as a threatening enemy. In facing one, men and women gladly die for one another. It is deep love.

Not much different from the answer Vince Lombardi gave to Lee Iacocca when asked what made a winning team: "Discipline, competence, and a love for one another." And the love is not the fruit of their similarities but the result of dedication to a common goal—to win the game. If the group does not have that love that binds them, it will never be an effective team. Winners!

Monks are not all that different. As diverse a lot as any monastery can be, the love that unites all is born of their common pursuit—the vision of God.

Any "contemplative identity" comes not so much from individual endowment as from the melding that follows on a common search. In the familiar terms of psychology, we would probably be safe in assuming most monks to be introvert, intuitive. It is not the practical aspect of the life that attracts them, but the inner experience born of dwelling on the mysteries of faith. Against a background of psalmody, work, reading, the celebration of the Christian mysteries of faith and a participation in the drama by way of one's life, is the power that unites. Even a group as restrained and unobtrusive as ours reveals a love that cannot be hidden and is obvious to all who are sensitive and responsive. It is the quest of God that unites. And it is a quest not through ministry and service to the people of God but a quest within. By some instinct, as it were, men so endowed come here. Tony Frank Higdon of New Haven knew the monks—his father worked here, his uncle was one of us—yet he joined Maryknoll and serves Bolivia's poor. He followed his own spirit and calling. Not ours. He may come later, of course. Some contemplative calls are not recognized or understood. Or mature late. Happens often enough.

The challenge, of course, is in response to the call and fidelity to it. When that weakens or fails, the love of all will soon wither, for there is nothing to sustain it. Such will walk out on the monks without difficulty. We do not love one another because we choose one another as friends. No more than soldiers choose their buddies in the corps, or players their team mates. It is the *pursuit* that creates love, nurtures and develops it. Call it a contemplative identity if you will, a certain cast of soul that prefers inner to outer, pondering to preaching, quiet to action. In a context of beauty and peace, barren of noise and strife, contention and confrontation, such people thrive. And it is the whole that matters: church, chapter, refectory, work, prayer, study, silence, solitude, seclusion. That's why Brother Joachim was right when he answered a questioning couple wandering in the woods, "What do you do?" "I am a monk." "We know that. But what do you do?" And Brother Joachim answered with that vehemence he is capable of, "I am a monk." So I pass the question to you: "What do you do?"

Amen.

Gethsemani
February 7, 1993

64
Abbot Timothy
Votive Mass of Sts. Robert, Alberic and Stephen
on the 20th Anniversary of the Abbatial Election
of Our Beloved Fr. Timothy Kelly, OCSO

*A*mericans proverbially do not know much geography, but Lake Superior flows into Lake Huron by way of Lake Saint Clair and the city of Detroit and another city called Windsor on the Detroit River. The river is indeed a bottleneck, since Great Lakes' traffic is heavy. It follows that a lighthouse as you approach Detroit-Windsor is functional even in days of sophisticated navigation.

One day, in August of 1958, the lighthouse keeper flew the flag on the station at half-mast. When a coworker shouted to him, "Kelly, what's the flag at half-mast for?," he retorted, "For my son. He has just buried himself alive in a monastery in Kentucky." That would be a typical instance of an Irish family pushing a son into priesthood and religious life.

Not that the mother was any different. She thought the life absurd, and when her son became abbot, she thought that was but the absurdity compounded. On a visit with two priest sons to the would-be monk, the two priests were putting the luggage into the trunk of the car, with the mother back of them, the monk gone into his abbey. Said one to the other, "Push the bags over so we've got room for Pat's" [Abbot Timothy was baptized Patrick, ed.]. The mother, as they knew she would, bit the bait and startled, asked, "He's coming home with us?" They chortled over their acerbic Irish wit and said, "Not yet, Ma. Not yet."

If the father was his own man, knew his own mind, the son can be said to take after him. If he ever drove you to the airport, you'll know what I mean—total commitment. As monk, as abbot, he has loved God and done as he liked. This formula can characterize holiness if you can pull it off. As 20 years the abbot, one can assume the man must be doing something right. And the absurdity of it never escapes him. And so he has kept a light touch.

Lest this be taken as mere incense-offering, I can say as much to each of you. You came here because you wanted to. It was your idea. And you stayed because you wanted to. And you are here this afternoon because you want to be here. All of this, of course, for the love of God, in the love of God, by the love of God. It is rather much an achievement of nature and of grace.

And so our gathering today is much an expression of gratitude that we have been able to pull something off as best we know how, which, by anyone's standards, is a beautiful thing. God knows that not all succeed. Why we seem to have succeeded as much as we have is a mystery of grace, given the poverty and frailty of humankind.

There are those who fancy that the service of God is to abandon any idea of being your own person, of having a mind of your own. The notion is wide of the mark. There is no better way of being who you are called to be, of being yourself, than to respond to a call from God with as full-hearted a gift as you know how to make, a gift that means being all you were meant to be, were created to be. Here is the grace of freedom from the false self, the worldly ego, the land of delusion and deceit. This is fulfillment with emphasis.

We focus our thanks on a commemoration of the men who founded the Cistercian way: Robert, Alberic and Stephen, three who followed the call of grace, did what they wanted to do in a fresh interpretation of an ancient Rule that has worn well through nine centuries. They, too, must have done something right. The Cistercians are a joy to the Church: a Church without them would be the Church impoverished. And heaven is more beautiful for the host of Cistercians there, not to say uncounted others because of them.

This, for sure, is reason for thanks. That the likes of us could be involved in so splendid an enterprise is a grace we can neither understand nor fully appreciate for the reason that we have but a modest grasp of the significance of being united with Christ for his glory and the common good. This is not to brag and prate, but rather to marvel in the mystery of a Providence that has dealt so magnificently with us.

Glorious thanks to God, then, for so much. And the much so wholly undeserved. We are so sad over failings, so overcome that they are not worse, and tender dear thanks and a humble petition that we may carry on to the end.

We thank the man who has served us these 20 years. Even to say that much is almost crude, yet we can do no better. His father was right: it is death for the cause of life. His mother was right: the whole business is absurd, with divine absurdity. The both see now how right they were. And we the while are cheered by example and inspired to get on with it and continue the original response we made so many years ago.

God be praised!

Gethsemani
March 15, 1993

65
Annunciation

*Y*ou can get a cup of coffee—to go—at McDonald's for 90 cents. By way of contrast, a monk's meal, by the figures released, averages 91 cents, or $2.73 per day of 3 meals. The meals for guests are a bit more since they are served meat: $1.11 per meal, $3.33 per day. But when you pay McDonald's 90 cents, you pay also for the handling, the building, the equipment, the help, the land and its improvement, and much else. Plus a little profit. Our costs, on the contrary, are selective. That is, we do not include equipment, refrigeration, transport, facilities: heat, light, power. Let alone help. It is selective pricing, simply a way of estimating, a way of comparing one year with another. The figures can be matched with other houses if they detail costs in exactly the same way. Otherwise, they are meaningless.

A similar selective process was found in the last *Britannica*, for example, in the article on the history of the Church. The early Church was never called *Catholic*, but *Christian*. The Catholic Church emerges only after the great schism of the Orthodox. Both branches are then viewed as developments of the earlier *Christian* church, now one Orthodox, one Catholic. When I wrote them, they explained they were not interested in theological arguments with various creeds. Their approach was selective . . . a view of the facts with a particular slant. The facts are fitted to need. Just as we might price a meal only by the cost of the food. The new edition of the *Britannica*, I might add, is quite different and more objective. They read their mail.

We can think of this when we approach today's feast, the Annunciation by the angel Gabriel to Mary, asking her assent to becoming the Mother of God. The feast is pivotal, basic, fundamental to our understanding of the mystery of our salvation. It is not mere piety and devotion. And the truth at heart is, of course, astounding.

The Holy Spirit does to Mary what a man does to a woman. He planted a seed: the divine seed by which she became the Mother of God. This is the most staggering event in history. It is unique, unfathomable in depth and beauty.

One consequence that follows immediately is that the act of conception is forever hallowed by God's direct involvement in it. From that time on, the union of man and woman becomes endowed with a holiness that is surpassingly marvelous for the fact that God, too, has entered the act.

It follows that the loving union which creates everlasting life acquires a holiness and glory all over again. Jesus Christ, Son of the living God, was born of woman who conceived of the Holy Spirit. Human love is now sanctified beyond our grasp by the act of God.

Love thus becomes holy. And what is holy cannot be violated, cannot be interfered with, degraded, humiliated by human deviance. Not without peril. For we then border on blasphemy. The consequences of irreverence are overwhelming evils. Our own generation has become well-schooled in the sequel to violating what is holy. A Pandora's Box of evil has been opened and spewed devastation on our society. You need no reminder.

The feast, then, is a call on us to renew our esteem for human love and human life. And a call, most of all perhaps, for courage: for the courage of responsibility and an understanding of the consequences of doing evil for a good reason.

The Virgin Mary was a humble woman. And it was her humility before God that graced her with the amazing courage it took to answer *yes* to the angel's request from God. She surely knew by intuition, born of grace in the Spirit, what *yes* meant. Otherwise, it is no *yes*. We ought, then, be inspired by that courage, and endeavor in the grace of God to trust humbly in him, that we too may say *yes* and mean it and do it.

If we, too, follow Mary and her Son in the virginal way of love, we are both fruitful in the Spirit for the salvation of the people, for the growth of Christ in us and in the world.

Our significance is far greater than we can imagine. And just as human love is to participate in eternal life, so our union with God, in fact, is to enter into the Kingdom for our good and the good of all. May we honor and revere human love. May we turn our own love to good account with the help of this wonderful woman, who this day conceived in her womb the very Son of God become human, become a man. We embrace this truth wholly and fully as the beginning of this greatest drama on earth.

Of her flesh he took flesh.
He does take fresh and fresh
Tho' much the mystery how,
Not flesh, but spirit now

And makes, O marvellous,
New Nazareths in us
Where she shall yet conceive
Him, morning, noon and eve.

G.M. Hopkins

Amen.

Gethsemani
March 25, 1993

66
The 36th Day
Sixth Sunday of Easter
John 14:15-21

*A*bout 50 years ago, a group of priests, Brothers and Sisters who had been spared Japanese war atrocities because of their remote locations decided to escape certain death by walking to the Highlands from the coast of Papua New Guinea - a formidable venture, difficult and hazardous. Like walking to Cincinnati, or better, to Chicago, by way of wandering native trails, through dangerous country of heartless ravines, rivers, gorges, up into a mountain valley of 6-7,000 feet altitude. A large group of natives went along to carry what was needed. Granted that they would have taken only what was essential, it is remarkable that the nuns also took along an iron, a large heavy piece that had a little door at the back that opened to an inner chamber where you inserted hot coals to heat it. This because they were nuns, and though they trekked in trousers and shirts, they were determined that when they reached a highland post, they could take out their habits and wear wimple and coif, starched and ironed, as an elemental necessity. They saw their identity expressed most emphatically in what they wore. So the U.S. Army photos, taken when they reached safety after several months, showed them in blue denim work habits, but with starched white linen very evident. Women of spirit. One is reminded of the Jesuits in early America in the forests in black cassocks, and in the canoes. And the friars in the Southwest, in brown. "Blackrobes" and "brown-robes," the Indians called them. No mistaking them for trappers or scouts.

We approach the departure of Jesus to His Father. The 36th day [after Easter, ed.]. A moment's reflection can awaken only amazement that the whole of our faith, our theology, our spirituality, all that was to become the Church at Pentecost, was entrusted to a handful of people, basically the Apostles. All in their hearts and minds. And astonishing is the first thing they did, the first action they took: they elected one among the group who had been with Jesus through his ministry to complete the Twelve who had been lessened by the departure of Judas. They chose Matthias. Somehow they thought it not only appropriate but essential that there be a basic body of Twelve who would constitute leadership in community service of the Gospel of Jesus. Not merely a matter of administration and even of pious memory, but in some way a necessary identity. This came first—before a word was written, an altar erected, a hymn composed.

We might be hard-pressed in determining what would be essential in our own eyes regarding our identity as monks. It probably would be close to the mark if we saw choir and altar, chapter and refectory as elemental. And soon to follow would be a cowl, something to make clear to our own eyes, more than the eyes of others, who we are.

It is one thing to stress that the contemplative life is an interior business, lived anywhere, in any context, and there is some truth in the matter. But the human is not merely an interior being. In no time at all, interiority is externalized. We cannot live in any other way.

When the central station of the north coast of New Guinea was warned by the U.S. Air Force that it was going to be bombed, the large group of missionaries there had to abandon an enormous complex from cathedral on down to housing, schools, workshops, wharves and what else. One wonders what they took with them to the hills. One thing is certain: altar and the makings of Mass would have been prime—the makings of prayer. There was little else they could do as they saw 50 years' work go up in smoke—it burned for four days.

It is good sometimes to think what is important. The complex that is Gethsemani is a marvel in many ways—a splendid gift of God and of those who preceded us. Yet it is not impossible to know what the heart of it is. And if it truly be a contemplative monastery, contemplation is not a visible entity. It is expressed in people and where they live, what they do, and what they have. If the whole be large and costly, we know well enough what it all means, what it is for.

If Sisters needed an iron to be Sisters, there are things we need to be monks, even if we had to carry them with us into the hills. The whole Church was present in the small gathering that received the Spirit 50 days after he rose from the dead. All that the Church is today and will be until the end of time was present there, even if only in embryo. If we as humans are no less marvelous for coming from so tiny a seed that contained us all, so the Church—the glory of God made manifest in sign and symbol.

God grant we may long continue to sing in choir, celebrate the mysteries, gather in chapter, and break bread together in the refectory in God's grace, for our good and the good of all.

May 16, 1993

67
How We Do Need Love
Eighteenth Sunday of the Year
Matthew 14:13-21

Who will separate us from the love of Christ?
Trial, or distress, or persecution, or hunger, or na-
kedness, or danger, or the sword?

Yet in all this we are more than conquerors because
of Him Who has loved us. For I am certain that neither death nor life, neither angels nor principalities,
neither the present nor the future, nor powers, neither height nor depth nor any other creature will be
able to separate us from the love of God that comes
to us in Christ Jesus, Our Lord.

Romans 8

This letter came in the mail. I read *all* my mail. So I did not miss this. You are likely to lose out if you do not look at what is called "junk mail." You can find gold.

She came to our front door Tuesday morning, dressed in dirty rags, holding a little aluminum paint can in her arms.

Whatever she did, wherever she went, the little paint can never left her hands.

When Kathy sat in the crisis shelter, the can sat in her arms. She took the can with her to the cafeteria the first morning she ate, and to bed with her that first night she slept.

"I'm sorry, this is mine," she told our counselors whenever we asked her about it. "This can belongs to me."

"Do you want to tell me what's in it, Kathy?" I'd ask her.

"Um, not today," she said. "Not today."

I've been around troubled kids all my life. Every kid has something—needs something—to hold. But a paint can?

"Would you like me to join you for breakfast?" I said.

"That would be great," she said.

Then I took a deep breath and plunged into it . . .

"Kathy, that's a really nice can. What's in it?"

For a long time, Kathy didn't answer. Then she looked at me, tears in her eyes.

"It's my mother," she said.

"Oh," I said. "What do you mean, it's your mother?"

"It's my mother's ashes," she said. "I went and got them from the funeral home. See, I even asked them to put a label right here on the side. It has her name on it."

"I never really knew my mother, Sister," Kathy told me. "I mean, she threw me in the garbage two days after I was born." (We checked Kathy's story. Sure enough, the year Kathy was born, the New York newspapers ran a story saying that police had found a little infant girl in a dumpster . . . and yes, it was two days after Kathy was born.)

"I ended up living in a lot of foster homes, mad at my mother," Kathy said. "But then I decided I was going to try to find her. I got lucky—someone knew where she was living. I went to her house."

"She wasn't there, Sister," she said. "My mother was in the hospital. She had AIDS."

"I went to the hospital and I got to meet her the day before she died. My mother told me she loved me, Sister," Kathy said, crying. "She told me she loved me." (We double-checked Kathy's story—every word of it was true.)[10]

How we do need love, someone, something even, to believe in. When love is lacking, the person breaks down beneath the assaults of reality. For most of the world, reality is rough, grim, tragic. Most of the world knows nothing of the world you and I live in. But even in our world of so few with so much, there is the rough, the grim, the tragic. Unless there be someone to believe in, the human can break. Even if that love be no more than the ashes of memory.

Yet we are unhealthy in our private world if we do not know the amazing power of the human to hang on, get through, begin again; a self-esteem surely rooted in experienced love. There being no greater love than the love of God, to establish ourselves in that love can be simply the best thing we can do for ourselves and others. For anyone.

St. Paul, in his letter to the Romans, describes God's love by proclaiming that there is literally nothing that can separate us from it. It is not that kind of love. And it is not difficult to line up the realities that would get between us and God, his love for us.

We come into this world uninvited—no one asked us—and we come tainted. Nor are we likely to forget it. Christ's redemption, and our share in it, is a matter of faith. We know this from experience.

That we be sinners is manifest in our sinning. Our sins confirm our conviction and establish it. This is a formidable block to God's love. It gets in the way, like a semi knifed across a thruway.

If that not be enough, the way the world goes is just as much an assault on our faith. Suffering, injustice, the haphazard and casual presence of malice, misfortune, catastrophe. The world seems often a merciless place. This is an enormous burden and block to faith.

Yet the truth remains. *Nothing* can separate us from the love of Christ. It is all a matter of appearances. No matter how devastating the scene, it does not change the ultimate reality.

Great consequences follow: we do not give up. We do not go under. We do not succumb. We do not hate and despair and reject. We believe in love because it is the only reality. You name it, come up with what you will, truth defies you, lays low your case. You do not have a leg to stand on. You color your life dark, but the color will not wash.

When flood waters deluge thousands of square miles of inhabited land, submerging towns and homes by the townsfull, faith in a loving Lord is sorely tried. It does seem a bit much to expect no murmur of complaint, no moment of doubt. Even for the elect, the meaningless tragic is hardest borne. *"So what have I done to deserve this?"*

You know this well enough if you've had your own flood waters. Giving up on faith is understandably common in our day. After all, turning in your ticket and getting your money back is routine; infidelity is standard. In the face of which, we hang on. We tap the enormous resources hidden in human depths, released through faith. We are capable of far more than we surmise, and too soon sell ourselves short for want of nerve. And thus there is no better enterprise for the good of the world than believing love, and that most of all in the worst of times. We don't need you when the sun shines overhead. We need you when the people are hungry and there is no more than five loaves and two fishes. We need you when we have only the ashes of past love to nourish the life of the future. The love is there. You'd better believe it. And there is nothing that can undo it, unsay it. Your witness to it might help keep the flickering flame alive in my heart. It just might. And in many hearts. A lot more than a can of ashes, a few loaves and a couple of fish.

August 1, 1993

68
Nobody Mentioned Rosary
Twenty-seventh Sunday of the Year
Mark 10:2-16

I was having a few words of pleasant chat with a monk before dinner when the Angelus rang. "Say the Angelus with me," I said. And he replied, "But I do not know it."

"So what do you do when the bell rings three times a day?"

"I don't do anything."

"Well, say it with me anyway. I'll show you how."

And while doing that, I wondered to myself: do you suppose he knows the Rosary? So when we were done, I asked him. No, he did not know how to say the Rosary. "That's odd."

And he said, "Four years Catholic high school, four years Catholic college, two years novitiate here. Nobody ever mentioned Rosary. You're the first."

With that, another bell rang within me: larger, deeper, more somber. And I knew I was getting older in a way I did not know before. Times have changed. Not that the Rosary is all that much.

It is not the faith, the Gospel, the liturgy, the Rule. Just a pious custom. Something like a fireplace in the living room. Who needs it? Yet who will deny the charm of a hearth and a fire and a quiet evening at home some winter night? Maybe fireplaces, too, have long gone. How would I know?

Times do change. A Princeton-based testing service just reported for the United States Department of Education that 80 million American adults are functionally illiterate. That's about half our grown people. I find it hard to believe.

One million children a year see their parents split up. "Split" being a rather cool term for a tragic event. No wonder Senator Daniel Moynihan calls ours a post-marital society. 4,500 abortions each American day seems even more incredible. And nearly a third of them are teenagers, some 400,000 a year. 60% of teenage mothers are not married. One baby out of four born in the United States is born out of wedlock. And to add a note, some 2 and 1/2 million adolescents will contact a sexually-transmitted disease before the year is out. Times do change.

And they will continue to change. For how long do you think a society of such a kind can last? And how long do you think people will put up with it? Only as long as they want to. But once the appalling amount of suffering comes home to them, once they experience the devastation of a violent society without grace or beauty, they will arise and say, "We can do better than this." And they can. And they will.

The evident lies in the very nature of things. I do not speak of a spiritual revolution, but a natural one. A human one. There are laws built into human nature, and when those laws are violated, there is hell to pay, here on earth.

Else, how do you suppose a primitive people can arrive at a way of living—after how many years—that makes life sufferable? They learned the hard way: that it must be one man with one woman for keeps. Nothing else works. That children must be reckoned a treasure. Nothing else works. That bothering another's wife is taboo. Nothing else works. And marrying within your kin is taboo. And doing harm to children. And the taboos bore a reprisal for failure to observe them: death. So there was no thieving in a primitive village. And it was share-and-share-alike in all things. And all of this surrounded by contact with the spirits that added another-worldly quality.

It sounds like paradise. It wasn't. The love of God was not there. Nor the love of Christ and one another in Christ. Christianity is the love of Christ and one another in Christ, not a code of ethics, a body of law, a cultural program. Christianity is the fear of hell, the love of heaven, to be one with Christ and His Father in the Spirit. It is human nature graced, for the good life here and the better life to come.

Therefore, have hope. Even in the midst of a disintegrating society. *"There lives the dearest freshness deep down things."* (Hopkins) Humankind has an amazing capacity for doing better, for beginning again, for renewing and starting over. Given by God. Praise God for it.

And God in Christ blesses and prospers such efforts. His Church promotes, supports, inspires and motivates all such movement. Does now and always has. And will continue to do so.

So mope not. And do not wring your hands that things are not as they once were. For they need not be as they are, either. They can be better. Your faith, your hope, your love can help. Meanwhile, have a little mercy with people overwhelmed by a plastic society that has betrayed them. They have been cheated, sold shoddy goods, been had. Let us help them in prayer and sacrifice to begin anew.

Gethsemani
October 3, 1993

69
Christmas Midnight Mass
Luke 2:1-14

*H*ere are a few lines from the poet, R.S. Thomas. He calls it "The Coming."

And God held in His hand
A small globe. "Look," He said.
The Son looked. Far off,
As though through water, He saw
A scorched land of fierce
Color. The light burned
There, crusted buildings
Cast their shadows: a bright
Serpent, a river
Uncoiled itself, radiant
with slime.

On a bare
Hill a bare tree saddened
The sky. And many people
Held out their thin arms
To it, as though waiting
For a vanished April
To return to its crossed
Boughs. The Son watched
Them. "Let Me go there," He said.[11]

If you are flying in a 747, so I read in the *Atlantic Monthly*, and the 747 takes to lowering its wings, one side or other in the night, you will not know it. Indeed, if the plane should continue to so fly, or even turn over on its back, you would not know that either. The attendant would still come down the aisle and pour you a drink. You do not think this is so because you never experienced it, and do not know as much about the mysteries of flight as you think you do. It's all a matter of going beyond, in this case going beyond the limits of gravity.

Going beyond has been what we have been doing from the beginning. Primitives in time long ago learned to span a river gorge with great vines from the forest, and made themselves a suspension bridge. They went beyond the limits of speech by learning to yodel, and so carried messages from one mountainside, across a valley, to another. They went beyond themselves in ecstatic song and dance, and so entered the world of spirit. We are never done going beyond limits. And the process has gone on for millennia and has reached fever pitch in our day.

It is practically impossible even to list in some brief summary what has been done in terms of going beyond our limits.

We can talk and be heard on the other side of the world. And that same talk can be recorded and preserved for time to come. Not merely talk. I can see you as you talk from across a continent, across a world. The limits of speech and of hearing are pushed far beyond their natural limits, not to say sight. For I can see and hear what happens thousands of miles away, and that in live color. And all that—no small matter—is but one modest dimension of human achievement in sight and sound and speech. See the splendor of what we build, the magnificent roads with traffic that span continents, the beauty of bridges that cross stream and river and mighty expanses of water. Not to mention tunnels beneath them. We build superb structures that defy reality in height. And these structures equipped with every facility that makes life not only liveable but pleasant in heat and cool and whatever comfort in food or drink or clothing. There is no end to a long catalogue.

Nor have we touched on beauty. What grace can compare with a speed skater on ice, a ski jumper flying through space? Think of ballet, of song and dance, or orchestra and symphony. Of the glories of art: in photography, in painting, in sculpture. All in some sense defy the laws of reality and move beyond their imposed limits.

All to the glory of God. And to the necessary conclusion: it cannot conceivably be that a people capable of such marvels should be destined to no more than a few dozen years on earth. They are certainly immortal. Any other conclusion is absurd.

Like the astronauts on the moon, watching the earth rise above the lunar horizon, we are overwhelmed with awe. How beautiful! How beautiful our world and the works that humankind can do in that world.

Alas. It is not quite so, not quite. In the midst of that glorious garden of beauty—for you have seen our parks, our cultivated fields, our national seashores—in the midst there is some power of darkness. Here stalk monsters of evil, terrifying and surely demonic. These mortals who have gone beyond so much and in so many ways—can write a word that is read in Hong Kong the next moment, can travel to the moon and back, can heal so marvelously—these humans: they kill, they maim. These people: they steal, they cheat, they defraud, they lust, they are greedy. They assault, they burn, they bomb. In the womb and out of it, young, old, male, female—no limit! How sad. How unutterably sad.

Sometime, somewhere, somehow, something went wrong. The astronauts could not see it from outer space. The world to them was a jewel. But the Son—he saw more when the Father showed him. He was filled with pity. And with compassion.

And so he said, "Let Me go there." And the Father let him. He knowing as well as the Son what would come of it. He could come among them and take the consequence of his goodness.

He is gone, but is still with us. He has come, but is still coming.

And we with him prepare for his coming again at the end, when the world will have reached its term. When all the hidden glory will make joyous forever the Kingdom of our kind—humankind—in Christ.

And we take part in that. We are involved in that, in ways hidden to us. Like a yeast hidden in the mass. And the mass will rise.

William Blake said it:

Did those feet in ancient time
Walk upon England's mountains green?
And was the holy Lamb of God
On England's pleasant pastures seen?

And did the Countenance divine
Shine upon these clouded hills?
And was Jerusalem builded here
Among these dark Satanic mills?

Give me my bow of burning gold!
Bring me my arrows of desire!
Bring me my spear, oh clouds unfold!
Bring me my chariot of fire!

I will not cease from mental strife
Nor shall my sword sleep in my hand
Till we have built Jerusalem
In England's green and pleasant land!

Well said. The chariot of fire is Christ in his Church. And in the chariot, we take the bow of prayer and the arrows of desire and engage in spiritual strife that is the conquest of darkness and evil with Christ the Lord. And we do not cease till we have built Jerusalem in our green and pleasant land.

Merry Christmas. God bless you.

Gethsemani
December 25, 1993

Endnotes

1. E.M. Forster, "What I Believe," in *Two Cheers for Democracy*. New York: Harcourt, Brace and World, A Harvest Book, 1951.

2. Constitution on the Sacred Liturgy, *Sacrosanctum Concilium*, 100.

3. Pastoral Constitution on the Church in the Modern World, *Gaudium et Spes*, 39.

4. *Gaudium et Spes*, 45.

5. Robert Hughes, *The Fatal Shore*. New York: Knopf, 1986.

6. Robert Fulghum, *All I Really Need to Know I Learned in Kindergarten*. New York: Villard Books, 1988.

7. Sophy Burnham, *A Book of Angels*, New York, Ballantine Books, 1990.

8. Sophy Burnham, *Angel Letters*, New York: Ballantine Books, 1991.

9. *Origins*, 9/24/92, Vol. 22, No. 15.

10. Excerpt from a letter from Covenant House, 346 West 17th Street, New York, New York 10011-5002.

11. R.S. Thomas, *Poems of R.S. Thomas*. Fayetteville: University of Arkansas Press, 1983.

Epilogue
Celibacy and the Gift of Gay

There are many kinds of men, there are many kinds of gay. There are many ways of explaining the genesis of what it is to be gay, just as there are many ways of living out that gift. The reflections that follow are one man's way, suggested perhaps as model, offered not professionally but personally, not just from what was read, but from what was lived.

It seems quite acceptable, surely since Freud and Jung, to see the human as more than one sex, the male as having a counter-side, the female a male side. It would seem, further, that the usual route for working out an integration that would accept the whole of one's being is in marriage, where male and female counteract on many levels, and where, hopefully, through exchange, each learns to accept all of the other, all of one's self. In that context of marriage, the male loves another, but the other he loves in some ways is a mirror of his own hidden side. And likewise, when it is a marriage made in heaven, she hers. It is in the discovery of the other, and ultimately of the full self, that makes marriage also much a journey into integrity.

But there is another way, for there are others in whom the polarity is more obvious, very obvious. Jung spoke of the other side of the man as his anima, the collective center of all we think of as feminine when we think as males. And this feminine is not merely pragmatic or diversional, but is also numinous, just as male-female love has overtones of immortality. It is this intense experience of the other side of man, the feminine side, that is basic—in my view—to an understanding of what it is to be gay. Not to be confused with effeminacy, of course, and yet very much a feminine presence, power, reality.

Such a man with an acceptable sense of his own being very much male, will have so vivid an awareness of all that is feminine that his attraction is not going to be toward the female, the feminine, woman. He already lives with her. His problem, to call life a problem, is how do I deal with this?

The first move in the dialogue as I see it, is to an acceptance of how good it is to have two live together in unity. It is a gift, a grace, if also expensive. Who has not been told how fruitful tension, conflict, dialogue can be, does not know that art and drama and poetry and craft are often tied to a center of confrontation of forces, the forces of male and female spirit?

If such men are not called to an outer marriage in virtue of their engagement with the inner, to what, then, if not a celibate state for a reason? Well, love of God, for example.

The man (and the woman, in the other court), who experiences some sense of call to celibacy is playing with a number of factors which may be much mixed in the beginning: he is lonely, he is different, he has a strong religious sense, he wants others, he wants a point and purpose and a reason to live. And he needs love. Merely assuming that a gay man seeks an integration of all that he is, does beg a question: Why bother? If most men are not consumed with questions of meaning and significance, and who says this is so, the gay man is most likely to be so, in depth, by reason of a bi-polarity experienced in measure. Opposing forces generate heat and light.

A companion in such a scene is to be desired, company in a lonely world. Company, comfort, may mean love, may mean sexual expression, may mean both. The search is not here just a reason why, but companionship in finding out.

Who by virtue of the gift of faith know the love of God, the service of God, do not surprise us by gravitating toward the celibate state, the consecrated life, since it unites the search for integrity and wholeness with a superb direction and purpose, the love of brothers, the spiritual context, God? Who better qualified for celibacy than the gay?

Not to say that all gays must be celibate, for that is not at issue here, but to say that being gay is grace indeed in following the celibate way. How puzzled I am at Church, churchmen, who write off being gay as disordered, when it appears that being gay is perhaps the most appropriate setting for one who would be celibate.

All men need the feminine. Most men need her in the obvious, realistic sense of marrying. Other men, found everywhere and always, *semper et ubique*, already have the feminine, need to know how to live with her, seek others who do the same, seek a reason for doing so.

A good theory, but only in a good society. If the society is sick, as ours may be, then the search for wholeness, the search for the complete self, the more so the self resonant with the eternal, must take place in a context hostile at worst, indifferent at best. A culture that has consistently idolized the masculine and pays women less for the reason that the feminine is worth less, is not going to rouse cheers for a man who sees integral humanity worth more than half of it. The gay by definition is cotton to an assessment of human nature that is taken as sick by the sick. The cards are stacked to begin with: the gay is condemned for being bigger than life, a judgment on a limp culture, a loner, a loser. Add to that a hunger for the Spirit, for God and what matters, and you put together a package few see as desirable. Yet it is, for all that. It is pure gift, society's blessing, the Church's hope.

Which makes it sound reasonable, sensible, easy. It is none of that. For gather a group even of all gay men in priesthood or religious or monastic life and realize at once how much of a piece they are in being so western, so capitalist, so male-oriented. See the problems they have in forming warm community, tender relationship, "Saint Aelred spirituality." Test the depth of self-loathing, self-hatred, self-contempt. They know by fruit of exposure to ridicule, hauter, disdain and dismissal.

But do not stop there, not if you know treasure when you see it. There is pure gold in these gays if you know how to refine it. And the refinement means true spirituality, smart discipline, a touch of beauty, fraternal love, and a good reason. These are all related and they are all significant, but it remains true that given our national climate it will take a while to let love loose. And then to let love grow, deeper, greater, wider.

I may as well make it clear: heterosexuals find all this very difficult, and given the number of heterosexuals in celibacy, given the basic male orientation of the social patterns and the cult given it, a heterosexual style of male love will be assumed normal. Which is fun when you are 20 with an unsure ego, dull by the time you are 30, and deathly in your 40s. Which is why so many heterosexuals abandon celibacy after a decade or two: they cannot handle it: they need an external woman to awaken the inner one, especially in our culture. Perhaps in a less divided one they do better.

For the gay must become comfortable with his being a human, two dimensional, tough and tender, strong and gentle. His search for wholeness is not a search for personality, but for Christ, who cannot be met by anything less than a person, let alone be loved. The love of God is possible in depth only to the whole person, at least the beginnings of one. From there on the limit is no limit.

The lonely life of so many diocesan priests hounds me. I know what it is. Communal love is a Godsend, be it formal or unstructured, yet only when men are free of the shackles that inhibit. And since those who tend to worry will worry here about sex, the answer is simple: sex is no problem. Love is. Where there is no love you can expect sex to emerge. All men want love, celibates too. Sex can be one way of loving, but it is absurd to say: no sex is no love, as absurd as saying sex is love.

A celibate priesthood, community, is a grace for the church, a sign of the Kingdom (where there will be no marriage, but all will be whole), and a joy for all in it. There are none more called to it, more capable of it, more created for it, than the people we call gay. They begin from day one a process of integration that others do not even have a hint of before they are 40. Bless them!

If I did not dwell much in these reflections on how this relates to women, to lesbian women, it is for lack of experience and knowledge, not for lack of courtesy or concern. Yet I do have a feeling that women do better with response to wholeness across the board, perhaps because the scene tolerates an integrated woman more willingly than an integrated man. In saying that much, I may betray ignorance. Basically, though, we deal with the same factors, the same endeavors. I do suspect that gays are more conspicuous than lesbians because the culture forces them to the surface for its own healing.

Finally, just as celibacy, especially as a consecrated state, is a health-promoting way in directing attention to the universal call to integration, so a well-ordered culture will foster a generous response to the call to celibacy: the same dynamics are involved.

Matthew Kelty, OCSO
Abbey of Gethsemani

Vita
Matthew Kelty, OCSO

Born Charles Richard Kelty 25 November 1915 in South Boston, Massachusetts, to Charles Richard and Mary Jane Watson Kelty. Young Charles grew up with two sisters and one brother.

Educated in the Milton, Massachusetts, Public Schools.

Entered the minor seminary of the missionary Society of the Divine Word (SVD), Duxbury, Massachusetts, in 1934.

Professed vows in the Society of the Divine Word in June 1941.

Ordained priest on 15 August 1946.

Assigned to SVD mission in Papua New Guinea from 1947-1951.

Assigned to SVD American headquarters in Techny, Illinois, as editor of the Order's magazine, *The Christian Family*, 1951-1960.

Entered the Abbey of Gethsemani, Trappist, Kentucky, in February 1960.

Professed vows in the Order of Cistercians of the Strict Observance at Gethsemani in June 1962.

Lived in a very small Cistercian community in Oxford, North Carolina from 1970 to 1973.

Lived as a solitary in Papua New Guinea from 1973 to 1982.

Returned to Gethsemani in 1982 and has since served as tailor, Mass office secretary, and Retreat House chaplain.